STUDIES IN THE YORKSHIRE COAL INDUSTRY

*Errata*

*Page* 114. The last four lines should read:

*What was Denaby Main like when you were a boy?*
In the 1890s there were only two taps in Denaby, one at the Denaby Lane end of the village and the other at the back of the second block of houses in Cliff View. Some women of the village got together and

*Page* 156. The first line of section VI should be at the foot of the page.

*To* CLARE *and* GEORGIE

J. BENSON *and* R. G. NEVILLE *editors*

# Studies in the
# Yorkshire
# coal industry

# Manchester University Press

Augustus M. Kelley   Publishers

© 1976 Manchester University Press

While copyright in the volume as a whole is vested
in Manchester University Press, copyright in the
individual papers belongs to their respective
authors, and no paper may be reproduced whole or
in part without the express permission in writing
of both author and publisher.


Published by
Manchester University Press
Oxford Road, Manchester M13 9PL

ISBN 0 7190 0643 0


USA

Augustus M. Kelley Publishers
300 Fairfield Road, Fairfield, N.J. 07006

**Library of Congress Cataloging in Publication Data**

Main entry under title:

Studies in the Yorkshire coal industry.

  Bibliography: p.
  Includes index.
  CONTENTS: Hopkinson, G. G. The development of the south Yorkshire
and north Derbyshire coalfield, 1500–1775.—Gray, G. D. B. The south
Yorkshire coalfield.—Ward, J. T. West Riding landowners and mining in
the nineteenth century. [etc.]
  1. Coal-miners—England—Yorkshire—History—Addresses,
essays, lectures. 2. Coal mines and mining—England—History—
Addresses, essays, lectures. I. Benson, John. II. Neville, Robert G.
HD8039.M62G7695  1976  338.2'7'209428  76–11778
ISBN 0–678–06793–7


Printed in Great Britain
by R. & R. Clark Ltd, Edinburgh

# Contents

# Notes on contributors

DR J. BENSON lectures in economic history at Wolverhampton Polytechnic.

DR BARON F. DUCKHAM is Senior Lecturer in Economic History in the University of Strathclyde.

G. B. D. GRAY was, until his retirement, headmaster of Long Eaton Grammar School.

DR G. G. HOPKINSON died in 1962, when he was senior history master at Swannick Hall Grammar School.

J. MACFARLANE is Lecturer in Industrial Studies in the Department of Extra-mural Studies of Sheffield University.

DR R. G. NEVILLE is a member of the staff of the Education Department of Leeds University.

J. T. WARD is Professor of Modern History at Strathclyde University.

# Foreword

Mining, like farming, is one of man's oldest occupations; and, like farming also, it is an industry of infinite variety. As soil and climate have shaped the evolution of agriculture, so the twin forces of geology and geography have determined the course of mining development; and because of this the history of coal mining is to be approached as much at the regional as at the national level.

Among the English counties Yorkshire has come to occupy a predominant place in the British coal industry. It was not always so. Though the history of mining in the county is long, reaching back to at least the thirteenth century, it is only within the last half-century that the West Riding has come to a position of unqualified ascendancy among the coal-producing counties of the United Kingdom. For decades Yorkshire was only one among the many areas of Britain contributing to the impressive record of nineteenth-century coal production, but from the final quarter of the century the penetration of the great concealed coalfields towards Doncaster marked the beginning of Yorkshire's emergence as the major region of British coal production.

The essays which have been brought together in this volume do not constitute a history of coal mining in the county. From one standpoint, indeed, they rather point to the wide territories still awaiting exploration; but at the same time they serve to illustrate the many-sided character of the industry's development not only in Yorkshire but in the nation at large.

This book may stand as a small tribute to the work of a distinguished labour historian whose major work lay in the fields of miners' trades unionism. Dr J. E. Williams supervised the early researches of the young scholars who have jointly edited this volume. Their continuing enthusiasm for the study of mining history testifies to the inspiring quality of all Jim Williams's work.

ARTHUR J. TAYLOR

# Acknowledgements

The editors wish to acknowledge the kind assistance and willing co-operation of the contributors, Dr Baron F. Duckham, Mr G. B. D. Gray, Mr J. MacFarlane and Professor J. T. Ward. For permission to reproduce material they acknowledge their debt to the editors of the *Transactions of the Hunter Archæological Society*, VII, 1957, pp. 295–319 (here chapter 1); *Geography*, XXXII, 1947, pp. 121–31 (here chapter 2); the *Yorkshire Bulletin of Economic and Social Research*, XV, 1963, pp. 61–74 (here chapter 3); and the *Bulletin of the Society for the Study of Labour History*, No. 25, 1972, pp. 82–100, and No. 26, 1973, pp. 39–42 (here chapter 6); and to David & Charles Ltd, *Great Pit Disasters*, 1973, chapter 6 (here chapter 4). They are also indebted to Professor A. J. Taylor of Leeds University, Mr J. Goodchild, curator of the Cusworth Hall Industrial Museum, Doncaster, and to Dr C. H. Thompson, formerly chief records officer of the National Coal Board. Dr Duckham wishes to acknowledge the kind assistance he has received from Mr T. R. Haynes, Borough Librarian, Barnsley; Mr A. B. Craven, City Librarian, Leeds; and the staffs of the Mitchell Library, Glasgow, and the Andersonian Library, University of Strathclyde.

# Introduction

From the earliest period of the industrial revolution the Yorkshire coalfield has been among the most productive coal-mining areas in the country. By 1880 Yorkshire, with only three exceptions,[1] produced more coal than any other region, and by 1913 only South Wales had a larger output. In 1931 the county overtook South Wales and became the premier coal-producing district in Britain, a position which it has since maintained.

Moreover Yorkshire holds a distinctive position in the history of miners' trade unionism. The South Yorkshire and North Derbyshire Miners' Association was the first permanent miners' union in the country, and the Yorkshire colliers also played a decisive role in the construction of a national miners' organisation. They helped to launch, and initially played a crucial part in, the affairs of the Miners' Association of the 1840s, and the establishment of the Miners' National Union at Leeds in 1863 was partly engineered by both the South and West Yorkshire Miners' Associations. In addition, of all the British coalfields, with the possible exception of Lancashire, Yorkshire contributed most to the formation of the Miners' Federation of Great Britain in 1889.

The Yorkshire coal industry has never lacked historians who have investigated a wide range of facets, though there are still significant areas which need serious attention. The seven essays brought together in this volume form a representative sample of the serious thought and study that has been concerned with the social, industrial and labour history of the coalfield. A select critical bibliography has been added to provide a survey of the present state of our knowledge and a catalogue of the major secondary works which are currently available.[2]

[1] Durham, south Wales and Monmouthshire and Lancashire, Cheshire and north Wales.
[2] December 1974.

The first two articles deal with the progression of the Yorkshire coal industry from the earliest times to the second world war. Dr Hopkinson traces the history of the industry from 1500 to the end of the eighteenth century, whilst Mr Gray concentrates on developments during the nineteenth and twentieth centuries. Although the evolution of the coal industry in the West Riding during the earlier period has been fairly adequately covered,[3] the period since 1800 has been less well served.[4] The absence of a major study of the development of the Yorkshire coal industry since the industrial revolution is a notable gap in our knowledge. This is one of several areas of study where the volume and depth of published and unpublished work fails to reflect adequately the large range of primary material available.[5] Indeed, there is also a need for a definitive national study of the coal industry since 1800 comparable to the authoritative works of J. U. Nef and T. S. Ashton and J. Sykes[6] which cover the period to the end of the eighteenth century.

Mining has always been an exceptionally dangerous occupation, although after the mid-nineteenth century the death rate per thousand men employed was gradually reduced by improved safety devices, stricter government legislation, more frequent prosecution of miners and mine officials as well as an increase in technology leading to more effective preventative measures. A hundred years ago, however, many Yorkshire pits were particularly hazardous places in which to work, for they were known as 'gasometers', being almost as fiery as those in Cumberland and the north-east. The terrible consequences which could result from these conditions were graphically illustrated by the Oaks disaster of 1866, which is the subject of Dr Duckham's paper.

[3]See select critical bibliography, Nos. 7, 30, 40, 49, 55, 60, 61 and 69. Less, though, has been written about the West Yorkshire than the South Yorkshire coalfield.

[4]Nos. 23, 30, 40, 49, 53 and 69.

[5]Important local repositories include Barnsley Library; National Union of Mineworkers (Yorkshire Area), Barnsley; Cusworth Hall Industrial Museum, Doncaster; National Coal Board Library, Coal House, Doncaster, and the Leeds and Sheffield City Libraries.

[6]J. U. Nef, *The Rise of the British Coal Industry*, two vols. (1932), and T. S. Ashton and J. Sykes, *The Coal Industry of the Eighteenth Century* (Manchester, 1929; second impression, with revisions, 1964). For the history of the Scottish coal industry in this period see B. F. Duckham, *A History of the Scottish Coal Industry*, vol. I, *1700–1815. A Social and Industrial History* (Newton Abbot, 1970).

Although explosions of gas usually caused the greatest number of deaths in any one accident, falls of roof and sides were far more common and produced a larger total number of fatalities over a longer period. 'Falls' caused over 50 per cent of miners' deaths in Yorkshire in, for example, 1881, while in 1894 and 1921 the figures were 56 and 59 per cent respectively.[7] In addition haulage or shaft accidents, among many other causes, were responsible for numerous fatalities.

The incidence of such injuries and fatalities in mining communities was so common that their effect raises the question of the extent of the compensation available to alleviate the inevitable hardships suffered by miners and their families. As the fifth article explains, the compensation which colliers or their dependants might receive for small-scale accidents was particularly inadequate, and indeed relief was in general seriously deficient in the years before 1900.[8] After the Oaks disaster there was an unsuccessful attempt in Yorkshire to provide a reasonable source of compensation for all pit accidents by the formation of a permanent relief fund. As this article shows, however, it was not until after the Swaithe Main disaster of 1875 that the climate of opinion was such that it was possible to establish successfully the West Riding Miners' Permanent Relief Fund.[9]

Although we now have regional histories of the miners' unions in most of the more important British coalfields, the employers' side of the industry has been much neglected, a truism that is clearly illustrated by the paucity of secondary works in this field. At the national level there is a need, for example, for much further research concerning the ways in which the great landowners promoted colliery enterprises and the transport systems to which they were linked; the social and economic power that colliery owners wielded over mining communities; and the history of the various employers' associations. Nonetheless in spite of these deficiencies we are able to reproduce in this volume three articles which explore some of these themes for the West Riding. Professor Ward examines the part played by Yorkshire landowners during the nineteenth century in exploiting the county's mineral wealth. Oral evidence

[7]*Reports of H.M. Inspector of Mines*, 1881 and 1894 (Yorkshire district) and 1921 (North Midland district).
[8]See also select critical bibliography, Nos. 2 and 49.
[9]For the only history of the West Riding Miners' Permanent Relief Fund see select critical bibliography, No. 64.

can present the historian with difficult problems, for time can distort the memory and it is not always possible to confirm the validity of the information obtained. However, oral history cannot be ignored, and if the necessary precautions are adopted much valuable information can be gained with regard to the coal industry during the twentieth century. Mr MacFarlane's article,[10] which is a good illustration of the undoubted significance of oral history, demonstrates the enormity of the power which a company like the Denaby and Cadeby Main Colliery Co. Ltd could use to influence, if not control, the miners' living and working conditions. The final article in this collection reveals the extreme measures which the Denaby and Cadeby colliery owners were prepared to take in an attempt to enforce their will. By 1893 the Yorkshire Miners' Association was the third largest British trade union,[11] and therefore when, only a decade later, a dispute involving the company jeapordised the very existence of the Association the issue was of considerable importance to the contemporary labour movement. This final contribution also considers the significance of the legal ramifications of the dispute and demonstrates the destitution and poverty which could accompany industrial struggles in early Edwardian England.

The literature relating to the history of the coal industry is vast in quantity but there is clearly room for further work in several areas, both in Yorkshire and elsewhere. The writers intend to explore the history of the Yorkshire miners up to the present day and to produce a history of the West Riding Miners' Permanent Relief Fund, while it is anticipated that other researchers will cover some of the remaining uncultivated ground. For the present, however, it is hoped that this, the first published collection of essays on the coal industry, will be of value to all those interested in economic and social history.

J.B. and R.G.N.

---

[10]The editors are especially indebted to Mr MacFarlane, who over a number of years has carried out extensive and thorough research into the history of the Denaby and Cadeby miners and plans to publish the results of his work. In these circumstances we are most grateful to him for allowing us to reproduce his paper alongside Dr Neville's article, which examines one aspect of this notable industrial dispute. Other, wider implications will be considered by Mr MacFarlane in forthcoming publications.

[11]The Amalgamated Society of Engineers was the largest, with the Durham Miners' Association second.

G. G. HOPKINSON

# 1 The development of the South Yorkshire and North Derbyshire coalfield, 1500–1775

The Yorkshire, Nottinghamshire and Derbyshire coalfield covers an area roughly oval in shape, with its longest diameter extending along the Trent between the Humber and the city of Nottingham. A bold escarpment separates the coalfield into two distinct regions —an eastern 'concealed' coalfield and a western 'visible' coalfield. In the latter area, bounded on the west by the moorlands covering the millstone grit and on the east by the fertile farmlands of the magnesian limestone, three important seams of coal outcrop between Barnsley on the north and Alfreton on the south, roughly parallel to one another and to the line of the gritstone. Furthest to the west the thinnest and poorest of the seams, known in Yorkshire on account of its association with deposits of fire clay as the ganister coal and in Derbyshire as the Alton seam by reason of its outcrop near the village of that name, bassets out from Wessington, through Ogston, Alton, Owler Bar, Millhouses, Stannington, Crookes and Loxley to Bullhouse, near Penistone. Farther east, basseting out through South Wingfield, Clay Cross, Chesterfield, Brampton, Staveley, Sheffield, Thorncliffe, Mortomley, Pilley and Silkstone is a five-foot seam, called after the last-named village and famous as producing a good house, gas and coking coal. Nearest to the magnesian limestone escarpment, outcropping from Blackwell, through Tibshelf, Sutton, Renishaw, Woodhouse Mill, Parkgate, Elsecar and Worsborough Park to Gawber, near Barnsley, is the most important of all seams in the region, the nine-foot Barnsley bed or, as it is known in Derbyshire, the Top Hard, yielding a coal which, when coked in open hearths, makes a hard coke, well suited to carrying a heavy burden in blast furnaces. In the Admiralty trials of 1849 it was adjudged the equal of the best Welsh and Newcastle coal for steam-raising, as it lights easily, burns freely and leaves only a small quantity of white ash and cinders.

In south Yorkshire the seams dip gently to the east, faulting being generally absent, except in the Don valley, where a number of seams basset out in a circle of some seven miles radius, centred on Rotherham. In north Derbyshire an anticlinal disturbance centered on Brimington throws up the coal measures on its flanks, so that coal mining in this area was particularly easy. Subsequent erosion of the coal measures here in the valley of the Rother and its tributaries again led to the exposure of the seams around Eckington and Staveley, once again facilitating mining operations. As a result, until the 1840s the South Yorkshire and North Derbyshire coalfield faced few of the problems of haulage, ventilation and drainage which confronted deeper fields such as the Lancashire and Durham coalfields.[1] Another great advantage it enjoyed was the concentration of land ownership in relatively few hands, as estates such as those of the Duke of Norfolk in Sheffield and Ecclesfield, the Duke of Devonshire at Staveley, the Earl of Effingham at Rotherham, Earl Fitzwilliam at Wentworth, the Marquis of Ormonde around Sutton Scarsdale, the Hunlokes at Wingerworth, the Cokes at Pinxton and the Morewoods at Alfreton enabled mining operations to be planned on a large scale without the distraction of the often exorbitant demands of the owners of intervening freeholds for underground or surface wayleaves or for the purchase of their coal at a price far above its real value.

## The sixteenth century

A number of deeds and accounts shows that coal mining was actively carried on in the area in the sixteenth century. In 1518 Ralf Constable, of Catfoss, Yorkshire, leased to Nicholas Hewett, described as of 'the Manor place of Barlborough', a pit in that village.[2] Sixty years later the wage book of Bess of Hardwick shows her making payments for ropes and other material for a colliery on her property. About the same time the Selioke family sold to Francis Rodes of Barlborough—one of the thrusting, ambitious lawyers characteristic of the Elizabethan age: serjeant at law in 1578, Queen's Serjeant in 1582, and Justice of the Common Pleas six years later—property there which included 'all and singular woods and cole mynes'. In 1587, when Rodes made his will, he left certain rent charges to his servant, Jeffrey Watson, on condition that the latter assisted Rodes's son, John, to mine coal and ironstone at Staveley, Watson being paid £6 13s 4d for the first 2,000 loads mined, with an extra five marks for each additional 1,000 loads.[3] In the same parish Peter Barley of

Barlow made a contract in 1578 with Henry Berresford of Nottingham whereby he reserved to himself the right to mine ironstone for his smithies and 'sea cole' for his house.[4] In the same year the Earl of Shrewsbury made an agreement with his tenants at Bolsover whereby both parties to the contract were to have the right to mine coal on Shuttlewood Common, the tenants, however, promising not to mine within ten poles of a sough put in by the earl for draining the seam. According to the Shrewsbury accounts, this colliery made a profit of £83 in 1586. On the same estate coal was being mined at this period in Handsworth, Gleadless and Dronfield. At the latter colliery, at Stubley, the agent reported that the 'colliers say they have for getting of coales in ye eye of ye pitt half of ye coales and my Lord ye other half and when they drive out of ye eye they have two parts and my Lord a third', declaring that the colliery would be worth to each of the two men employed there twenty pence a week.[5] Across the county boundary the earl was also mining coal in Sheffield.[6] Farther south, in Derbyshire, Godfrey Foljambe in his will of 1595 left to his wife, Isabella, the right to mine ironstone and coal on his Walton property, outside Chesterfield, on consideration that she paid £4 3s 4d annually to Dame Constance Foljambe for wood and coal.[7] In the same parish a lease of the manor of Linacre, made in 1544, specifically mentions the right to mine 'sea cole'. According to a customary of this manor, freeholders could mine coal on the common. Near by the right of mining coal on Beeley Moor was sold in 1560 for £1 2s 3d a year.[8] In the southernmost parish of the hundred of Scarsdale Edward Holte of Stanton had sold the pits at Greenhill in Alfreton in 1593 to John Tenery of Stapleford. It is obvious enough that certain features of the industry which were to remain characteristic of coal mining throughout the period in question—sough drainage, piece work and the dominance of the land-owning class—were already well established in the Tudor period.

*The seventeenth century*

For the next century more evidence has survived in the form of deeds, rate assessments and mine accounts to show how widespread coal mining was in the area. Judged by rentals, a fair enough guide, the most important pits in south Yorkshire and north Derbyshire were those in Sheffield Park. In 1619 the coal under this property, then in the hands of the Earls of Arundel and Pembroke, was leased at £76 annually, an amount which had been increased to £200 a year on the eve of the Civil War. After the Restoration this colliery was leased by John Eyre, a Sheffield ironmaster, at a rent of £145. When Eyre became bankrupt the colliery came into the hands of George Bamforth, one of the lords of the manor of Owlerton. In 1692 Richard Richmond, a London merchant, leased for twenty-one years, at a rent of £140, the coal mines in Sheffield Park within the Great Lawns and the Nunneries. He, however, sub-leased the colliery to Richard Bagshawe of Castleton, one of the leading lead mine owners in the Peak, who worked the pits until 1700.

Outside the town collieries were much smaller in size. To the west of Sheffield, on the outcrop of the Alton seam at Crookes, the coal under the Norfolk property there was being mined at the end of the century by a partnership which included Henry Bromhead, yeoman, of Fulwood, and two lawyers, each at some time agent to the duke, Thomas Chappell and Joseph Banks. This group paid £40 a year and a fifth of the profits as rent for the colliery. On the other side of the town Stephen Bright, of Carbrooke, one of the leading lead merchants of Sheffield, leased a colliery from Lady Grace Cavendish at Handsworth in 1635 at an annual rental of £66. At the end of this century this colliery was leased to Samuel Shepley, a small freeholder on this manor, at £30 a year. Two other men of much the same social class, William Fenton and John Savage, were working small pits in the same area in the reign of Charles II. Another small landowner, Randolph Ashenhurst, was selling coal in Sheffield from a colliery at Intake in the reign of William III.[9] To the south of the town the coal on the Bright property at Ecclesall was rented during the Commonwealth at £5 a year, an amount which had increased at the end of the century only to £6 a year, when it was worked by Henry Bromehead, mentioned previously as a partner in the pits on Crookes Moor.

North-east of Sheffield the largest collieries were in the Don valley at Kimberworth and Whiston on the Effingham estate. During the Commonwealth these were in the hands of Lionel Copley, the most important ironmaster in south Yorkshire at the time, who rented them at £100 and £55 respectively. Another colliery at Kimberworth was worked at this time by the Hurt family of Ickles Hall.[10] The pits near Barnsley—known, according to the topographer Blome, as 'Black' Barnsley on account of its connection with coal mining—were also in the hands of ironmasters after the Restoration. The coal under Barnsley Moor was leased by William Simpson, a member of the Spencer group which dominated the iron industry in the region. Simpson, however, sub-leased the coal to Gamaliel Milner, of Burton Grange, another member of this group of ironmasters. In 1676 the lease passed to the Hon. Sydney Wortley, who again sub-leased the coal to Valentine Hurt of Ecclesfield at a rent of £40 per annum. Twenty years later Wortley acquired another lease of this Crown property and, after buying out the other royalty owners on the Moor, leased the colliery to William and John Rooke and to Peter and John Shippem, members of two well known Catholic landowning families in the area.[11]

Evidence of coal mining in north Derbyshire during this century is much more complete than that for south Yorkshire, and it is apparent that although the material is scattered chronologically there were collieries at work in almost every parish of the hundred of Scarsdale during this period. Aided by seams of good coal at a shallow depth, the Derbyshire coalmasters sank a multitude of small pits, and it is likely that, however tiny may have been their individual output, cumulatively they may have equalled the less numerous but larger South Yorkshire mines in productivity.

A rate assessment made during the Commonwealth shows that there were coal mines at work at Alfreton, Bolsover, Brimington, Eckington Heath, Staveley, Walton, Dore, Sutton and Tibshelf.[12] Other material amplifies this information. A lease drawn up in 1649 of a farm at Shireoaks included, as part of the rent, the obligation on the part of the tenant 'to fetch one waine load of cole—from Barlborough pitts to Gateford Hall'. The mines at Barlborough were then worked by the Rodes family, as may be seen by a letter written in 1677 by Dame Martha Rodes, then hard at work trying to pay off the heavy debts incurred by her late husband, to Andrew Clayton of Romeley, a wealthy lead merchant, appealing for a loan. This expressly states that 'This money is for Manageing of ye Coal Delph for Colliers must be paid or els their is no enduring'. A Chancery petition of her creditors of much the same date states that Dame Martha 'hath for several years last past sold great quantitys of Cole—amounting to the sume of £500'. Evidence in a case as to the ownership of certain commons near Eckington shows that coal was mined there during the Cromwellian era, as one witness testified that 'Major Bolton had about twenty-five years ago purchased the King's right in the Manor of Eckington from the then Commonwealth and he directed Mr Godfrey Bright to sink a cole pitt—which he did and went forward until they were driven out by water'. A Parliamentary survey of this particular manor made in 1650 shows that there were pits on Bramley Moor, leased by Francis Stephenson, a landowner in Unstone and on Mosborough Moor and at the Marsh, worked by Richard Taylor of Durrant Hall, a Chesterfield lead merchant.[13] To the north of Barlborough John Ogilby's map 'Illumination of the Kingdom of England' marks in a 'Moore with a great many cole Pitts'. On the Yorkshire border a rate assessment for 1697 shows William Newbold and Robert Haslehurst, two farmers, mining coal at Beighton.

To the west another assessment for Dronfield, dated 1667, includes, among the property rated, collieries at Dore, Coal Aston, Unstone and Sommerwood Common. In the same parish a petition from a number of farmers on the Newcastle estate in the reign of Charles I shows that Godfrey Outrem and George Calton, both members of the class of minor gentry, had opened an open-cast working at Hill Top, fifty yards broad and ten deep, from which they had carried away a hundred loads of coal. In the adjoining chapelry of Barlow the accounts of the headborough for 1643–44 show him buying coal in that village for the Royalist garrisons at Wingfield Manor and Bolsover Castle. His disbursements for the next year include payments for coal bought at Dunston for the Puritan troops billeted in Chesterfield. In the same parish John Frecheville leased the coal under the common and enclosed grounds at Eastwood in Staveley to John Hewett of Beightonfield in 1659 on a forty-one-year lease for £46 annually. During the reign of James II German Pole, of Park Hall—like Hewett, one of the few Catholic gentry in this part of Derbyshire—leased the coal in Staveley Westwood for seven years from Lord Conyers at an annual rent of £30. The Court Baron records for this manor, now at Chatsworth, contain many entries ordering miners to fill up coal pits near the highways through Staveley West Wood. When, in 1647, the Parliamentary Committee for Compounding sold the property of the greatest supporter of the King in the north of England, the Earl of Newcastle, Cosse Manor and the right to mine coal on Shuttlewood Common were sold to William Newton, a later mayor of Chesterfield.[14] In the same area a trust deed devising property on his daughters by William Woolhouse, lord of the manor of Glapwell, shows that family mining coal there, and another deed forty years later—in 1695— shows them leasing coal from other landowners in the vicinity.[15] Within a few miles of Glapwell the Devonshire family were mining coal continuously through the century on their Hardwick property.

On the western side of the coalfield the Earl of Newcastle had leased the coal in the manor of Newbold to Anthony Eyre of Rampton in 1637. Eyre, however, sub-leased the coal to Gabriel Wayne, one of the lords of the manor of Whittington. Wayne put in four soughs down to the river Rother, and by 1688 almost all the coal under Newbold Great Moor had been extracted.[16] On the east of Chesterfield, at Spital, where the Rother had exposed the coal measures, the Jenkinson family of Walton Hall were mining coal after the Restoration. Another Brampton family mining coal on the moors beyond Chesterfield were the Clarks.[17] In the same area Plot records an explosion in a colliery at Wingerworth which not only badly burned the miners but also, 'going forth of the mouth of the pit like a Clap of Thunder', blew out the windlass at the top of the shaft.[18]

South of Chesterfield the existence of coal mines at Tibshelf, Blackwell, Pinxton and Normanton is shown in a letter written by John Twentyman, vicar of Tibshelf, in 1673, appealing for a reduction in the assessment on his colliery.[19] The coal rights on the Coke property in the last two places were leased to Godfrey Haslehurst of Teversall, described by the Heralds in 1687 as 'A great dealer in Coles, thought to be worth £10,000'.[20] Another parson with coal-mining interests was William Sleigh of Shirland, who was accused by his successor, John Towne, in a suit over dilapidations of having impoverished the glebe by getting the coal under it. The coroner's inquests for the hundred of Scarsdale include one for two colliers killed at Stretton in 1694, when they fell off pick shafts inserted in the haulage ropes while descending the shafts. Two estate surveys give further information as to coal mining in this locality. One, now at Chatsworth, mentions coal mines on the Cavendish property at Hardstoft and Pentich in 1610. The other, of the Duke of Norfolk's Derbyshire estate, made in 1684, includes amongst the Wingfield property a coal delph at Ufton Fields. Finally, the Turner family, having bought all the minerals in Alfreton from the Crown and from the Zouches of Codnor Castle, were mining coal continuously in that parish throughout the century.[21]

It is obvious that both in south Yorkshire and in north Derbyshire coal mining was largely in the hands of the land-owning class. A new feature in the industry during this century is the appearance of the lead merchant and the ironmaster, who were taking a leading part in the development of coal mining. Capital from at least one other source flowed into the industry: the Turners of Alfreton, who were probably the most important family of coalmasters in the hundred of Scarsdale during this century, were originally mercers.

The typical coal lease of the seventeenth century contained both a fixed annual rent and restrictive covenants drawn up in the interest of the landowner to prevent more than the customary output of coal. For example, when the Earl of Newcastle leased a colliery at Henpit Leyes in Barlow in 1632 the lessees were restricted for nine months of the year to working one pit at a time, employing a maximum of four hewers, two drawers and a barrowman. For the other three months of the year, when the roads were dry enough to bear heavy traffic, they could work two pits with double the number of men.[22] The lease previously referred to between Hewett and Frecheville in 1659 limited the former to the working of two pits with full companies from the end of September to the beginning of February, but allowed four pits to be worked for the remainder of the year. The same type of restriction may be seen in the lease of the Sheffield Park coal by Richmond in 1692, whereby he was not to get coal at more than two pits at a time nor to employ more than ten getters. In addition the lessee contracted to carry on work on the deep of the seam equally with the basset and to leave two pits in working order at the expiration of the lease.

The technique of coal mining throughout the area seems to have varied little from colliery to colliery. In south Yorkshire mining methods can best be studied at the Handsworth pits, worked by Sir John Bright.[23] Bright took over this colliery, valued at £1,800, in 1651, at a rent of £30 a year, from the Countess Dowager of Arundel. To drain the coal a sough was dug at a cost of £265 'beside our labour'. In February 1651 the colliers began to sink three pits, which were completed a year later. Ventilation was provided at this stage by 'trunks', or wooden pipes, through which air was forced by bellows. One pit was on the outcrop of the coal and the other on the deep, so that the intervening seam could be extracted by driving benks into the coal and then mining the seam between each pair. Such an arrangement provided natural ventilation. As the life of each pit was short, a third was usually being sunk while coal was being extracted from the other two. The coal was hauled along the workings in baskets placed on sledges. During the first year, when construction work was it its heaviest, thirty-two men were employed. Later payments were made to six getters, so that it may be assumed that, together with the manager, Thomas Stacey, and a banksman, the total regular labour force was about fifteen. Annual output during the third quarter of the century averaged about 1,000 loads a year.

Further information as to the technique of mining can be gained from a study of the accounts of Heath and Beightonfield collieries, the former worked by the Duke of Devonshire and the latter by Henry Bowden, who had acquired this property of the Hewetts by inheritance. The Heath coal book for 1697, when the colliery produced 259 horse loads, contains an inventory of the colliery equipment. This included a wheelbarrow, five new mandrels, three new hammers and twenty-four wedges with which to bring the coal down, three new spades and one new mattock and, most interesting of all, a new fire pan, showing that artificially induced ventilation was in use in north Derbyshire at the end of the century. The Bowden accounts show that at Beightonfield almost all mining operations were done on piece work, as may be seen from the following agreement, typical of others drawn up between the coal-master and his colliers.

2 Oct 1699. Bargained with Henry Ryall to gett coales till Feb ye 2nd and was to give him 10*d* 2 qrs a 3 Quart he allowing me one att ten to make good ye stack; for any bye work or if it run in he is to bear his share. I am to allow 8*d* a score for punches getting and 12*d* a yard for heading.

These accounts, incidentally, are almost unique among those so far discovered in that they contain details of profits—the coalmaster made £25 in 1698 and £33 the following year, in addition to clearing the whole cost of pit sinking and equipping the two new pits sunk.

Markets for the coal produced around Sheffield are indicated in a letter written by the banksman of the Park colliery in 1630, when he reported a diminished demand from cutlers, brewers and house-holders as one of the reasons for a fall in output. In Derbyshire great houses such as Chatsworth and Hardwick consumed large quantities of coal—the latter, for example, was supplied in 1666 with 975 loads from a colliery on the estate at Hardstoft. It is probable that, apart from its use for heating and cooking at Hardwick, coal was used there for malting, as this part of Derbyshire was already well known for its production of barley. Other markets taking increasing amounts of coal were brick making and lime burning. Brick only slowly replaced stone as the traditional building material of the region, but houses such as Swanwick Hall, built by the Alfreton coalmaster John Turner on the occasion of his marriage to Elisabeth

Thoroton, daughter of the famous historian of Nottinghamshire, in 1672,[24] and a house in St Mary's Gate in Chesterfield erected by the lead merchant, Richard Youle, show the trend of architectural fashion away from the old halls, with their walls of native grit or sandstone. The Welbeck estate accounts show building in brick towards the end of the century.[25] In Yorkshire an agreement of 1640 in connection with a brickworks at Ecclesfield, specifying that both coal and wood were to be provided for the use of the burner, shows an early use of coal in this industry in the area.[26] Traditionally the first brick house to be built in Sheffield was erected in Pepper Alley in 1696.[27] Peak District rentals show an increasing amount of lime burning during this century, and odd leases specifying the quantities of lime to be used on farms by tenants, and entries in estate accounts, point to its increasing use in agriculture. Another market for coal was in the manufacture of pots—the first big pothouse in the area seems to have been set up in Crich by Thomas Morley, a Nottingham potter, in 1698. In addition to these internal markets coal was supplied from the pits on the eastern edge of the field into Nottinghamshire and from those on its southern perimeter into the counties of Leicester, Rutland, Northampton and Lincoln.[28]

*The pre-canal age*

Three rivers penetrate the Yorkshire, Nottinghamshire and Derbyshire coalfield—one, the Don, in its central section and the other two, the Calder and the Trent, on its flanks. In the seventeenth century these two latter, unlike the Don, were naturally navigable to points within the coalfield. As a result the coal on the northern and southern edges of the coalfield, at places such as Sharlston, near Wakefield, and at Strelley and at Wollaton, outside Nottingham, was more extensively exploited than that in the central area of the field, the greater part of which was many miles from a navigable river.[29] Improvements on the Don, initially as far as Aldwark in 1733 and subsequently as far as Tinsley in 1751, placed the South Yorkshire coalfield on an equality with its competitors as far as transport facilities were concerned, leading to a spectacular expansion of the industry in the Don valley as it responded to the stimulus offered by the demands of a rapidly expanding market. By 1732 South Yorkshire coal was effectually competing with Durham coal in the Humber estuary and the valleys of the Trent and Ouse.[30] During the '60s coal mined around Rotherham penetrated the Trent valley as far south as Newark and along the Fosse Dyke to Lincoln, from which the adjacent parts of the county were supplied, as a result of the temporary exhaustion of the collieries around Nottingham and the inability of the South Derbyshire mines at Heanor, Shipley and Langley to compete in this market as the roads between them and the Trent were in such poor condition.[31] It is probable that the introduction of the atmospheric engine into the Nottingham coalfield and the turnpiking of the Bramcote road between the Trent and the Erewash valley coalfield led to the capture of the market for coal in the lower Trent valley by the southern portion of the coalfield once again, but a traveller in Lincoln in 1772 noted that the supply of coal in this county was chiefly from Yorkshire collieries.[32] The South Yorkshire pits, however, had no monopoly of this market, as it was fiercely contested by coal brought by barge from the mines along the Calder near Wakefield.[33] Another extensive market for coal mined in south Yorkshire was along the Derwent Navigation to Malton in the East Riding, an inland navigation controlled by the Marquis of Rockingham and leased by the most important coalmasters on his estate, the Fenton family. Altogether it was estimated that the total coal traffic down the Don in 1772 was some 10,000 waggons—probably between 80,000 and 90,000 tons.[34]

The extension of the Don Navigation to Tinsley, within a few miles of Sheffield, with which it was later connected by a turnpike, led to a considerable expansion in the trade both of Rotherham and Sheffield. When Arthur Young visited the former town in 1769 he noted the foundries there making ploughshares, boilers and pans, a pottery making earthenware, and two collieries supplying these with fuel. He also noted the great prosperity of Sheffield, where during the previous twenty years the number of forges had increased by seven, tilts by two, grinding wheels by eleven and the number of troughs by 262. As most operations in Sheffield industry consumed coal, this expansion in business activity necessarily led to an increase in the demand for coal. Technological change, particularly the substitution of coke for charcoal in forges, also led to an increased demand for fuel. Increased industrial development and the growth of population brought an increased amount of building in their train, a considerable proportion of which was in brick. Both the Norfolk and Bright rentals show the construction of new brickyards in or around Sheffield. The Wentworth Woodhouse rentals show the establishment of brickyards at Greasborough and Wentworth and tileworks at Swinton. To meet the demand for glass new glasshouses were built at Bolsterstone and Catcliffe, at each of which small collieries were worked by the owners to provide the necessary fuel.[35] An increase in the number of houses led to an expanding market for domestic fuel—visitors to the area were astonished at the cheapness of coal and the amount burned by householders.[36] The increase in population stimulated agricultural development, and, led by such landowners as the Marquis of Rockingham and the Duke of Leeds, landlords began to enclose waste and common land on a considerable scale. Lime was a necessity to bring this under cultivation and to keep it in good heart. Young, on his northern tour, noted that farmers in Ecclesfield used four quarters of lime per acre. As the river Don cut consecutively through the magnesian limestone formation and the coal measures between Doncaster and Sheffield, it was easy to transport both along the river and to burn the stone down to lime. The Don company established lime kilns at Conisborough in 1733 to stimulate its use; the Marquis of Rockingham worked lime kilns at Hoober, Wentworth and Kilnhurst in conjunction with his collieries on the Wentworth property; Young noted lime kilns in Rotherham, and other documentary evidence shows lime kilns at work at Sprotborough, Warmsworth and Tinsley during this period. Two other coal-consuming industries which underwent considerable expansion in south Yorkshire at this time were the manufacture of malt and of cloth.

This combined internal demand and export trade led to a massive development of coal mining in the first three-quarters of the century in that section of the Don valley where the river cuts through the coal measures. The rentals stipulated in coal leases of this period show a vastly increased scale of output. In 1723 John Hirst leased two collieries on the Wentworth estate at Swinton and Greasborough with a combined rent of about £200 a year. Two years later William Spencer, of Bramley Grange, a Yorkshire landowner with considerable interests in the Derbyshire lead industry, leased a colliery at Kimberworth from the Earl of Malton at an annual rent of £245 and another at Greasborough for £63. These latter pits were taken over by the Derbyshire coalmaster John Bowden, of Beightonfield, in 1742 for the same rent, but output at Greasborough rose so rapidly that this was soon increased to £240 a year. The account books of this estate show Richard Bingley paying a rent of £124 at this time for a colliery at Brampton Linthwaite, lower down the river. These rents are, however, dwarfed by that paid by

Thomas and William Fenton, who leased the coal under the Wentworth estate at Basingthorpe in 1757 at a rent of £324 for the first two years of their lease and of £648 for the remaining nineteen years. By 1773 their sales down the Don were more than 20,000 waggons—about half the total amount of coal sold downriver.

Coal mining naturally developed around the terminus of the Don Navigation at Tinsley, near the outcrop of the Barnsley bed. At Darnall a colliery was opened by a local landowner, Joseph Alsabrooke. At his death the colliery came into the hands of his son-in-law, Joseph Swift, who in 1760 entered into a partnership with Walter Oborne, a Hallamshire merchant and a leading committee man of the Don Navigation, and with Joseph Clay, of Bridgehouses, the most important of mid-eighteenth century Sheffield lead merchants. By 1762 competition from this colliery had become sufficiently acute in Sheffield for the Duke of Norfolk to take legal advice whether, as lord of the manor of Attercliffe, he could prevent traffic crossing the common from the colliery to the town. Ten years later Darnall was supplying half the house coal used in Sheffield, as it had the advantage of good road communication with Sheffield, whereas the Norfolk pits had to bear the cost of heavy repairs on what were then private roads through the Park. Coal from this colliery was also exported down the Don.

Despite competition from Darnall Colliery, mining in the Park at Sheffield expanded rapidly under the dual stimulus of increasing industrial and domestic demand. At the beginning of the century, after the expiration of Richmond's lease, the Sheffield lawyer Banks took over the colliery for a period of twenty-one years. A rate assessment of 1716, however, shows the colliery then to have been in the hands of Robert Clay, a Walkley yeoman, the owner of a lead-smelting mill at Dore. After his death the colliery was leased by John Bowden of Beightonfield at a rent of £400 a year and a fifth of all sales in excess of £2,000 annually. Payments in the cash books of the Norfolk estate show that in the last six years of his lease, which ended in 1758, Bowden paid £1,377 in excess rents. No further records of mining in the Park have been discovered until 1774, when a twenty-one years' lease was granted to Townshend and Furniss whereby they undertook to pay a minimum rent for Sheffield Colliery of £100 per annum and in addition a royalty of £2 4s 0d for every tenn (forty-four loads) of coal mined over 600 tons. This partnership also took over the Manor Colliery at a minimum rent of £50, with an additional royalty of eight pence per cart load on all coal mined in excess of 4,400 loads. This partner-ship invested £3,200 in improvements, and, with the advantages of shallow pits and plenty of the hard coal demanded by the cutlers easily accessible, increased output here to the extent that they were paying the Duke of Norfolk, at the end of the period, over £1,000 a year in rent and royalty.

Although no river penetrated north Derbyshire, improved road communication with the lead-mining areas of the Peak and the agricultural districts of Nottinghamshire widened the market for coal. There is ample evidence to show that during the first half of the century coal transport was confined to a comparatively short season between hay making and the corn harvest, and that after the end of October the roads were almost useless for heavy traffic. The creation of a road system usable throughout the year must have been a big advantage to the collieries. A primary motive in road improvement was to facilitate coal traffic. The Turners of Swanwick rebuilt the road from their pits to Matlock at their own expense in the '30s.[37] The chief purpose of the turnpike road from Little Sheffield to Buxton, via Grindleford Bridge and Hucklow, and to Sparrowpit via Hathersage, Hope and Castleton, was to enable coal mined around Heeley to compete with coal mined in Cheshire, carried along the Sherbrooke Hill trust's road from Chapel en le Frith toll-free.[38] In the next year, when the road between Baslow and Calver bridges was turnpiked, one clause of the Act stipulated that coal brought from Baslow colliery by the owners of the lime kilns at Calver or by the Duke of Rutland's tenants should pay only half toll. Another road turnpiked in 1759, that connecting Chester-field with Mansfield, was improved with the object of facilitating the transport of coal from the pits at Heath, Barlborough and Staveley to Worksop and Mansfield and other parts of Lincolnshire and Nottinghamshire.[39] A third road turnpiked in that year, largely through the influence of Anthony Tissington, the trustee of the Turner property at Swanwick, the Newhaven turnpike, connecting the collieries at Alfreton with the Winster, Matlock and Ashbourne districts, gave waggons carrying coal a concession of one-third of the toll. An Act passed the next year, turnpiking the road from Chesterfield to Matlock Bridge, exempted all coal traffic entering the road from a side gate from paying toll. In 1764, when the road from Alfreton to Mansfield was made into a turnpike, the Bill contained a clause whereby coal from Blackwell colliery would only pay half toll. Two years later, when the High Moors turnpike was made over the East Moor, concessions were once more given to coal traffic. In the same year a cross-country road from Ashover to Temple Normanton was made into a turnpike, largely through the efforts of the Quaker Lead Company, which wished to improve communications between the pits along the Mansfield turnpike and their Bower's Mill lead-smelting plant.[40]

There is no doubt that coal traffic between the Derbyshire coalfield and the lead-mining areas in the Peak was heavy, even before these roads were turnpiked. One reason for this was the introduction of the Newcomen engine to clear the deeper mines of water. There were three such engines at work at Winster in 1730.[41] Shortly after this time, according to Farey, usually a most accurate witness, there were ten of these engines working at lead mines in the Peak.[42] Another was installed at Foolow by William Soresby, a Chesterfield lead merchant, in 1748.[43] The Gregory Mine partnership bought another of these engines in 1768. As the efficiency of the machines was low, their high fuel consumption must have greatly stimulated coal production. Another technical innovation was the introduction of the cupola, which used coal instead of kiln-dried wood, to smelt lead. The first of these was built at Ashover by the Quaker Lead Company, but others were constructed during the period at Kelstedge, outside Ashover, on the Sir William turnpike, and at Barber Fields, on the moors between Hathersage and Sheffield. The intensive development of the Alton seam, on the eastern margin of the coalfield, must be largely ascribed to these new markets in the Peak.

Turnpike development and increasing population undoubtedly did much to stimulate the enclosure of common land in the hundred of Scarsdale and of the wastes in the Peak. Lime was needed to bring both under cultivation. Arthur Young, on his eastern tour in 1771, noted that it was customary to use a hundred bushels of lime per acre around Chesterfield. On the infertile grits twelve horseloads per acre were used for wheat growing and as much at 350 bushels per acre was used to destroy the ling on the newly enclosed land between Chatsworth and Tideswell. As the coalfield was flanked on both east and west by limestone formations, it was easy to take fuel to the quarries and burn the stone down to lime. To the west there were kilns at Ashover, Hockley, Calver and Stoney Middleton, and to the east at Cleasby and Worksop. These kilns, in addition to supplying lime for farming, also supplied it for building.

Brickyards also provided another market for coal. Brick, as may be seen from the advertisements in the *Derby Mercury*, was replacing stone as the principal building material of the region. Successful lead merchants, such as William Soresby, who built himself 'a capital mansion house' near Saltergate in Chesterfield, and Isaac Wilkinson, who built Tapton House, outside the town, both built in brick. Even smaller houses, such as the delightful little house erected for the use of a master at Dronfield Grammar School, were built in this material. The construction of the Chesterfield Canal, for which three million bricks were made at Harthill for lining Norwood tunnel and another million at Shireoaks for building locks, must have led to a considerable demand for coal in this area at the end of the period.

Brewing was another industry which expanded during these years. Mansfield had become an important malting centre, supplying markets in Cheshire and Lancashire, and Alfreton was noted for its beer.[44] A German professor, J. F. K. Ferber, who visited Derbyshire at the end of this period described the process of making coke for malting. The coal was placed in piles about seven yards long and a foot high, with the lumps loosely packed so that the air could circulate through them. The heap was then ignited by throwing lighted coal down holes left for the purpose. The pile was then allowed to burn until it was considered that all the coal had been turned into coke, when the heap was broken up with iron bars and the fire put out.[45]

This expansion in demand was not met, as in south Yorkshire, by an enlargement of existing collieries so much as by an increase in the number of collieries at work. The pattern is similar to that of the previous century, with pits at work in almost every parish. The majority of these, where production figures are available, seem to have had an annual output of 1,000 to 2,000 tons a year. Whereas the construction of the Don Navigation tended to canalise mining along one narrow sector of the coalfield, the development of the turnpike system in Derbyshire, crossing and crisscrossing the coalfield, tended rather to open up new pits and to decentralise rather than concentrate production.

The pattern of ownership during these seventy-five years is clear. Coal mining was still dominated by the land-owning class. The part played by the aristocracy was, however, a minor one when compared with that of the gentry. These, as elsewhere in the country, were recruited both from the families whose names appear in the Tudor and Stuart heralds' visitations and from the new men, investing the profits of trade and industry in land. Both these classes provided men working collieries in the eighteenth century. Typical of them was John Bowden, who, apart from the collieries already mentioned on the Norfolk and Wentworth estates, had other pits on the Portland property at Shuttleworth, on the Duke of Leeds's estates at Todwick and on the Devonshire property at Beightonfield, Hollingwood and Inkersall in Staveley. This Catholic, descended from two of the best families in the county—his mother was an Alleyne of Wheston Hall, near Tideswell—called himself 'yeoman' and registered himself with the Derbyshire quarter sessions as owning land worth a mere 6s a year, but had considerable landed property in the hands of trustees bonded to him for rents. Altogether he must have been a very rich man, and his son, in times more peaceable for Catholics in the second half of the century, was able to acquire a large landed property in Clowne, where he built Southgate House. Of equal importance as coalmasters as the Bowdens, although the major part of their coal-mining interests was in the south of the county, were the Fletcher family. In the seventeenth century they can be traced as yeomen, living at Kilburn. In 1684 Robert Fletcher was offering Francis Stanhope, the owner of the important Zouch coal royalty at Heanor, £70 for the lease of a pit there. His two sons, John and Robert, had a lease of the coal there in 1715 for sixty-three years, and the family worked this colliery until 1766.[46] During the next half-century the brothers extended their mining operations, working collieries at Hartsay, Denby, Smalley, Shipley, Langley, Ripley and Pentrich.[47] John, who lived at Stainsby Hall, had a grant of arms in 1731; Robert, of Heanor, married the daughter and heiress of William Richardson of Smalley, another South Derbyshire coalmaster. This family first became interested in coal mining in the hundred of Scarsdale in 1728, when they leased the coal on the Coke property at Pinxton. Later, in 1758, they took a further lease of the coal on this property at South Normanton.

Other members in this same social class working collieries in Derbyshire were the Rodes of Barlborough Hall, with pits at Nitticar Hill and under the open fields of that village; the Hunlokes of Wingerworth Hall, the leading Catholic family in the district, who had a colliery alongside the Derby turnpike; the Wraggs of Stretton Hall, who were working coal on the Hunloke and Wood-yeare estates near Clay Cross; and Thomas Thoroton of Scriveton, MP for Newark (according to Reynolds, the Derbyshire antiquary, writing in 1760) after having inherited the Turner property in

Swanwick, received 'a large income from the coal mines there'.
Three other land-owning families who were mining coal at this
period, all with their roots in lead mining in the previous century,
were the Brights of Chesterfield, with a colliery at Eckington,[48] the
Gladwins of Stubbing Court, with pits at Boythorpe,[49] and the
Milnes of Dunston, with a colliery on their property there.[50]

The same situation can be found across the county border in
Yorkshire. In Handsworth three families which had risen into the
ranks of the gentry by wealth derived from either coal or lead
mining—the Staceys, the Nodders and the Fentons—were all mining
coal under their own land. The Fenton collieries on this property
and one rented from the Duke of Norfolk came by marriage into
the hands of John Rotherham of Dronfield, a member of a family
which, starting as mercers in the previous century, had become
agents to the Duke of Portland, and lead smelters and lead merchants in the early eighteenth century, investing their profits in the
purchase of the manor of Dronfield. North of Sheffield the Phipps
family were mining coal in Ecclesfield in the '40s, selling it to
Wortley Forge.[51] In the upper part of the Don valley, a series of
disputes between the Duke of Norfolk and the Bamforths of Owlerton show the latter family mining coal in the early part of the
century at Loxley, on the common between Bradfield and Wadsley.
In the middle section of the river, where it was navigable around
Rotherham, another family of landowners, the Hirsts, in possession
of a colliery advantageously sited near the Don, were selling some
15,000 waggons of coal down stream in 1774. Near Barnsley coal
mines were being worked in the first quarter of the century by such
local families of gentry as the Shippems, the Archdales and the
Elmhirsts.

The class below the gentry, that of the small landowner and
tenant farmer, too, provided much of the capital and initiative for
developing coal mining, In 1770 Peter Browne, a Staveley yeoman,
leased the pits, later held by John Bowden at Westwood, for £30 a
year and another colliery at Eastwood for £100 for the first year
of the lease and £70 annually for the remaining four years. Nine
years later, as shown by another lease at Hardwick Hall, he took
over the coal at Beightonfields, on the deep of Mastin Moor, for
£100 a year. Another family of this class, the Allwoods, had
collieries on the Devonshire property at Heath and on that of the
Earl of Scarsdale at North Wingfield. More important than either
of these in the long-term development of the Derbyshire coalfield

were the Barnes family. Joseph Barnes of Linacre Farm was mining coal on the Oxford estate at Barlow and Brampton in the first half of the century. A second member of the family, another farmer, Edmund of Leadhills, was at the same time buying coal rights in Brampton. The real founder of the family fortunes, however, was John Barnes of Holme Hall, a man with a multitude of business interests in addition to coal mining. He farmed land—both his own and rented—on a large scale at Holme Hall, Ashgate, and Chander Hill in Ashgate. According to a memorandum written by one of his descendants he exchanged coal against an equal weight of bones, which he crushed at a windmill on his farm. In addition, he was a timber merchant, buying and felling standing timber and selling bark to the local tanners—of which there were a large number in Chesterfield, Sheffield and Rotherham—and sawn timber to local joiners and wheelwrights. Finally, to add to this total, he ran a brickworks. In the '40s he was mining coal at Barlow on the Oxford estate. In 1756 he bought seventy acres of land at Ashgate and another thirty at Newbold, under which to get coal; in 1763 he leased another pit at Barlow; in 1765 he leased from the Duke of Devonshire 'that delph of coal lying within and under the North side of Chatsworth Park' and in the same year he leased another colliery from the duke at Heath. The deeds of the Coke family of Pinxton contain a number of coal leases to farmers on this property; John Stones, a tenant farmer on the Oxford property at Brampton, rented a colliery on his farm; on the Wentworth property in Yorkshire leases show William Beaumont, husbandman, and Farham, a tenant renting over 150 acres, in possession of pits at Tankersley and at Westwood respectively.

Compared with these classes, the production controlled by the aristocracy was small indeed. The Duke of Devonshire was working a colliery on the Hardwick estate during the first half of the century which, when leased in 1749, was valued at £300. Over the Yorkshire border, the Duke of Leeds took over a colliery on his property at Woodall Moor from a local farmer who had gone bankrupt and found himself in York gaol in consequence. Its output in 1740–41 was 2,500 loads. At a later date two more collieries worked by the duke at Todwick Common and at Wales had a total sale of coal in 1765 of £430. On the Wentworth estate the policy during the first half of the century was to lease the coal, but in 1752, after a visit to the Duke of Bridgewater's colliery at Worsley, the Marquis of Rockingham took over a small colliery at Elsecar, largely for the purpose of burning the lime which was brought down the Don to Kilnhurst from the magnesian limestone scarp near Brotherton. Other lime kilns at Hoober were supplied with coal from a number of shallow pits at Braithwaite and Swinton Common. In 1763, on the death of the lessee, the marquis began to work a larger colliery at Law Wood. At this time twenty-two colliers were employed here and eight at Elsecar. Coal from Law Wood was also used to burn bricks and pantiles for estate use. Of interest, if not of any real economic importance, were the efforts of the marquis to supply his town house in Grosvenor Square and his estate at Higham in Northamptonshire with coal mined on his Wentworth property. The coal was first sent by barge to Thorne, where it was placed in larger keels for shipment to Hull. There it was forwarded by collier to London or Lynn. These areas were normally supplied by the north-eastern coalfield, and as these shipments were from the cost standpoint uneconomic they can be regarded as a relic of feudalism, the determination of a great nobleman to use the products of his own estate, rather than an attempt to break into new markets.[52]

The colliery lease underwent considerable change during this period. In the early years of the century the typical lease on the Devonshire, Manvers, Portland, Norfolk and Newcastle estates[53] contained a fixed rent without any reference to the amount of coal mined. The interest of the landowner, however, continued to be protected by clauses stipulating the maximum number of hewers to be employed and the number of shafts to be worked at any one time. As an example, the lease between the Duke of Devonshire and Peter Browne, drawn up in 1700 for the colliery at Staveley Westwood, may be quoted. Browne was restricted to working two shafts at any one time, limited to employing not more than the usual number of men and bound by a bond of £600 not to use any mining methods whereby 'the said mines may be sooner wrought out or rendered the less beneficial'. With the expansion in coal output brought about by the improvement in communications, landowners and their lawyers began to draft leases under which there was some definite relationship between output and the royalty paid by the coalmaster. The normal practice on the Wentworth property in the second half of the century was a fixed payment per hewer. This varied from colliery to colliery. The amount stipulated was probably arrived at by a consideration of all the factors which governed profitableness—the thickness and number of the seams, the depth worked and the situation of the colliery in relation to markets and communications. The royalty on each hewer at Fenton's Basing-thorpe colliery, situated alongside the Don, was £40 10s 0d in 1762. At Richard Bingley's Law Wood colliery, where although there was a thick seam of good coal the pit was a considerable distance from water transport, the payment per hewer in that year was seventeen guineas. At Parkin's Bolsterstone pit, working a thin seam in a sparsely populated district, it was only £3 10s 0d. On the Coke property at South Normanton, probably influenced by what was customary practice in south Derbyshire and Nottinghamshire, fifteen acres of coal were leased to Goodere Fletcher in 1758 at a royalty of 1s 6d a stack.[54]

The fairest system—and one which virtually replaced all others during the early railway age—was that in which royalties were calculated on the acreage of coal extracted. In addition to the virtue of fairness between the two parties it offered another advantage in that it was both cheap and simple to operate, the only operation needed being an annual scaling by a surveyor. The first example discovered of this type of lease is one for coal under the Ogston estate, dated 1742, in which the lessees were to pay £42 for each acre of coal mined. This lease is also of particular importance in that it contains a clause whereby a minimum annual payment of £45 was stipulated, a practice which again became general during the early railway age. Another example, twenty years later, between Anne Cartledge of Dronfield and Anthony Gallimore, whereby the former was to sink two shafts and make a sough at Dore, provides for a coal rent of £60 per acre.[55] In 1765 John Barnes of Ashgate leased the Top Hard seam on the Hardwick estate and a poorer coal at Brampton from the Duke of Portland. In the first case the royalty to the Duke of Devonshire was £120 per acre and in the second the coal rent was £40 per acre. Despite its advantages, the acreage lease did not, however, completely replace the older type, examples of which can be found at a much later date.

In a few cases the landowner agreed to meet a part of the initial costs of mining development. On the Wentworth property, when Richard Bingley leased Elsecar colliery in 1752, he was allowed to work the coal free of royalty for two years provided he cleaned out a sough, constructed by a previous tenant, as far as Elsecar Green and continued it as far as 'the foot of the coal now lying . . . in a certain close . . . situate in Hoyland . . . called the great arm royd'. In the same year another collier submitted a proposal to the Marquis of Rockingham to make a boring for coal at Hooton Roberts, in which it was suggested that he should not pay any rent for the first two years. On the same estate £50 was paid in 1761 to the tenant of Elsecar Colliery towards the cost of extending a sough. In the 1765 lease mentioned above between Barnes and the Duke of Devonshire the latter was to pay the cost of the sough for draining the Hardwick coal. In his other lease of the same year Barnes was allowed to mine six acres of coal without payment as an allowance towards driving a sough from the bottom of Brampton Moor.

Information as to the amount of capital engaged in coal mining is, unfortunately, sparse. It is conspicuously absent for the more important owners, such as the Fentons. What exists relates almost entirely to the smaller collieries. In 1716 Thomas Wentworth leased to John Green of Swinton, yeoman, the coal on the west side of Wath Common at a rent of £15 for the first year, when only one pit employing three men and three boys was to be at work, and of £30 for the remaining six years of the lease, when two pits would be in operation. Green sub-leased the two pits to working miners, but the lease had to be surrendered when the sough became stopped up. An inventory made at this time shows the meagre equipment needed in the early decades of the century for coal mining—thirty pit props, four corves, three pairs of turnstakes, a fire pan, trunks and a pair of bellows for ventilation, a hurrying hook, planks and footboards—the whole valued at about £9. An inventory of Woodall Moor Colliery, made in 1740, at the time of its transfer to the Duke of Leeds, shows the amount of capital invested in a colliery capable of producing well over 2,500 loads a year—corves, sledges, hammers, mandrels, dressers, axes, saws, wedges, a fire pan and bank hooks were valued at £85, pumping machinery at £63—a total, with other items, of about £200. In 1754 a colliery on the Wentworth property at Braithwaite was sold for £115. Three years later, when the coal on the north side of Swanwick Hall was worked out, Anthony Tissington estimated the cost of sinking a new colliery on the south side of the house at £700, with an additional £1,100 for a Newcomen engine.[56] In 1767 another colliery working the Alton seam at Barber Fields, outside Sheffield, was sold for £57.[57] John Barnes spent £130 on sinking pits and making a sough at Heath Colliery before it came into production in 1767. It is obvious that the capital needed to begin coal mining during this period was not large, a fact which largely explains why the industry was so much in the hands of individuals, whereas contemporary lead mining and iron smelting, which demanded much larger initial investment, were almost entirely in the hands of partnerships.

Information as to the profits made during this period, again, mostly relates to the smaller collieries. One owned by the Duke of Leeds at Kiveton, selling coke as well as coal for making bricks, made a profit of £125 between September 1718 and February 1719. A much larger concern, that in the Park at Sheffield, was, according to the Duke of Norfolk, selling coal in 1725 to the value of £1200, and £400 of this was profit. In 1730, when the colliery was worked by the duke, almost exactly the same amount of coal was sold but the profit realised was only £276.[58] The Bowden account book for Todwick colliery shows that sales averaged £400 to £500 annually from 1720 to 1734 and that the pits made about £80 a year profit. In 1747, when D'Ewes Coke, the owner of the Pinxton property, was heavily in debt, he drew up a balance sheet of his assets, in which he included the value of his colliery, which he estimated at that time to bring in £400 a year. As part of his plan to free himself from his encumbrances and to settle the property on his son George he proposed to lease the colliery to Goodere Fletcher, who was to expand production to 4,000 loads annually, which, it was estimated, would bring in a profit of £1,000 a year. Near by, at Swanwick, Anthony Tissington, when planning his new colliery there in 1757, considered that it would make an annual profit of £600. On the Wentworth estate Law Wood Colliery, in 1753, cleared £140 in selling 558 pit loads—about 2,800 tons; in 1756 Elsecar sold 2,200 dozen cf coal—about 4,500 tons—and made a profit of £160; a colliery on Swinton Common made a profit of £200 on 1,521 dozen in the first eight months of the next year; and at the end of the Seven Years' War Law Wood and Elsecar realised £777 profit. At Heath John Barnes, in the years between 1768 and 1775, just cleared his expenses. His methods of accounting, however, hide a substantial profit in that he charged the colliery with a management fee of £20, drawn by himself, as well as 5 per cent interest on the capital he had invested in sinking the colliery initially, and on the money employed as circulating capital in the business during these years. There is, therefore, every reason to believe that coal mining was a most profitable activity in this period.

Coalmasters such as Barnes, the Fletchers and the Bowdens obviously managed their own pits. The only example of a paid manager discovered during this period is Thomas Smith, employed on the Wentworth estate at a salary of £20 in addition to the wages of an ordinary workman. Generally speaking, the mining problems encountered could be dealt with by men native to the coalfield. On two occasions at least, however, engineers had to be called in from outside to solve problems too difficult for the Derbyshire or Yorkshire miner. In the early part of the century the collieries belonging to the Archdale and Shippem families on Barnsley Moor ran into serious trouble with water. Wortley, the ground landlord, who had big mining interests on the north-eastern coalfield, called in two Durham viewers to advise on draining the pits.[59] In 1771 the steward of the Townley collieries in Lancashire came to Sheffield to advise on the future development of the Duke of Norfolk's Handsworth colliery, then leased to the Rev. Mr Stacey of Ballifield.

In general the technique of coal mining shows little advance on the methods in use during the previous century until the end of this period. There was in fact little necessity for any change, as coal could still be mined in large enough quantities to satisfy the demands of the market from shallow pits. The shafts at Whittington Moor Colliery were only six yards deep; those at Hardstoft were eight yards; at Barnes Heath Colliery they were sixteen yards and at Beightonfield they were twenty yards deep. Across the Yorkshire border, in the third quarter of the century, the pits at Elsecar, Ecclesall and Basingthorpe were fifteen, fourteen and twenty-five yards deep respectively. As a result it was more economic to mine coal by sinking a large number of shafts than to drive long headings into the coal. 'A Scratch of Jonathon Swift's Colliery' at Darnall, drawn probably at some date prior to 1750, shows five shafts; the same number are shown on a plan of Elsecar Colliery made in 1757;[60] another of Westwood Colliery at Tankersley, made in the same year, shows the whole of the wood scored with the remains of old shafts;[61] seven pits were sunk at Ecclesall in 1758; the accounts of the Duke of Leeds' collieries at Wales and Todwick show that nine pits were sunk there in 1765; a map of Sheffield Park, now in the Norfolk estate office, shows seven pits at work in 1765; a plan of Fentons' Basingthorpe colliery, drawn in the same year, shows four pits in operation, and another plan made in 1776, after a Newcomen engine had been installed to drain the coal to a depth of eighty yards, shows the whole area to be one mass of old pits which had been filled in, with coal then being mined from ten separate shafts.[62] Evidence from Derbyshire tells a similar story. Bowden, for example, sank seven pits at Beightonfield between 1703 and 1707; John Barnes, in evidence against William Soresby, who amongst his many business activities was agent to the Oxford property in Derbyshire and who was accused of having abused his position to grant himself advantageous leases, declared that he had sunk no fewer than eighty-five pits at Barlow between 1726 and 1743;[63] six shafts were sunk at Heath Colliery from 1766 to 1770. It seems, indeed to have been normal mining practice to begin to sink a new shaft immediately production began in its predecessor.

Leases and accounts of workings suggest that most collieries were worked by two shafts, one on the basset and the other on the deep of the coal. In the larger collieries two or more pits were worked simultaneously. Such a layout made ventilation simple, especially where a fire lamp was employed. Where levels were longer, separate wind pits were sunk to the workings. The first chimney built on top of the air shaft to improve ventilation was probably at Beightonfield as early as 1700. Gas does not seem to have been a serious problem at this period, and when met with it was driven out by installing trunks—pipes constructed out of wooden boards—through which air was blown by bellows into the pit.

Coal was extracted, as is shown by the numerous references to benks, endings and gobs in colliery accounts, by a method which was to disappear only in the Victorian era, known as narrow work.[64] In this a bord or level was cut transversely to the grain of the coal and from this endings or roads were cut at intervals of thirty yards against the end of the coal. When these endings had been carried the requisite distance on either side of the main level, a communication was established between their extremities and the coal worked by short faces, leaving behind a goaf—or, as the accounts write it, a gob. In Derbyshire, at least at the beginning of the century, some coal was mined by the board and pillar method, as is evident from the remarks of Celia Fiennes when visiting the Chesterfield district[65] and from an account of land to be sold at Newbold Fields c. 1720, which declares that it was the normal Derbyshire practice to 'leave about a third of the coal to support the roof'. It seems probable, however, that most Derbyshire collieries were adopting the more economic 'narrow work' at the end of this period. Explosives do not seem to have been widely used, although there are references to their purchase in the Bowden accounts in 1700 and in an inventory of Swanwick Hall in 1744. After the hewer had extracted the coal, the coal baskets or corves were filled by his mate and then 'hurried' to the bottom of the shaft —sometimes through post holes, i.e. roads cut diagonally through the ribs of coal separating the benks—by a barrower. In a few of the

Barnsley Bed collieries, where a nine-foot seam was being worked, horses were used to drag the corves or sledges to the pit bottom. Gins, in most cases driven by horses, were used to haul the coal up the shaft. Sometimes these were in charge of girls, who seem to have been restricted to this work alone on the coalfield. Barnsley Colliery seems to have been unique in its use of water power for raising coal, if the 'water gin, house and ropes' mentioned in an inventory of 1713 refer to a haulage engine.

Drainage throughout the period was mainly by sough. Little information is available as to the cost or extent. John Barnes, in the case previously referred to, declared that he had spent £500 on a sough at Barlow; proposals were put forward to construct a sough at Barnsley Moor in 1716, 900 yards long and costing £1,000, but it is doubtful if anything came of the plan; Sheffield Colliery was drained in 1773 by a sough a mile and a half long, flowing into the Sheaf. Barnsley Colliery, again, seems to have been unique in its employment of a wind gin for pumping. This, however, was not sufficiently powerful to drain the pits on the moor, and Shippem suggested to Wortley that he should install a 'Newcastle gin' for this purpose. These is no evidence that it was ever erected. Probably the first Newcomen engine to be erected in south Yorkshire was that which William Spencer of Bramley Grange contracted to build in 1735 'for the draining and recovery of the coals' at Carr House 'as well as those lying within the Precincts of Kimberworth as those coals also which lye within Greasborough Bierley' by raising water from the Thick Coal to a sough driven through to the Don.[66] As the only 'fire engine' shown on Dickinson's 'New and Current Map of the South Part of the County of York' published in 1750 is at Carr House, and as Bowden, who took over Spencer's colliery in 1742, is included in a list of three Newcomen engine owners at Greasborough, printed in the *Gentleman's Magazine* in 1763—the others were Hirst and Fenton—it may fairly be assumed that Spencer did fulfil the terms of his contract in this respect. It is probable that another Newcomen engine was installed at Darnall Colliery about the same time.[67] Evidence as to the introduction of the 'fire engine' into the North Derbyshire section of the coalfield is, unfortunately, as indirect as that for Yorkshire, but it seems from a comparison of the first accurate map of Derbyshire to be printed —Burdett's Survey of Derbyshire, 1762-67—and Brindley's survey for the Chesterfield to Stockwith canal made in 1769, that the first was installed at Staveley at some time between those dates. It is

highly probable that it was erected by either John or Henry
Bowden, as the former had leased the Devonshire coal there in
1756. Another Newcomen engine was at work at what a German
visitor to the county described as one of its largest collieries, at
Alfreton, in 1775.[68]

The miner himself remains, during this period, a shadowy, in-
distinct figure. One thing, however, is certain, that in numbers he
was not, as he was to become during the railway age, the dominant
social type in the region. The number of hewers at various collieries
—two at Westwood, four at Cortwood and four at Bolsterstone in
1755, and twelve at Carrhouse, seven at Law Wood and sixteen at
Basingthorpe in 1759—shows that throughout the area the miner
was everywhere outnumbered by the agricultural population.
Indeed, an examination of the land system of the coalfield and a
comparison of it with that of the magnesian limestone district
to the east bring out the high proportion of very small holdings
throughout the coalfield, suggesting that the collier, like the nailer
and the edge tool worker, was probably a landholder himself. It is
certain that the majority of the miners were natives of the area in
which they worked, as the Poor Law certificates in such typical
mining parishes as Attercliffe, Staveley, Brampton and Barlow show
only a thin trickle of movement into these parishes, and in almost
all cases such migration was from a narrowly restricted region.

Almost everywhere the collier worked as a member of a group.
The 'butty system', whereby one man contracted with the coalmaster to drive headings at so much per yard or to get coal at so
much per ton, was strongly established. As an example, at the Duke
of Leed's Todwick Common Colliery in 1765, Allen & Co. were
paid 3s for each three quarters of coal got, 3d a yard for filling pits,
half a crown a yard for driving headings and a penny each for recovering pit props. Wages were paid either fortnightly or monthly.
Such a system renders it almost impossible to ascertain a collier's
real wages or to compare them with those of other workers. In addition, the miner enjoyed many perquisites. The sinkers were given sod
ale when a new shaft was started and pricking ale when it reached
the coal; ale was also given when a gin was moved; a colliers'
feast was an annual event at Elsecar; colliery accounts contain items
for Christmas presents; many coalmasters provided flannel for pit
clothes; free coal, coal at reduced price or a money payment in
lieu were everywhere provided. Probably many coalmasters felt, like
Bowden, that it was all an intolerable burden and that colliers, like

other workmen, should be satisfied with wages, but, as he wrote in his account book, there was no evading it or 'else they pretend their custom'.

## Acknowledgements

I should like to thank all who have made this article possible. Major T. Wragg, Keeper of the Collections at Chatsworth, made it possible to see material there and at Hardwick. I owe much to the kindness of the staff at the Norfolk estate office in Sheffield. Mr Stitt, then archivist at Shire Hall, Nottingham, facilitated access to sections of the Portland MSS, then uncatalogued. As always, Miss Meredith and the staff in the Local History Department of Sheffield City Library have aided my work in every way possible. Finally, I wish to thank the Earl of Wharncliffe and the Trustees of the Fitzwilliam Settled Estates for permission to use their MSS deposited at Sheffield Library.

## Notes

1  Water did not become a serious problem on the South Yorkshire coalfield until 1877; *vide* H. Saul's articles, 'Water levels for mine drainage', *Colliery Engineering* (1936), pp. 203-6, 'Outcrop water on the South Yorkshire coalfield', *Trans. Mid. Institute Mining Engineers* (1937), pp. 64–67.

2  Barlborough Hall MSS.

3  Crewe muniments, No. 372, Sheffield City Library.

4  Portland MSS, 73/1, Shire Hall, Nottingham.

5  Ronksley MSS, No. 12110, Sheffield City Library.

6  Lawrence Stone, 'An Elizabethan coal mine', *Economic History Review*, III, 1, pp. 97-106.

7  Star Chamber proceedings Jas. I, 139/20.

8  *Collecteana Dakeynæ*, X, p. 345, Derby County Council offices.

9  T. Walter Hall, *The Park in the city of Sheffield*, p. 100.

10  Sir George Reresby Sitwell, *The Hurts of Haldworth*, ch. XI.

11  Wharncliffe deeds, Nos. 344–53, Sheffield City Library.

12  'A breviate of the survey of the 31 townships within the hundred of Scarsdale, 1641–61', Portland MSS, Shire Hall, Nottingham.

13  T. Walter Hall, *Worsborough, Sheffield and Eckington*, p. 71.

14  Calendar of Committee for Compounding, p. 1735.

15  Glapwell MSS, Derbyshire County Council offices.

16  Newbold case for arbitration, 1688, No. 1701, Derby Borough Library.

17  W. Senior, 'Plans of the estates belonging to Wm. Cavendish, Earl of Newcastle, 1629–32', Welbeck Abbey MSS.

18  *Natural history of Staffordshire*, pp. 135–6.

19  *D.A.J.*, XXXI, pp. 221–3.

20  'A Derbyshire Visitation manuscript, 1687', *D.A.J.*, XXXII, p. 69.

21  R. Johnson, 'An ancient Swanwick coal mine', *D.A.J.*, LXXIII, pp. 114–21.

22  Barlow leases, No. 34, Portland MSS, Shire Hall, Nottingham.

23 Sir John Bright's papers concerning Handsworth, Wentworth Woodhouse MSS, Br. 52/6, Sheffield City Library.
24 Reynold's Derbyshire notes, Bagshawe collection, 12/2/17, John Rylands University Library of Manchester.
25 Andrew Clayton *v.* Duke of Newcastle concerning the administration of the Welbeck estate, D.D. 2.P. 24/73, Portland MSS, Shire Hall, Nottingham.
26 Wentworth Woodhouse MSS, Br. 45, Sheffield City Library.
27 John Bigland, *History of the County of York* (1811), p. 817. (The statement has been challenged.)
28 Richard Blome, *Britannia* (1673).
29 Sharlston Colliery was leased by Thomas Stringer in 1664 for a period of seven years for a rent of over £1,000 annually; the Strelley colliery made a profit of over £10,000 from 1654 to 1667; the importance of mining at Woolaton is shown in HMC, Middleton MSS.
30 Journals of the House of Commons, XXII, 456, 458 and 467.
31 Journals of the House of Commons, XXIX, 712, 796, 915 and 971.
32 *A Short Tour of the Midland Counties of England performed in the summer of 1772*, pp. 41–2.
33 'List of common carriers of coal to the river Calder', Bretton Hall MSS, Yorkshire Archæological Society, Leeds.
34 Bundle 116 (Barnsley Canal), Bretton Hall MSS.
35 Ronksley collection, No. 1587, Sheffield City Library.
36 *Magna Brittannia et Hibernia*, VI, p. 448 (1730), and *Travels in England*, letter II (1761), MD, 1769, Sheffield City Library.
37 British Museum, Add. MSS, 6692, p. 180.
38 'The Humble Petition of the Town of Sheffield' in Tibbitt's collection, No. 362, Sheffield City Library, and 'Petition respecting the Chesterfield turnpike', in Bagshawe collection, 13/3/296, John Rylands University Library of Manchester.
39 'Case on behalf of the Bill . . . for repairing the road from Chesterfield in Derbyshire to the town of Mansfield', n.d.
40 A. Raistrick, *Quakers in science and industry*, pp. 184–5.
41 'Dr Clegg, minister and physician', *D.A.J.*, XXXV, p. 28.
42 Farey's *Agriculture and Minerals of Derbyshire*, I, p. 338.
43 Wheat collection, 530/5, letter dated 10 June 1748, Sheffield City Library.
44 *The Universal Magazine*, October 1748.
45 J. F. K. Ferber, *Versuch einer Dryktographie von Derbyshire* (1776), p. 43.
46 Charlton of Chilwell MSS, Shire Hall, Nottingham.
47 John Fletcher *v.* Francis Barber, 'Accounts for sale of coal, 1713–55', parcel CXCV, Bemrose collection, Derby Borough Library.
48 Eckington rental, D 46, Fairbank collection, Sheffield City Library.
49 Crewe MSS, No. 1139, Sheffield City Library.
50 Beauchief MSS, No. 905, Sheffield City Library.
51 Accounts of carriage, No. 27, Cannon Hall MSS, Sheffield City Library.
52 Wentworth Woodhouse muniments, R 174/23, 'Calculation of the expences attending a chald. Coals from the river Humber to Lynn and thence to Higham up the Nothampton river'.

53  Rents of the Duke of Newcastle, 1737–74, British Museum, Add. MSS, 33165.
54  A stack was 74 in. long, 46 in. high and 57 in. wide.
55  Deed No. 37/2, Brookhill Hall, Pinxton.
56  Turner MSS, Flintham Hall, Nottinghamshire.
57  Tibbitt's collection, No. 830, Sheffield City Library.
58  William Ellis's account for Sheffield Colliery, 1730–1, deed box 25, Norfolk estate office, Sheffield.
59  Barnsley Moor Collieries, 1705–26; Wharncliffe muniments, No. 114, Sheffield City Library.
60  F.B. 12, pp. 58–65, Fairbank collection, Sheffield City Library.
61  F.B. 12, p. 67, Fairbank collection.
62  F.B. Supp. 40, pp. 2–7, and F.B. Supp. 46, p. 4, Fairbank collection.
63  Henrietta, Countess Dowager of Oxford v. W. Soresby, Jackson collection, No. 1285, Sheffield City Library.
64  Parkin Jeffcock, 'On coal and iron mining in south Yorkshire', *Proceedings of the Institute of Mechanical Engineers*, (April 1862).
65  *The Journeys of Celia Fiennes*, ed. Morris, p. 96.
66  Wentworth Woodhouse deeds, No. 1727, Sheffield City Library.
67  John Needham's map of the colliery on Darnall Common, Wheat collection, No. 1751, Sheffield City Library.
68  Ferber, *op. cit.* p. 40.

G. D. B. GRAY

# 2 The South Yorkshire coalfield

*The evolution of coal mining*

1. *Medieval coal mining.* Historically, the exploitation of coal came much later than that of either lead or iron. It is likely that the presence of this mineral was betrayed by some plough or else was seen as a black band along the foot of a scarp face. In any case the coal seams crop out along the valleys of the many streams for the region shows a marked degree of dissection. Whether the Romans worked coal here matters little. Much later, however, there was a deliberate attempt to work some of the seams. In 1293 two men lost their lives mining coal near Rotherham, whilst another unfortunate labourer was killed in a primitive form of bellpit at Silkstone, near Barnsley in the early years of the fourteenth century.[1] About 1370 several leases and grants for coal working at Cortworth, near Wentworth, were given to the Fitzwilliam family.[2] Again, in 1491 the Cluniac monks of Pontefract acquired a coal pit at Barnsley for £8 and the life of the mine was estimated at sixteen years.[3]

A word of caution is here necessary for south Yorkshire is not exceptional in having historical proof of early coal workings. With the opening of the thirteenth century most of the British coalfields were being scratched on the surface. One must, therefore, guard against producing a distorted picture from the many scattered references in the past. Indeed, the industry of medieval times was simply for local use and the output would amount to a few thousand tons at the most. It is almost certain that the method of working was by a short adit, a day-hole or later by a shallow vertical shaft. The actual mining itself was frequently a seasonal occupation when the men and horses were free after harvest. Following Mumford and Geddes we can call this the eotechnic stage of development during which period the major seams were being probed.

2. *Coal mining in the early seventeenth century.* It is now a well known fact of economic history that during the period 1550–1650 there was a minor 'industrial revolution' in Britain. Coal output for the whole country has been estimated to have increased from 200,000 tons to about 3 million tons. By this time techniques had improved and adits reached 200 yards in some cases, whilst shallow mines of 120 ft were quite common. South Yorkshire likewise shared in this expansion and there are many references to mines and coal workings near Barnsley, at Silkstone, Cudworth, Ardsley and Thurnscoe, as well as near Rotherham and Sheffield.[4] These have been plotted on fig. 2.1 for both West and South Yorkshire.

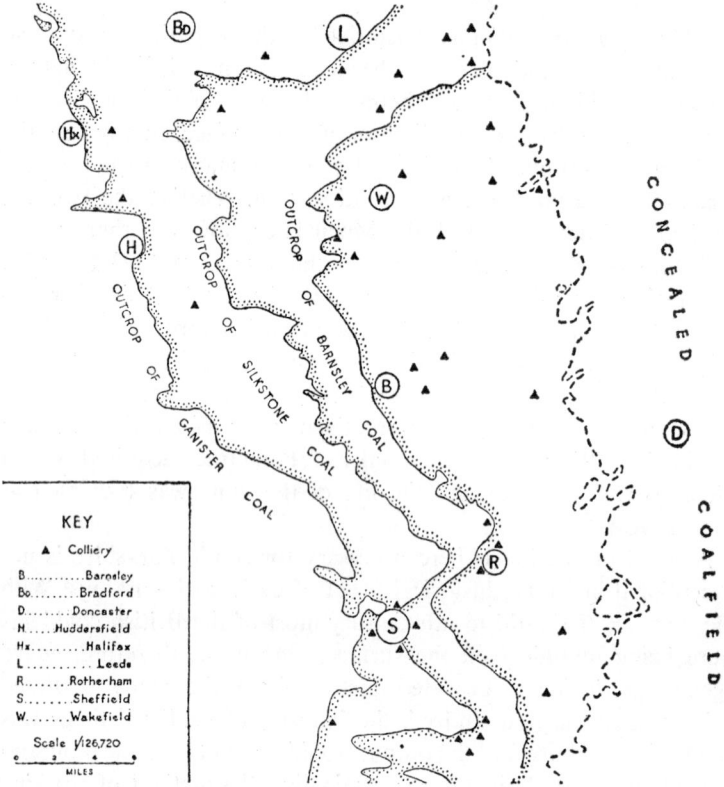

Fig. 2.1   Yorkshire collieries in the seventeenth century

In the seventeenth century the region fell within the category of 'landsale' districts for it had no navigable waterways and no seaports. The Don and Dearne were useless because as yet there were no canals. The coal was consumed locally and went by land on the back of a pack-horse or in a cart. Working took place along the outcrop which suggests that 'day holes' or open-cast working was the rule. Shafts were being dug, and 5,000 tons was a large tonnage from one shaft. As a matter of fact, 'certain cole delphes lying in Waleswood', south of Rotherham, had an output in 1599 of 2,000 tons. This tonnage can be drawn in one day at a modern mine. It is worthy of note that the collieries farther south near the navigable Trent at Wollaton and Strelley had very much larger outputs (30,000 to 50,000 tons). West Yorkshire too had more mines and probably a greater output.

Perhaps this period has been stressed in the past as one of a search for the technique of using coal to smelt iron. This was only part of a greater problem, that of using coal to refine and heat metals and to burn in the home as well as to smelt ores. Wood and charcoal were much in use and the Weald was not the only part of Britain to suffer from deforestation. Harrison in his survey of the manor of Sheffield in 1637 speaks of trees being cut down in the Park. The Steward's account for the previous year for the Norfolk estates contains an item for 'cutting and rivinge old roots and other old wood into cords', and money disbursed, 'for the newe cole myne on the Park Hill topp and thereabouts, more than the profitts of the coles there come to this year £8 19s 6d'.[5]

As yet, the steel makers relied on charcoal, but coal could be used for heating wrought iron. Generally speaking, this period sees the slow transition from the eotechnic to the palaeotechnic stage.

3. *The industrial revolution of the eighteenth and nineteenth centuries.* Prior to this phase, coal mining had left but a faint trace on the geography of south Yorkshire. It was during the eighteenth and nineteenth centuries that larger and deeper mines came into existence and worked the main seams of the exposed part of the coalfield.

Development depended on three factors during this period:

1 The improvements in the techniques of mining.
2 The increased demand for coal by a growing coal industry and by the homes.
3 The development of better communications, which widened the market of south Yorkshire.

Developments in mining technique in south Yorkshire kept pace with those in other coalfields. A Newcomen engine was introduced at Fenton's Colliery, near Chapeltown, in 1753. Underground haulage improved and some pioneer work was carried out by John Curr, the viewer at the Duke of Norfolk's Sheffield collieries. He invented, in 1787, wooden corves to replace the wicker baskets in the winding shaft; fitted guides to prevent the corves from bumping against the sides. He later introduced a flat winding rope. Interesting though it is, we cannot pursue this fascinating subject here.

During the early part of this period the demand for coal increased for both industrial and domestic purposes. Prior to 1820 the Duke of Norfolk had the monopoly of coal in Sheffield. In 1728 the duke sought to raise the price of coal, but since the road was 'intolerable bad' he first desired to mend it. This created a riot, for the Sheffielders of the day naturally thought the cost would fall on them. Later in 1774 cries were again raised against the high price of fuel.[6] These the duke sought to placate by conveying coal from the Park colliery by a 'railway'. The cost was £3,000, but the scheme was denounced and the track wrecked, though later it was relaid and used. Incidentally there is a striking commentary on the state of the roads at this time, for in 1795 leading coal merchants opened a colliery at Dore House, Handsworth, only three and a half miles from the centre of Sheffield, but after a few years it had to be closed on account of transport difficulties. A great demand for coke was created by the cast-iron phase of the metallurgical industry between 1750 and 1850. Firms like Samuel Walker of Masbrough, Rotherham, and Newton Chambers of Sheffield and later Chapeltown are associated. Coal was turned into gas and coke and used to smelt the coal-measure ironstones and thereby produce cast iron. By 1857 there were sixteen blast furnaces in south Yorkshire, with eleven in blast. They were located at Chapeltown, Elsecar, Rotherham and Parkgate. Actually Samuel Walker moved from Sheffield to Holmes, Rotherham, in 1746 and was therefore nearer to the bell pits of the ironstone outcrop. Newtown and Chambers fired their first blast furnace at Chapletown in 1795, and the foundry moved from Sheffield to Chapeltown in 1802. They found coal and ironstone in close proximity and subsequently transformed the Blackburn valley and the Chapeltown district. These local ironstones were being raised as late at 1875, when the output from Elsecar and Chapeltown amounted to over 50,000 tons.

Better roads were built during the turnpike era (1740–1826) in south Yorkshire. As early as 1726 the Doncaster–Tinsley canal Bill was passed, and the Don navigation was improved to Tinsley by 1751. The short distance from the Tinsley Wharf to Sheffield (three miles) was completed in 1819. The Dearne and Don canal Bill passed in 1792, and both the Dove valley at Worsborough and the Elsecar valley had canals about 1800. The opening of these canals and the development of new roads saw the opening of more collieries, and the coming of the railways in the middle of the nineteenth century improved transport facilities still further.

It was in 1838 that the Sheffield to Rotherham railway was built to meet the North Midland Railway, which was eventually constructed from Leeds to Derby via Rotherham in 1840. Between 1850, when the Great Northern entered King's Cross, and the year 1864 there was a veritable freight war between the Great Northern and the Midland as they both competed for the transport of South Yorkshire coal to the metropolitan market.

*Distribution of collieries in 1855*

A clear picture of the distribution of the collieries can be obtained for this date, since the statistics of the Home Office, kept by a certain J. Hunt, are available. As many as eighty-one collieries are listed in our area, and these have been plotted on fig. 2.2. It can truly be said that Barnsley was the coal capital at this time, and by far the greatest number of pits are situated between the Barnsley and Silkstone outcrops. Actually, half the total output of 2·8 million tons came from these two seams (1·1 million tons from the Barnsley seam and 0·43 million tons from the Silkstone). Other seams which were worked at this time were the Thorncliffe, Lidgett, Flockton and Swallow Wood (Haigh Moor). Looking more closely, the mines were actually to be found some three miles east of the Barnsley outcrop, which shows a distinct 'down the dip' movement of coal undertakings, and the deeper mines at this time were about 1,000 ft in depth. Comparing this map with one showing the railways, roads and canals of the period, it is apparent that the mines are all placed very closely to some means of communication. To facilitate this a 'waggon line' was constructed in some cases. Many of these are marked on old maps along the many side valleys of the district, as, for example, along the subsequent valley which flows eastwards into the Don at Kilnhurst and along both the Blackburn brook and the Greasbrough valleys.

A further point to notice is that the deeper parts of the field—the Frickley and Maltby troughs—were avoided at this time for a combination of technical and financial reasons. Prior to this date no

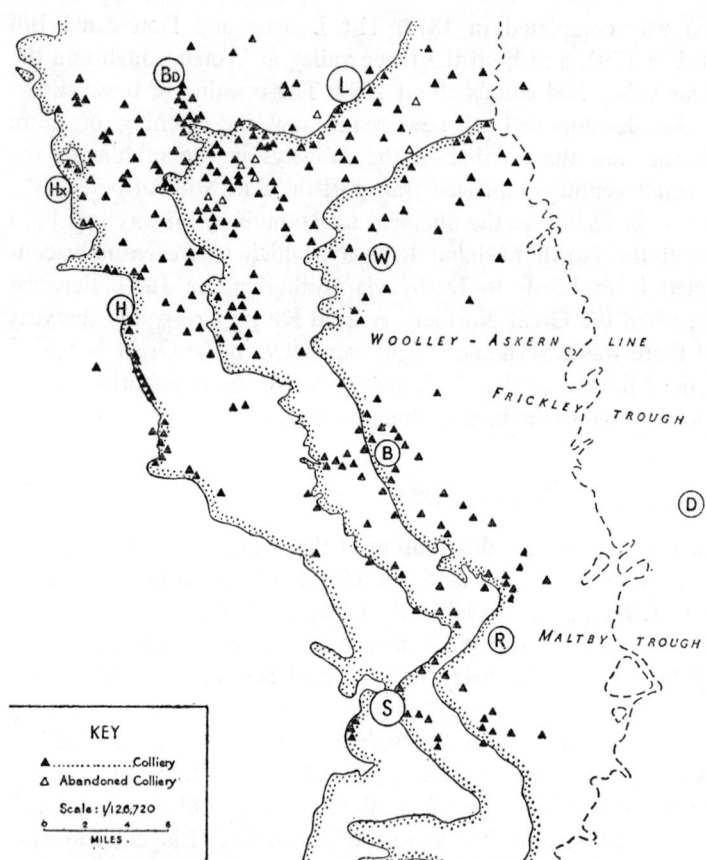

FIG. 2.2 Yorkshire collieries in 1855

mines had been sunk into the concealed coalfield of south Yorkshire, although the Duke of Newcastle had found the Barnsley seam
at 1,530 ft and about 3 ft 10 in. in thickness at Shireoaks, near
Worksop, in 1854. It is also worth noticing that a number of small
workings are seen to be dotted along the outcrop of the ganister
coal, where thin coal, clays and ganisters were worked.

Finally it may be pointed out that the Woolley to Askern zone
can be discerned at this period. Incidentally, west Yorkshire stands
out as a most important field, for it had in 1855 as many as 252
mines which produced 5 million tons, an output almost twice that
of south Yorkshire.

By 1870 the industrial momentum of south Yorkshire showed a
marked increase by over 60 per cent to a total of 4·4 million tons

from 108 mines. Many of the collieries of the exposed coalfield, which are even today large producers, date from this period— Manvers Main, 1870; Denaby, 1866; Cadeby, 1893. In comparison, west Yorkshire still led, having 308 mines and an output of 6·25 million tons, as against 4·4 million tons for our region.

## Distribution of collieries in 1895

A glance at figs. 2.2 and 2.3 definitely shows several changes between 1855 and 1895:

1 A most pronounced eastward shift, the newer mines being deeper, hotter and requiring greater capital expenditure.
2 Mines are situated in the deeper part of the Frickley trough.

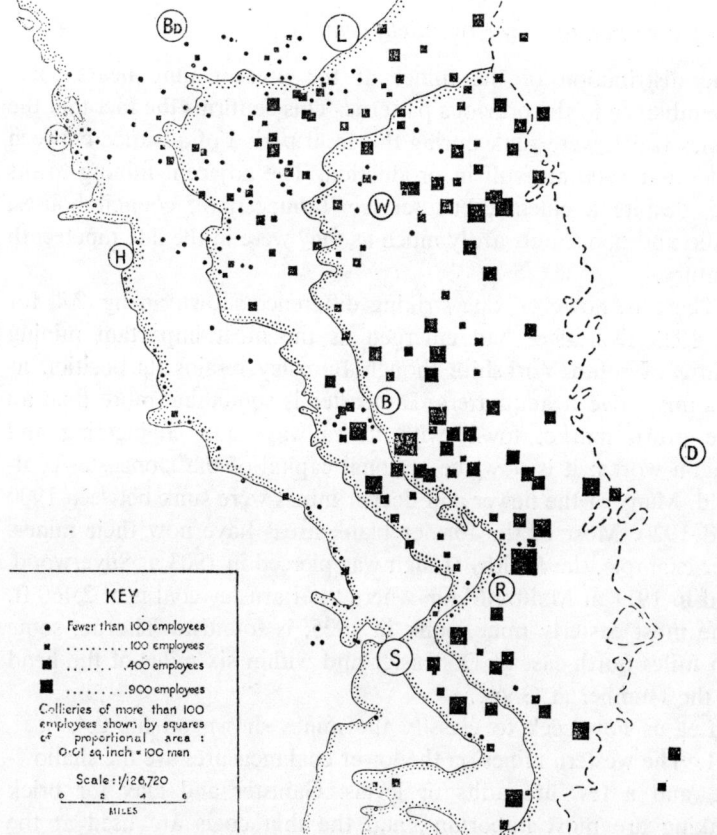

FIG. 2.3   Yorkshire collieries in 1895

3 A great number of mines are to be found dotted along the outcrop of the ganister coal. The reason for the latter feature is obvious when it is recalled that after 1856 the Bessemer process of steel manufacture was demanding ganister as a refractory. It is possible to show the number employed in 1895, and it would appear that mines in the middle coal measure tract of the field were in their heyday at this period. Many of these enterprises still appear on the present-day map, but they are usually working deeper seams. The blank areas on fig. 2.3 are to be seen near Ecclesfield and Norton to the north and south of Sheffield, for these are both regions underlain by the unproductive lower coal measures. The other noticeable blank area coincides with the Maltby trough, as yet undeveloped.

*Deep coal mining in the twentieth century*

The distribution of the mines at the present time bears some resemblance to the previous patterns. This confirms the fact that the mines which were sunk during the great period of advance between 1850 and 1900 are still in production. The adjacent mining towns are, despite a cinema, bus service, tarmacadam, council houses, radio and pools, outwardly much as they were in the late nineteenth century.

There is, however, one striking difference shown on fig. 2.4, for by 1935 Doncaster had emerged as the most important mining centre of south Yorkshire though Barnsley retains its position as administrative headquarters. Doncaster is something more than an overgrown market town, with its railways and engineering and wagon works; it is now the regional capital of the Doncaster coalfield. Many of the newer and deeper mines were sunk between 1900 and 1920. Most of the former blank areas have now their mines. For example, the Maltby trough was pierced in 1903 at Silverwood, and in 1911 at Maltby Main, where the Barnsley coal is at 2,460 ft. The most easterly mine, sunk in 1925, is found at Thorne, some ten miles north-east of Doncaster and within six miles of the head of the Humber at Goole.

Let us now seek to classify the mines shown on fig. 2.4.

1. The western mines on the lower coal measures are the shallowest, and a few are adits or levels. Ganister and clay for brick making are most important, and the thin coals are used at the brickyards or turned into briquettes. Such ganister workings are to

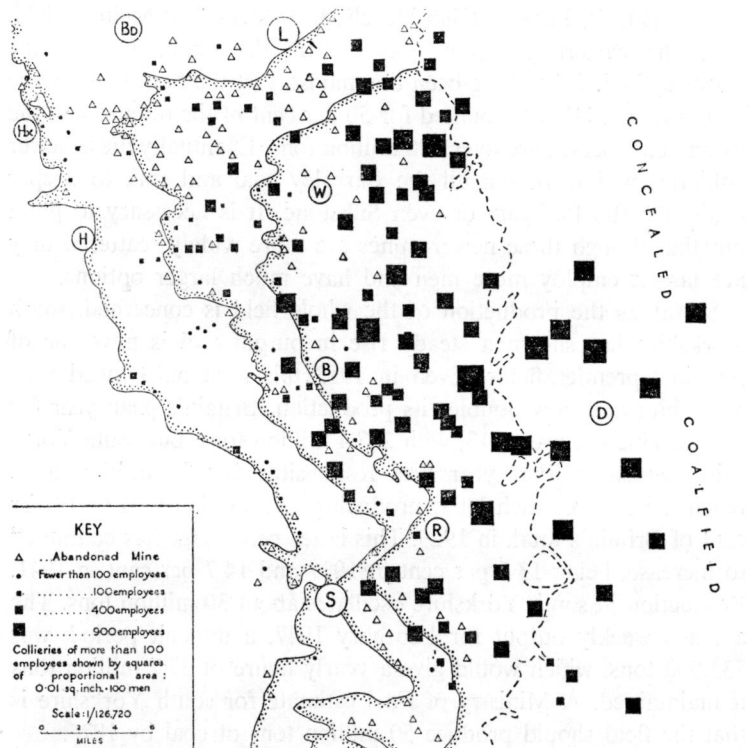

FIG. 2.4 Yorkshire collieries in 1934

be found at Deepcar, Wharncliffe, Stannington, Dungworth and Bradfield. The Whinmoor coal is worked in the Silkstone district.

2. The western group of collieries in the middle coal measure tract began by working the Silkstone seam, and it remains their main seam. In the Dearne valley some mines have now deepened their shafts to it. Other and thinner coals which are mined comprise Walker's Thin or the Thorncliffe.

3. The central group of collieries have generally all worked the Barnsley seam and have now extended their shafts to the Parkgate. Many thousands of tons of this coal have been raised, but much still remains. In 1938 about 22 per cent of the total of South Yorkshire coal came from the Parkgate. It is also worked at Brodsworth in the concealed field and will later be developed by other collieries in the eastern group. A fairly large number of comparatively minor seams are now being worked at pits previously dependent on the Barnsley and the Parkgate: the Fenton, Flockton, Swallow Wood (Haigh

Moor), Dunsil, Lidgett, High Hazels, Beamshaw and Melton Field.
4. The eastern group of pits are, in the main, working the
Barnsley bed. It has long been the mainstay of the South Yorkshire
field and in 1938 it accounted for 50 per cent of the output, and the
estimated reserves are over 700 million tons. Eventually these newer
collieries will work out all the Barnsley coal and sink to deeper
coals like the Parkgate or even Silkstone. It is necessary to point
out that though these newer mines are more widely scattered they
are larger, employ more men and have much larger options.

So far as the production of the whole field is concerned, south
Yorkshire has shown a steady rise in output and is now one of
Britain's premier fields. Even in 1913 this area outstripped west
Yorkshire and now doubles its production. Britain's peak year for
coal production was 1913, with 287·4 million tons, but south Yorkshire, which in that year was responsible for 27 million tons,
reached its peak much later, producing 33·5 million tons or 13 per
cent of Britain's total, in 1929. This latter percentage has continued
to increase, being 13·5 per cent in 1937 and 14·7 per cent in 1941.
Production in south Yorkshire oscillates about 30 million tons. The
average weekly output for February 1947, a difficult period, was
533,000 tons, which would give a yearly figure of 27·7 million tons
if maintained. A Ministry of Fuel estimate for south Yorkshire is
that the field should produce 50 million tons of coal by 1975.

Leaving aside conjecture and the possibilities of atomic fission,
certain qualitative changes are recognisable, though perhaps of a
minor order. The chief seams are gradually being worked out or else
becoming more difficult and more expensive to work. For example,
between 1938 and 1943 production from the Barnsley seam declined
from 48·5 per cent to 42·6 per cent of the total, and that from the
Parkgate from 21·3 per cent to 15·6 per cent. This may seem a small
decline, but it is symptomatic. Regarded from another angle, the
percentage of first-class coal with a relatively high ash and sulphur
content increased from 14·4 to 17·7 per cent between 1938 and 1943.

On the other hand, the stage is being set for increased production,
since most of the mines are now quite highly mechanised. Several
pits in the central group which are about fifty or seventy years old
and employ 1,000 to 1,500 men are valiantly keeping pace with
the more modern collieries of the concealed field, which employ
from 2,500 to 3,000 workers. There has, in fact, been a decided
change since 1929. In that year only 13 per cent of the coal was
cut by machines in south Yorkshire; this increased to 36 per cent

in 1934, 56 per cent in 1938 and as much as 76 per cent in 1944. Now this figure exceeds the national average for mechanisation, which stood at 71·6 per cent in 1943. Not only more coal cutters but more conveyors and more electric motors have been installed; so much so that 82 per cent of the coal is mechanically conveyed in south Yorkshire at the present time.

When considering industry in its modern or neotechnic stage of development it is necessary to guard against becoming immersed in purely economic questions. Nevertheless certain aspects are worthy of mention. South Yorkshire still largely depends on land sale. The natural outlet for waterborne coal is via the Humber. In fact 13·5 million tons were shipped from there in 1923. This figure, however, fell to 7·2 million tons in 1935. In 1943 24 per cent was utilised by public utilities; 23 per cent coking and gas; 17 per cent industry; 14 per cent locomotives; 18 per cent households; leaving 3 per cent for export and coastwise.

One further feature of South Yorkshire collieries is that many of them are parts of composite undertakings. They are associated with coke ovens and by-product plants. Some have blast furnaces, steelworks and brickyards, e.g. Newton Chambers' at Chapeltown and Manvers Main near Wath on Dearne. Much surplus gas is fed into the South Yorkshire coke-oven gas grid, created in 1930, which supplies local industry and public utilities. Another feature is the low-temperature carbonisation and Coalite plant at Barugh, near Barnsley.

Finally reference must be made to the latest development on the face of the country—the present phase of open-cast working. It will be recalled that the increased demand on the coal-mining industry led to the creation of the Directorate of Open-cast Coal in 1942. By 1943 over 4·4 million tons had been won by open-cast working. The total tonnage from all regions in Britain had reached 34·10 million tons by the end of April 1947. This is equivalent to the best annual tonnage from the deep mines of south Yorkshire.

After preliminary boring and contouring of the coal seam from outcrop to about 60–80 ft below ground level a frightening army of engineers and their machines move on to the site, putting up screening plant and hutments and making access roads. The general method of open-cast working is to make a series of cuts parallel to the coal outcrop, the useless overburden from a given cut being cast into the previous cut from which the coal has already been dug. Of course, the first cut is piled beyond the excavation area and finally tipped into the last cut. A considerable number of American machines are now used. There are drag-line excavators, some with 150 ft jibs, which cast the overburden aside. Some of these actually walk. The seam is thus laid bare and mechanical face shovels pick as much as five cubic yards of coal and place it into seven- or ten-ton lorries.

It is obvious that as the seam is traced deeper and deeper the overburden becomes excessive and eventually uneconomic. The limiting height of the 'high wall' depends on the thickness of the seam. The thicker the seam, the higher the final high wall. The mean 'economic ratio' is 7 : 1, i.e. seven cubic yards of overburden can be economically removed to obtain one ton of coal.

It is apparent from fig. 2.5 that the open-cast working in south Yorkshire is considerable. In fact Yorkshire as a whole had produced 10 million tons in aggregate between 1943 and March 1947, or about one-third of the total open-cast coal of Britain. Perhaps the Wentworth Woodhouse site has attracted most publicity, and incidentally, has been the most productive. Here the Barnsley seam is over 10 ft in thickness, and more than 1,000 tons per day can be transported from one small site. The Wentworth group of sites have produced 34,000 tons in one week. The overlying Barnsley rock has to be blasted, and, needless to say, the aspect of the workings is somewhat terrifying, but the work of restoration has to be seen to be believed. The fields are levelled and the topsoil previously stripped off by mechanical scrapers is replaced, and, after fencing, crops are planted and the land is handed back to the landowner or tenant farmer. Whether the soil profile and texture have been radically damaged will take time to assess, but when demands for coal are as great as at the present much can be justified.

In south Yorkshire the three main seams have been worked open-cast in addition to minor seams like the Flockton, Whinmoor and Fenton. When seams of about 1 ft 6 in. are worked and are friable and weathered near the outcrop, justification seems more difficult. Actual analysis is, however, necessary to determine the degree of weathering. Thus in south Yorkshire there is a similarity of technique between the medieval 'day hole' and the modern open-cast site. There is, however, a difference, for the pick and shovel are replaced by diesel drag-line and mechanical shovel, and we truly appreciate that a neotechnic phase is slowly passing over the landscape in the space of five or six years instead of in two to three hundred.

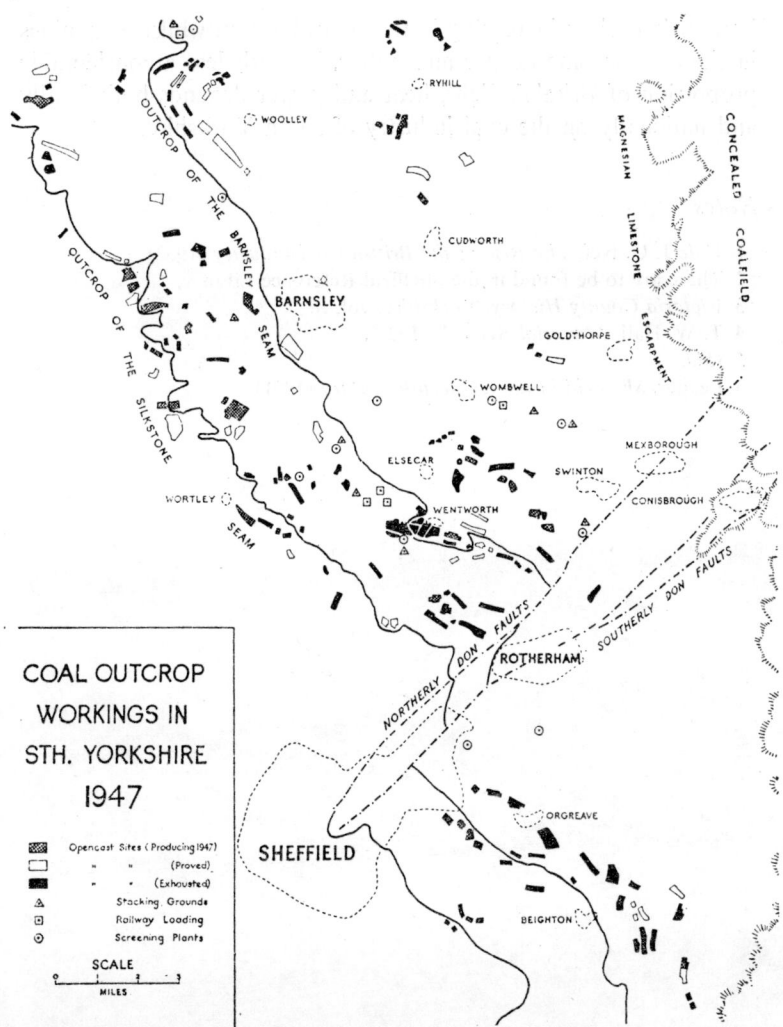

FIG. 2.5   Coal outcrop workings in south Yorkshire, 1947

In conclusion, we may state that south Yorkshire is one of the foremost of Britain's fields because it is endowed with rich main seams with good sandstone roofs, a low angle of dip and few faults. The region possesses coals eminently suited for coking and gas making, as well as having good house coals like the Silkstone. Transport is now available by rail and to a smaller degree by road and canal. The future may show a greater reliance on poorer and thinner seams, and, of course, the length of haulage to the pit bottom is rapidly increasing in the central group, whilst new mines in the east become deeper and hotter. Nevertheless a considerable proportion of Britain's light, heat and power depends both locally and nationally on the coal industry of south Yorkshire.

## Notes

1  *Vide* J. U. Nef, *The Rise of the British Coal Industry* (1932).
2  These are to be found in the Sheffield Reference Library.
3  *Victoria County History, Yorkshire*, vol. II.
4  T. W. Hall, *Manorial Records* (1924).
5  *Ibid.*
6  Leader, *Sheffield in the eighteenth century* (1901).

# 3 West Riding landowners and mining in the nineteenth century

In many nineteenth-century estate accounts, sums received from mining operations held a significant place. Some examples are well known: the Marquess of Londonderry, the Earls of Durham, Lonsdale and Crawford, John Bowes and Lord Ravensworth owned famous and lucrative mineral properties. Many West Riding landowners also shared to some extent in the prosperity created by mining developments. During the nineteenth century the Yorkshire and North Midland coalfield became the largest in Britain, extending from Leeds to Nottingham; by the first world war its proved area was over 1,300 square miles, with partially proved reserves of 760 square miles. Annual production in 1851 and 1852 was estimated at 8 million tons (and later 7·5 million tons) and by 1869 had reached 10,829,827 tons. The 'Yorkshire and Lincolnshire district', producing nearly 17·5 million tons in 1880, exceeded 24 millions in 1897 and ten years later reached over 35 millions. In 1913 the whole coalfield yielded almost 73 million tons, a figure still maintained in 1930, when Yorkshire's individual contribution was about 44·5 million tons.[1]

Mining was not a new industry in the West Riding; it had an ancient, though somewhat obscure, history. The medieval religious houses provided the first entrepreneurs. The Augustinian priory of Nostell had coal land at Crofton and Houghton, and the Benedictines of Monk Bretton owned Cudworth property. Byland monks worked iron at Emley, Denby, Whitley and Flockton; and Rievaulx and Fountains shared their interests.[2] Enterprising squires and merchants continued the monastic ventures after the Reformation. By the end of the eighteenth century Yorkshire and Lancashire industry was estimated to use about 1·5 million tons of coal annually; and John Hardy of Bradford claimed that 'no less than 150,000 to 200,000' acres could be worked around Leeds, Wakefield, Barnsley and Bradford.

In the early nineteenth century Yorkshire coal was used largely by local consumers. Coal was still being imported in 1829, at Whitby, Scarborough, Bridlington, Hull and Goole, although almost similar consignments were shipped from Hull and Goole.[3] The shipments soon passed the stage of being mere ballast; in the 1850s the average export was over 2·6 million tons, and in the following decade over 4·4 million tons, and very large quantities were also moved by canal and railway. Two distinct districts developed—the West Yorkshire, extending 'from Lord St Oswald's estate at Nostell almost in a straight line following the valley of the Calder on towards Mirfield', and the South Yorkshire, with its rich Barnsley, Silkstone and Parkgate seams from Barnsley to the south.[4]

The purpose of this paper is to examine the connection between this industrial growth and the landowners of the West Riding.

# I

As the owner of the minerals beneath his property the landowner had a natural interest in the extraction of his underground wealth. For many years owners leased mines for a share of the coal, but by the eighteenth century money rents were general, sometimes in addition to the provision of coals and an understanding that the site should be cleaned up when operations ceased—an arrangement stated in 1890 to have 'been used as a very severe whip upon lessees'. Rents might be fixed annually during the period of the lease, but as leases lengthened rents tended to be agreed for longer terms. The annual rent, variously called the 'fixed rent', 'dead rent', 'certain rent' or 'mineral rent' was generally high in south Yorkshire. But landowners increasingly demanded extra payment, directly or indirectly related to the quantity of coal mined.

The royalty on coals extracted was the landowner's second source of income. This might be a fixed charge on the tonnage raised or acreage worked, or might depend on a sliding scale adjusted to selling prices. In Lancashire, Yorkshire and the Midlands royalties were usually charged on the acreage, and were often regulated by the thickness of a new seam. By the late nineteenth century average charges were £120–£375 per acre for the Barnsley bed and £25–£30 per foot per acre for Silkstone coal in south Yorkshire, and £50–£300 per acre or £20–£40 per foot per acre in west Yorkshire. Owners might demand guarantees against failure to work the mines fully, or might restrict operations to conserve supplies. When an annual royalty fell below the fixed rent the lessee was obliged to pay 'shorts', which he might be allowed to recoup from later overworking. The average Yorkshire rate was 6d per ton in the 1890s, and Yorkshire landowners were estimated to have received £549,401 in 1889. By 1919 the average South Yorkshire royalty was 5d and in the newer districts at Doncaster and in the west 4d.⁵ Royalties might amount to very large sums. The largest coal owners, the Ecclesiastical Commissioners, received about £410,000 from mineral properties in 1917, and about £300,000 in the 1890s, including some £8,500 from Yorkshire. Durham, Scottish and Welsh estates also received big payments: Lord Durham had nearly £53,000 in royalties in 1913 and over £35,000 in 1918, and on average the Duke of Hamilton received some £113,000 in 1908–18, the Duke of Northumberland over £69,000 in 1913–18, and Lord Tredegar £74,000 and the Marquess of Bute £109,000 in 1912–18.⁶

A third type of income arose from various wayleaves. Considerable sums were charged as outstroke rents for transporting coal under property, wayleave rents for transferring it to shafts, shaft rents for raising it, and surface wayleaves for further passage. Waterleave might be charged for drainage, and airleave for ventilation. But wayleaves, charged by the acre, were generally moderate in Yorkshire. In the 1890s they were estimated to affect only a quarter of production and to yield about £10,000.⁷

Some owners faced legal difficulties in granting leases. Before legislation of 1856 a tenant for life of a settled estate was usually limited in his granting powers to a period of twenty-one years. The resulting inconveniences led to further reforms, especially the Settled Land Act of 1882, which permitted sixty-year leases, while providing that a portion of the rent should be capitalised for the benefit of others entitled under the settlement. This remedial measure opened the way to longer-term mining ventures; but trouble still arose where the surface and minerals had different owners, especially when there was surface damage. 'A cantankerous small owner' might also be a great nuisance to promoters.⁸

Some landowners operated their own mines. In the north-east Lord Durham had ten mines, worth £540,000, in 1835, and eleven in 1871; in 1896 he sold fourteen collieries and nineteen steamers to Sir James Joicey. Earl Vane had seven collieries in 1871, including several previously managed by his mother, the Marchioness of Londonderry. The Bridgewater trustees owned nineteen Lancashire collieries; and in Staffordshire the Earl of Dudley's industrial empire included twelve mines, nine blast furnaces, ninety-six puddling furnaces and ten rolling mills. Yorkshire also provided examples of the landowner–industrialist: in 1890 'probably one-eighth of the whole output was worked by proprietors of the coal' in west Yorkshire.[9]

## II

The two wealthiest West Riding estates, the properties of the Duke of Norfolk and Earl Fitzwilliam, both lay above the South Yorkshire coal seams. The ducal estate consisted of 19,440 acres in and around Sheffield. In 1873 the 'New Domesday' survey estimated the gross rental of 15,270 acres at £231,354, noting that the duke, as ground landlord only, received much less. The fifteenth duke himself gave the gross annual value of the full acreage as £39,897, excluding mineral and shooting rights. Many mineral ventures had been developed by the ninth, tenth and eleventh dukes in the eighteenth century. Several collieries were operated by the estate, and leases were granted at Whiston, Chapeltown, Sheffield, Attercliffe, Ecclesfield and Herringthorpe, and for ironworks at Chapeltown, Wadsley and Attercliffe.[10] The area was famous for its 'beehive' coke manufacturing ovens.

In the 1770s the ninth duke appointed the famous John Curr (1756–1823) as his viewer. Curr introduced Durham practices and his own inventions. In 1774 he built a wooden railroad, to carry coals to Sheffield, and when it was smashed by mobs complaining of high prices he laid cast-iron plate rails. He introduced underground rails and four-wheeled trucks, and from 1788 fitted conductors in the shafts to allow safe and rapid surfacing of the corves. In 1798 he patented a flat winding rope, and in 1805 he used stationary engines to haul wagons, at Birtley, near Gateshead. Curr was keenly interested in the development of steam engines, though he also used underground canals, at Sheffield. Nevertheless the mines faced serious difficulties, and the eleventh duke, who succeeded in 1786, called in the celebrated John Buddle, who advised extensive draining and the closing of Attercliffe. Curr's troubles persisted—there were irregular seams, floods and competition from a sick-club colliery from 1793. In 1801 Curr was suddenly dismissed, though his foundry and ropeworks continued to serve the duke.[11]

After a price war the rival colliery failed. More successful was the Low Manor lessee, who obtained 159,000 tons annually in the 1830s and made vast profits. The dukes ceased to operate mines but continued to draw large revenues. In 1805 Attercliffe was leased to the former agent, Vincent Eyre, now a banker. The twelfth duke supported the Manchester and Sheffield railway, sanctioned in 1836, but opposed the Sheffield and Rotherham line of 1837 because of its pledge to reduce coal prices. But the dukes were highly regarded by mining concerns. In 1875 the fifteenth duke let some 1,300 acres of Barnsley coal at a minimum rent of £5,000 and a footage royalty of £50. The lessees broke their contract during the depression, but the duke remitted the rent, and when operations were resumed in 1883 he reduced it to £3,000 and the footage to £30; the hard-pressed undertaking was extremely grateful.[12]

The Fitzwilliam estate at Wentworth Woodhouse contained 19,164 acres in 1873. It had been developed in the previous century by the second Marquess of Rockingham: collieries, ironworks, blast furnaces, ironstone pits, a china works and a tar works were in operation. Several coal and iron concerns were run by the estate, though most were leased. In 1801 the 'industrial' income was little more than a sixth of the total, and thereafter varied considerably. By the mid-century, when the failing iron concerns were sold, minerals accounted for about a fifth of the income. As technological and transport problems were solved the collieries were rapidly developed, and at the end of the century mineral payments from twenty-one companies, with £13,701 from the estate mines, more than doubled farm and general rents.[13]

Successive earls interested themselves in the local industry. Fashionable parties from the great house visited the sloping futterils at Elsecar and Rawmarsh. The estate's operations were well equipped with a Newcomen pumping engine, and Nasmyth steam hammer and shaping engine. The earls were represented at trade meetings, and often spoke on mining affairs. In 1847 the third earl supported demands for efficient inspection, to improve ventilation and prevent explosions. In 1851 he exhibited Barnsley coal at the Great Exhibition. The earls were regarded as benevolent employers, providing good housing, free coal, sickness, widows' and injury benefits and occasional feasts. Certainly the third earl disliked trade unions, and in 1858 his son fought the union. But, maintained a local journal,

His Lordship's collieries have long been noted for exemption from serious disorders, and the good understanding that has prevailed between employers, managers and employed.

The strikers soon returned, and left the union until 1872; the union itself made little effort to recruit Fitzwilliam's men, and when they struck in 1873 it ordered them back and apologised to the earl. The fifth earl was particularly interested in mining engineering; but when, as lord mayor, he attended the 1910 TUC conference in Sheffield, during a strike, there was some disturbance.[14]

The Fitzwilliams were well served by a remarkable family of viewers, Joshua Biram (c. 1765–1835) and his son Benjamin (1804–57). Joshua was a well known Barnsley mineral surveyor, and Benjamin achieved some fame as an inventor. Yorkshire owners were long axious to improve ventilation, to allow deeper sinkings, and in 1842 Biram patented several rotary ventilators, including his celebrated anemometer—later used for measuring air currents and perhaps 'the best instrument of this kind known'—in 1852. Biram and Nicholas Wood (1795–1865) of Hetton, a leading northern viewer and owner, advised the coroner after a catastrophic explosion in Darley Main Colliery in 1849; both favoured mine inspection, which began in the following year. In 1852 Fitzwilliam's pits were the first to use Nasmyth's straight-vaned fan, and in 1853 Biram experimented with a fan with tangential blades. Biram also invented an unsuccessful safety lamp in the late '40s.[15]

TABLE 3.1. *Earl Fitzwilliam's Wentworth estate income* (£)

| Year | Mineral income | Total rents, etc |
|------|----------------|------------------|
| 1801 | 4,214 | 26,135 |
| 1831 | 2,576 | 32,396 |
| 1841 | 11,082 | 43,489 |
| 1850 | 8,991 | 44,356 |
| 1871 | 37,210 | 71,281 |
| 1901 | 87,743 | 130,585 |

*Source.* Wentworth Woodhouse muniments.

Like the Norfolks, the Fitzwilliams generally leased their coal; and deeper pits brought increased royalties and shaft rents. Lessees might assign leases to others only with special consent and possible rent increases. But the earls continued to work their coal, at Elsecar, Park Gate and Stubbin. Their mineral income gradually grew much larger than agricultural revenues. The final chapter was reached after the second world war, when the coal under the park of Wentworth Woodhouse itself was worked by a messy open-cast process.

## III

Landowners who did not manage their own mines nevertheless enthusiastically supported mining developments, which might greatly augment their agricultural incomes. At Bretton Hall, near Wakefield, the Beaumont family owned some 9,000 acres and considerable coal. In 1829 eleven mines paid only £1,470 in rents and royalties, three paying nothing, while agricultural rents totalled £13,105. By 1844 fifteen collieries paid some £1800, though some were in arrears, and the farms and cottages added about £13,500. Twenty-two years later fourteen concerns were working, in 1873 seventeen and in 1874 twenty-one. The 1874 peak in mineral income was followed by a long fall in receipts from both mines and farms, and in 1882 over £3,800 were lost when the Thorpe firm at Darton went into liquidation.[16] The Beaumonts, however, owned some 15,000

TABLE 3.2. *W. B. Beaumont's Bretton estate income (£)*

| Year | Mineral income | Total rents, etc |
|------|----------------|------------------|
| 1866 | 6,727 | 18,896 |
| 1873 | 7,136 | 19,544 |
| 1874 | 9,280 | 21,651 |
| 1880 | 5,950 | 18,624 |
| 1885 | 3,830 | 13,753 |
| 1890 | 3,215 | 11,586 |
| 1894 | 3,505 | 10,855 |

*Source.* Bretton Hall rentals.

Northumberland and Durham acres around the Blackett family's old seat at Bywell. With the land they inherited the Blacketts' Allendale lead mines, and Wentworth Blackett Beaumont, later first Lord Allendale, leased the Weardale mines from the Ecclesiastical Commissioners. Beaumont also owned smelting mills, and in 1855 started the Blackett Level in east Allendale. In the '60s he was 'reported to be one of the wealthiest commoners in the country'. His grandfather, T. R. Beaumont, was a vice-patron of a society for preventing mining accidents, at Sunderland, in 1813, and W. B. Beaumont was a patron of the North of England Institute of Mining Engineers.[17]

Among other patrons of the pioneer Newcastle Institute was the first Earl of Wharncliffe, whose 9,000 West Riding acres produced over £15,700 in the '70s; his total Yorkshire estate of 22,544 acres was worth £34,440. The land included iron and coal around Wortley Hall, and the family had old connections with industry. Sir Francis Wortley ran an ironworks near Bentley Grange in the sixteenth century, and Barnsley Moor collieries were leased in Stuart times. But the Wortleys were also engaged in the north-eastern coal trade. Sidney Wortley, who assumed the name on marrying the natural daughter of the last baronet, was a signatory of the 'Grand Alliance' to control Durham coal production with Sir Henry Liddell and John Bowes, in 1726. His son Edward was second only to Liddell in his production allotment. By marriage with Edward's daughter the third Earl of Bute inherited the northern estates, the Yorkshire land passing to his second son, James Archibald, who passed it to his son, the first Lord Wharncliffe.[18] The Wharncliffes took a considerable interest in mining affairs. In 1849 the second lord presided over a select committee to examine the prevention of accidents; it sat for eighteen days but reached few conclusions, apart from recommending inspection. Wharncliffe's old rival, the seventh Earl of Carlisle, passed the Act establishing inspection in 1850. By the end of the century Wharncliffe's son was renting Carlton minerals at £50—£163 per acre, half-yearly. Six months' rents at Wortley, New Hall and Carlton totalled £6,628 in 1891 and £6,038 in 1898. Between July 1901 and October 1902 the second earl received £19,624; but arrears totalled almost £10.000.[19]

Many smaller owners increased their incomes by mineral rents and royalties. When the third Earl of Mexborough died in 1860 it was reported that he had 'been for a long time in pecuniary difficulties'; Methley Hall was let to Titus Salt, the manufacturer. But his son prospered through mining developments, and in 1896 the sixth earl extended the estate by buying Arden Hall. On the nearby Swillington estate the Lowther baronets emulated their relations, the Earls of Lonsdale, the great Cumbrian mine owners, though not operating their own mines, as the earls did for some time. Sir John, first baronet of the new creation, was the brother of the first earl. His second son, Sir Charles, the blind third baronet, drew the bulk of his income from coal mining—which eventually caused the subsidence of Swillington House itself.[20] At Kirklees Park Sir George Armytage, fifth baronet, also owned valuable coal land. His son, Sir George John, the chairman of the Lancashire & Yorkshire Railway, was a member of the Royal Commission on Coal Supplies in 1901–05. Henry Frederick Beaumont had some coal on his ancient Whitley Beaumont estate near Wakefield, where mines had been let since the eighteenth century. Edmund Calverley of Oulton Hall, Thomas Davison Bland of Kippax Park, James Milnes Gaskell of Thorne House, John Hatfield of Thorp Arch Hall and Skellow Grange, F. J. S. Foljambe of Osberton Hall in Nottinghamshire, T. H. S. Sotheron-Estcourt of Darrington Grange, C. S. A. Thellusson of Brodsworth Hall and J. W. Torre of Syndale Hall all shared to some extent in the prosperity created by coal.

Landowners in many parts of the Riding were affected. The Edmunds family of Worsborough Hall had valuable coal under their 1,462 acres near Barnsley, which produced £10,322 for W. H. Martin-Edmunds in 1873. The Fullertons of Thrybergh Hall drew three-quarters of their income from coal around Denaby, Kilnhurst, Mexborough and Thrybergh. The Radcliffe baronets of Rudding Park, who owned much more land than the 2,872 acres credited by the 1873 return (which gave a rental of £7,271), leased minerals at Royton, Butterworth, Oldham, Denby Dale, Liversedge, Darton, Elland and Mirfield on their Lancashire and Yorkshire estates to nineteen concerns. Thomas Edward Taylor of Scaftworth and Dodsworth Halls had land at Barnsley, Silkstone and Darfield in the colliery districts. The Thornhills of Fixby Hall owned several mines, over which some controversy was raised in the '40s by the activities of the former agent, Richard Oastler, the factory reformer.[21] On the Fryston Hall estate the Milnes family had coal at Fryston and Bullhouse, which produced £916 for a half-year in 1881 for Richard Monckton Milnes, first Lord Houghton, including a rent of £750. Some 5,400 acres then paid over £8,500. Houghton's son, the first Marquess of Crewe, later lent substantial sums to Midland and Yorkshire collieries during their lean years.[22] The Earls of Cardigan, whose 5,583 acres included urban land at Leeds, Batley and Dewsbury, also owned some coal; in 1883 the dowager countess received £20,588. The sporting fourth Lord Hawke had some 6,000 acres at Womersley Hall, which produced over £8,000 for his widow in 1873. The estate passed to his daughter, who married the fourth Earl of Rosse, already the owner (through his mother) of the Field family's estate at Heaton, where there were two collieries. In 1883 the Earl of Effingham, lord of the manor of coal-rich Rotherham, received £3,013 from 1,445 acres.[23]

Some estates had been mining centres for centuries. Coal had been mined at Godfrey Wentworth's Woolley Park estate since Edward I's reign. In 1873 some 5,000 acres paid £13,000. The family had owned further unentailed land, but the failure of their banking business in 1825 necessitated its sale; coal land at Hickleton and Darton was sold to T. R. Beaumont and Sir Francis Wood, second baronet, in 1829.[24] F. W. T. Vernon-Wentworth of Wentworth Castle owned an estate of similar size in an intensive mining area bounded by Barnsley, Wortley, Wentworth, Penistone and Wombwell. Some Worsborough coal and iron workings dated from the seventeenth century; William, Earl of Strafford, gave leases in 1663. Even in 1814 colliery rents amounted to £1,023, plus a charge on coal mined over 15,000 tons. The family gave financial help to local collieries in difficult periods.[25]

Several of the Riding's largest owners also benefited from mining. The Meynell-Ingrams of Temple Newsam had long connections with various entrepreneurial ventures and now increased already large rentals; in 1873 some 8,200 acres paid over £27,800. Andrew Montagu of Ingmanthorpe Hall owned coal in both Yorkshire and Nottingham—where 3,254 acres paid £12,200 in 1883. The Dukes of Leeds had coal at Kiveton, Barnsley and Wakefield; the estates, excluding Wakefield, produced over £10,400 in 1809 and £12,500 in 1820. The income gradually rose, despite the alienation of the land of the baronies of Darcy and Conyers; the twelfth Lord Conyers inherited Doncaster and Sheffield mineral rights and nearly 1,800 acres (producing £5,400 in 1873), which passed to his daughter, the wife of the fourth Earl of Yarborough. But the dukes were reluctant to work their Wakefield land, where an enclosure Act of 1793 caused legal difficulties over surface rights. Another large

TABLE 3.3. *Reported incomes of some West Riding landowners*

|  | Acreage of estate | 1873 (£) | 1883 (£) |
|---|---|---|---|
| Sir George Armytage | 3,274 | 17,064 | 8,700 |
| H. F. Beaumont | 5,219 | 11,907 | |
| T. D. Bland | 4,320 | 10,126 | 8,500 |
| C. G. Fullerton | 3,331 | 13,000 | 13,000 |
| Sir Charles Lowther | 2,855 | 14,543 | |
| Earl of Mexborough | 6,969 | 31,309 | 31,309 |
| Andrew Montagu | 20,700 | 28,384 | 35,234 |
| Henry Savile | 16,000 | 23,402 | 35,000 |
| W. C. C. Thornhill | 2,611 | 9,111 | |
| F. W. Vernon-Wentworth | 5.111 | 15,240 | 15,240 |

*Sources.* 1873 return; Bateman (1883 edn.).

mineral estate was owned by the Lumley-Savile family. The eighth Earl of Scarbrough left vast Yorkshire and Nottinghamshire estates to his natural son, Henry Lumley Savile, including urban property at Dewsbury and Batley and traditional coal areas around Emley. But despite this large alienation the ninth earl inherited valuable lands in Yorkshire, Lincolnshire and Durham, including coal near Sandbeck Park; some 8,600 West Riding acres produced over £10,300 in the '70s.[26]

West Riding landowners were not concerned only with coal mines, however. John Yorke of Bewerley Hall owned lead mines at Appletreewick, which paid handsomely for some time. In 1813 the Yorkes' 12,000 acres paid only £5,081, but in 1873 Yorke's son received some £7,500 from 9,700 acres, and ten years later his second son had £11,000 from 14,500 acres. The seventh Duke of Devonshire's industrial energies were mainly spent in creating the town and industries of Barrow; his 31,366 West Riding acres were largely moor and agricultural land. But until 1869 he also ran Wharfedale lead mines around Grassington, which had been developed by the Earls of Burlington, along with a smelting mill founded by the Devonshires in the mid-eighteenth century. Foreign competition eventually made the industry uneconomic,[27] but such ventures typified energetic landowners' attitudes to industrial development.

## IV

Some landowners had especially close connections with mining, through their own colliery operations. They were not all great proprietors: Charles Winn had a 'home colliery' on his 2,461 acres at Nostell Priory. The Listers of Shibden Hall had several pits—which were later let—in the eighteenth century. Around Hudders-field the Earls of Dartmouth owned large coal rights which they let from the early eighteenth century; the fourth earl's 8,000 acres paid £20,520 in 1883. But the Legge family's home was on their Staffordshire estate, where 7,316 acres produced £16,356. The fourth and fifth earls were benevolent landowners around West Bromwich, where they had two collieries. In 1842 the fourth earl tried to arbitrate on local colliers' complaints; and his son was still testing bore holes in the '60s.[28]

The Charlesworths of Chapelthorpe Hall, whose 2,169 West and North Riding acres produced £7126 in 1883, were leading mine

owners. In 1809 Joseph Charlesworth ran seven pits, through col-
lective agreements with mining gangs. He bought Chapelthorpe in
1814. His son, John Dodgson Charlesworth, extended the business,
despite several famous disasters. By 1853, when 2,500 miners
celebrated a wage increase at Stanley Hall, there were six West
Yorkshire and four South Yorkshire collieries; Charlesworth then
condemned unionism, but he did not victimise strike leaders.
Industrial relations were bitter during the 1858 lock-out, but after
the acceptance of unionism there was 'the most perfect friendship
and good feeling'. In 1869 the firm had twelve collieries around
Dodsworth, Barnsley, Rotherham, Leeds and Wakefield; and
through mining the family joined the ranks of the Victorian gentry,
two members sitting in Parliament.[29]

More surprisingly, several mines were operated by Sir John
Lister-Kaye, second baronet, of Denby Grange. Since the Reformation his family had owned the Byland monks' iron and coal lands
at Denby, Flockton, Emley and Whitley, and some of the old
Rievaulx land. The baronet's property was small; in 1873 his
executors had 1,713 acres, producing £5,377. But Sir John had
collieries on the Wharncliffe and Bretton estates and at Wakefield
and Thornhill; in 1869 he was still operating three mines around
Wakefield, but the 'Needle Eye' at Denby Grange had been sold.
His daughter later ran the Flockton colliery and the Wharncliffe
mine.[30]

The Brandlings of Gosforth House in Durham were an old
landed family with six collieries in the Great Northern Coalfield.
Charles John, brother-in-law of Thomas Creevey, sat in Parliament,
while Robert William led the northern coal trade until his death in
1846; Robert Stephenson was his engineer for some time. In the
eighteenth century Ralph Brandling of Tilling had inherited by
marriage the Leighs' 1,200-acre Middleton Hall estate near Leeds.
The estate colliery was an important local supplier, and a private
Act of 1757 allowed Charles Brandling to construct a railway to
the town. Despite an explosion in 1758 the venture grew, and a
Newcomen engine was installed in 1780. In 1801 Charles John
appointed the celebrated John Blenkinsop (1784–1831), the cousin
of his northern viewer, Thomas Barnes, as viewer at Middleton.
An Act of 1803 sanctioned an iron railway, and in 1812 Blenkinsop
demonstrated his locomotive to Leeds crowds. By 1808 the colliery
employed ninety hewers and sixty putters. It passed, on C. J.
Brandling's death in 1826, to his brother, Ralph Henry, vicar of

Rothwell, who had three pits in 1835. Middleton had 'nothing like the expense of working the Tyne Collieries', Robert told a Lords committee in 1830; coals were then delivered in Leeds at about 7s 1d per ton, while similar Newcastle coals were shipped at about 8s 9d.[31] However, profits declined and debts mounted; the colliery was handed to trustees in 1834.

Several mine-owning families were related. C. J. Brandling's second wife was a daughter of Sir George Armytage. C. G. Fullerton's son John married the only daughter of Robert Couldwell Clarke of Noblethorpe Hall. In 1873 the Clarkes' 2,310 acres produced £5404; but the family were primarily mine owners. R. C. Clarke and his father Jonas had leased Silkstone Common coal from John Spencer-Stanhope and other owners for twenty-one years at £210 per acre early in the century, promising to repair damages and compensate landowners. By 1824 there was a long controversy over the amounts mined, and Joshua Biram and Andrew Faulds took four years to arbitrate on the question. Clarke's Old Silkstone Colliery was later the scene of bitter disputes, on one of which Walter Spencer-Stanhope arbitrated in 1869.[32]

One of the most astonishing entries in the 1873 return was that for William Day of Monk Bretton, whose sixteen acres had a rental of £6353. Day owned the Mount Osborne and Old Mill collieries near Barnsley. Samuel Fox of Stocksbridge, credited with 800 acres worth £5,624, owned a colliery and various other undertakings. Michael Stocks of Upper Shibden Hall, an owner in Caithness, Norfolk and the West Riding, had a total of 16,490 acres; but 1,020 Yorkshire acres paid £5,652 of his £9,206 income. He owned the Crooked Lane, Shaw Lane and Shugden collieries near Halifax.[33] Thus several landowners were also sizable industrialists.

## V

At the opposite end of the scale were the rural estate owners. But even they cherished periodic hopes. The Greenwoods of Swarcliffe Hall, originally Keighley merchants, bought their land in 1805, and by 1873 had some 6,000 acres worth over £9,200. The predominantly agricultural estate stretched to iron-ore land in Cleveland, and coal had often been found near Birstwith, though generally 'of indifferent quality'. John Greenwood optimistically sank a shaft at Meg Yate in 1820, and ten years later a mining concern started three shafts, but without success. Thereafter the only operations were those of an illegal digger, one Bill Ward, who was eventually driven away.[34]

The Greenwoods' neighbours, the Earls of Harewood, owned an agricultural estate of 21,090 acres in the West Riding and 9,078 in the North Riding, producing £26,788 and £10,432 respectively in 1880. But the third earl, when selling property at Lea Gate in Craven in 1849, carefully reserved the mineral rights. To the east George Lane-Fox owned the 15,000-acre Bramham Park estate, which produced almost £20,000 in 1837, nearly £22,000 in 1873 and £17,000 in the '80s. This agricultural estate included the great Allerton Bywater Colliery, which James Lane-Fox leased to one Thomas Fenton in 1797 and 1802. Part was conveyed to Thomas Davison-Bland in 1820, but when the surface was sold in the 1830s the coal was retained, until it was exchanged with Davison-Bland in 1856. Mining opportunities were fostered; Rimmington lead mines were let to John Tomkinson and Henry Hayes for twenty-one years in 1822, interests were acquired in Silkstone, Wrenthorpe and Haigh Moor collieries, and in 1823 the land at Bramham Park itself was surveyed for minerals. Coal rents amounted to £750 in 1846 and £1,156 six years later.[35]

The Spencer-Stanhopes of Cannon Hall owned land near 'Black Barnsley' itself. The Spencers had established their fortunes as South Yorkshire ironmasters in the late seventeenth century, but eventually settled as country squires; in 1786 Walter Spencer-Stanhope refused to buy Low Moor, whose ironstone and coal brought rich dividends to his more venturesome agent, John Hardy. A small mine on the Stanhope estate at Horsforth failed disastrously in 1806. And the discovery of coal under Silkstone Common in 1800 brought little reward to the Spencer-Stanhopes, the principal owners; from 1824 to 1828 the agent, John Brackenridge, argued over terms with Jonas Clarke's executors. The estate remained principally agricultural; by the 1870s the 11,357 acres paid £11,070.[36]

At St Ives, near Bingley, the Ferrand family owned almost 4,000 acres early in the century, and this size was recorded in the 1873 return; but the estate had expanded, and was locally estimated at about 10,000 acres. The rental was £6,193 in 1846, £5,023 in 1857 and £7,698 in 1883. William Busfeild Ferrand also owned some coal and ancient collieries at Wilsden and Allerton. In 1852 he leased Clayton coal to Joseph Briggs & Co. for sixty years, at a rent of £90, but the lease was surrendered in 1856. The Allerton and Wilsden mines were more profitably let to the Bowling Iron

Company (which had twelve collieries in 1869) and Wood & Co.
In 1874 Wilsden paid a rent of £450, plus royalties.[37]

Some landowners only started to benefit from mining after about
1885, as the industry moved south-eastwards, ravaging—but often
financially saving—more rural estates. But other owners remained
far beyond the blessings and curses of industry.

## VI

Nineteenth-century mining obviously had far-reaching effects on
many Yorkshire estates. For some it subsidised agriculture through
lean years. It sometimes provided an important prop for heavily
mortgaged properties. And it paid for grandiose building and
'improvement' schemes elsewhere. To some owners it provided
large unearned increments, with all possible losses prevented by
complicated leases, but it roused others into energetic surveying;
in 1850 William Aldam of Frickley Hall was advised of possible
coal on his land by a barely literate miner.[38]

Very little Yorkshire coal was produced by estate-owned mines.
Consequently there was little direct investment in the industry,
except by such landowners as Fitzwilliam and Lister-Kaye. However, several owners gave financial help, either by remitting payments or by lending money, during depressions. Many more were
led to take further interest in transport problems: South Yorkshire
squires were among the leading promoters, planners, directors and
users of the railway network in the colliery districts, as their fathers
had been of the turnpike trusts and canals.[39]

Aristocratic ownership allegedly had 'social' advantages, which
were stressed by Thomas Tancred, in his report on South Staffordshire mines, in 1842:

It appears a legitimate deduction . . . that the rank and wealth of the
employers of mining labour has an important influence upon the welfare of the working men . . . . It is not unreasonable to imagine *a priori*
that men of rank and capital will not condescend to adopt the shifts
and expedients to which an inferior class of proprietors are as it were
driven to resort . . .

Tancred illustrated the theme with northern and midland examples;
the traditions of aristocratic paternalism seemed to have passed
from agriculture to mining. There were exceptions. In 1852 Inspector John Dickinson agreed that large collieries were generally
'better managed than the smaller ones', but insisted that 'some very

large and wealthy colliery owners' were too interested in cheap production. However, larger owners were 'more amenable to public opinion' and took much more care over safety than did small operators. In Yorkshire Fitzwilliam appears to have been regarded as a benevolent employer.[40]

Despite complaints in other districts, mine owners were generally satisfied with Yorkshire landowners' terms. Most local coalfields, declared J. D. Ellis (chairman of the South Yorkshire Coal Owners' Association and of John Brown & Co. Ltd) in 1890,

are in the hands of large landed proprietors such as the Duke of Norfolk, Earl Fitzwilliam, the Earl of Effingham and Mr Foljambe; they are all of them most liberal, honourable landlords, and I scarcely ever hear the slightest complaint made by anyone.

B. P. Broomhead, chairman of Thomas Firth & Sons, favoured certain legal changes; but he 'would very much prefer to be in the hands of a man like the Duke of Norfolk', who had treated him well, than under 'some wretched middleman and speculator', as in Spain, where minerals belonged to the State.[41] Such statements by leading industrialists were scarcely conventional politenesses; in some coalfields royalty charges were bitterly resented.

Mineral ownership does not appear to have affected landowners' party allegiances. Through most of the century the Fitzwilliams, Norfolks and Beaumonts continued to be Whigs, while the Wharncliffes, Lowthers and Mexboroughs were generally Tories. Both groups followed traditional allegiances, at least until the closing decades of the century.

Yorkshire lessees were usually held responsible for agricultural damage and sometimes for subsidence; after trouble over early agreements to raise maximum amounts, leases prescribed the pillars to be left in the pits. There were occasional arguments over terms, especially where ownership was divided. But in 1893 a Royal Commission decided that royalties had not retarded development; the system evened differences, and many owners helped collieries in difficult periods. Ellis found owners 'generally . . . quite willing to meet the tenants as far as they possibly could'. Furthermore comparisons with agricultural leases were invalid; as Broomhead pointed out, 'a lease of coal was in effect not a lease at all, but a sale of part of the hereditament'. Although some owners demanded and received large sums (especially as the agricultural depression developed), there was often a debit account of agricultural dislocation. Certainly landowners did not hold back the industry's growth: the number of Yorkshire collieries rose from 276 in 1854 to 413 in 1869.[42]

While members of the ancient territorial families benefited from the rise of 'King Coal', the growing industry was creating new dynasties of wealthy entrepreneurs who hastened to gain social status and approval by entering the landed gentry. Royalties and mineral rents buttressed the traditional wealth of fortunate squires, but simultaneously helped to change the social order of the country-side.[43]

Since this paper was originally published in May 1963 there have been several additions to the literature on landed estates' involvement in mineral ventures. These include: B. F. Duckham, 'Some eighteenth-century Scottish coal-mining methods', *Industrial Archæology*, v (1968); 'Life and labour in a Scottish colliery, 1698–1755', *Scottish Historical Review*, XLVII (1968); 'The emergence of the professional manager in the Scottish coal industry', *Business History Review*, XLIII (1969); intro-duction to R. L. Galloway, *A History of Coal Mining in Great Britain* (Newton Abbot, 1969 edn.); *A History of the Scottish Coal Industry*, I: *1700–1815* (Newton Abbot, 1970). G. S. Hudson, *The Aberford Railway and the History of the Garforth Collieries* (Newton Abbot, 1971). F. C. Mather, *After the Canal Duke* (Oxford, 1970). T. J. Ray-bould, *The Economic Emergence of the Black Country: a Study of the Dudley Estate* (Newton Abbot, 1973). Eric Richards, *The Leviathan of Wealth* (1973); 'The industrial face of a great estate: Trentham and Lilleshall, 1780–1860', *Economic History Review*, second series, XXVII (1974). T. C. Smout, 'Scottish landowners and economic growth, 1650–1850', *Scottish J. Polit. Econ.*, XI (1964). David Spring, 'Agents to the Earls of Durham in the nineteenth century', *Durham Univ. J.*, LIV (1962); *The English Landed Estate in the nineteenth century: its Administration* (Baltimore, Md., 1963); 'English landowners and nine-teenth-century industrialism', in J. T. Ward and R. G. Wilson (eds.), *Land and Industry* (Newton Abbot, 1971, 1974). R. W. Sturgess, 'Land-ownership, mining and urban development in nineteenth-century Staf-fordshire', in Ward and Wilson, *op. cit.* J. T. Ward, 'The saving of a Yorkshire estate: George Lane-Fox and Bramham Park', *Yorkshire Arch. Jour.*, XLII (1967); 'Ayrshire landed estates in the nineteenth century', *Ayrshire Arch. and Nat. Hist. Soc. Collections*, second series, VIII (1969); 'Some West Cumberland landowners and industry', *Indus-trial Archæology*, IX (1972); 'Landowners and mining', in Ward and Wilson, *op. cit.*

## Notes

1 'Report from the Select Committee on coal mines' (*Parliamentary Papers,* 1852, v) p. 50; 'Report of the Commissioners appointed to inquire into the several matters relating to coal . . . ' (*P.P.,* 1871, XVIII), III, p. 63 and appendix; H. S. Jevons, *The British Coal Trade* (London, 1915), p. 64; A. M. Neuman, *Economic Organisation of the British Coal Industry* (London, 1934), pp. 513–5.

2 J. U. Nef, *The Rise of the British Coal Industry* (London, 1932), II, p. 441; D. A. Wray, *The Mining Industry in the Huddersfield District* (Huddersfield, 1929), pp. 9–16.

3 'Select Committee of the House of Lords on the state of the coal trade', second Report (*P.P.,* 1830, VIII), p. 263 *et* pp. 266–7.

4 1871 Report, III, p. 92 *et seq.;* 'First Report of the Royal Commission appointed to inquire into the subject of mining royalties' (*P.P.,* 1890, XXXVI), p. 51 *et* p. 180.

5 1890 Report, pp. 51–88 *et* pp. 180–3; 'Final Report' (*P.P.,* 1893–94, XLI), p. 3 *et seq.;* 'Coal Industry Commission reports', 1919 (Cmd. 360), II, p. 671; see J. Clark, 'Minerals', in R. C. Walmsley, *Rural Estate Management* (London, 1948), pp. 323–33; T. S. Ashton and J. Sykes, *The Coal Industry of the Eighteenth Century* (Manchester, 1929), p. 175 *et seq.*

6 1890 Report, pp. 1 *et* 146; 1919 Report, II, pp. 584–657.

7 1890 Report, pp. 52 *et* 58; 'Final Report', pp. 8–11; 1919 Report, II, p. 671.

8 1890 Report, pp. 52 *et* 58–9 *et* 74; 'Final Report', p. 23 *et seq.;* *Digest of Evidence given before the Royal Commission on Coal Supplies* (London, 1905), I, p. 18 *et seq.*

9 See D. Spring, 'The Earls of Durham and the Great Northern Coalfield, 1830–80', (*Canadian Hist. Rev.,* XXXIII, 3, September 1952); 1871 Report, appendix 27; 1890 Report, p. 51.

10 'Return of owners of land, 1873' (*P.P.,* 1874 LXXII), II, West Riding section (hereafter cited as 'Return'), p. 71; J. Bateman, *Great Landowners of Great Britain and Ireland* (London, 1879 edn.), 327; Ashton and Sykes, *op. cit.,* pp. 176–82; J. Wilkinson, *Worsborough* (London and Barnsley, 1872), p. 255.

11 F. Bland, 'John Curr . . .', *Trans. Newcomen Soc.,* XI (1930–31); W. Green, 'Chronicles and records of the northern coal trade', *North of England Institute of Mining Engineers' Trans.,* XV (1866); R. L. Galloway, *A History of Coal Mining in Great Britain* (London 1882), pp. 116–19 *et* 186, *Annals of Coal Mining and the Coal Trade* (London, 1898), I, pp. 321–5 *et* 369; Ashton and Sykes, *op. cit. passim;* G. P. Jones, 'Early industrial development', in D. L. Linton (ed.), *Sheffield and its Region* (Sheffield, 1956).

12 Galloway, *Annals,* I, p. 474; 1890 Report, pp. 77–8.

13 'Return', *loc. cit.,* 35; Wentworth Woodhouse muniments in Sheffield City Library, by courtesy of the Earl Fitzwilliam and the trustees of the Fitzwilliam settled estates; see my article, 'The Earls Fitzwilliam and the Wentworth Woodhouse estate in the nineteenth century', *Yorkshire Bulletin,* XII, 1, March 1960.

14 *Trans. Newcomen Soc.,* XI (1930–31), 132; Galloway, *Annals,* I, p. 474,

II, p. 385; *Sheffield Independent*, 16 October 1858, *et seq.*; F. Machin, *The Yorkshire Miners* (Barnsley, 1958), I, pp. 28–9, *et* 51–5 *et* 279–89 *et* 393–4; J. E. Williams, *The Derbyshire Miners* (London, 1962), pp. 253–4.

15 *N. of Eng. Inst. . . . Trans.*, X (1862), pp. 216–7; 1852 Report, vii; Galloway, *Annals*, II, *passim*. I am indebted to Mr J. Bebbington, Sheffield City Librarian, for information.

16 Bretton Hall accounts, by courtesy of the Viscount Allendale, K.G., C.B., C.B.E., M.C.; see my article, 'The Beaumont family's estates in the nineteenth century', *Bulletin of the Institute of Historical Research*, XXXV, 92 (November 1962).

17 T. Sopwith, 'On the lead-mining districts of the north of England', *N. of Eng. Inst. . . . Trans.*, XIII (1864); *The Times*, 14 February 1907.

18 'Return', *loc. cit.*, p. 107; Bateman (London, 1883 edn.), p. 473; Wray, *op. cit.*, p. 13; *N. of Eng. Inst. . . . Trans.*, XV (1865–66), p. 202; P. M. Sweezy, *Monopoly and Competition in the English Coal Trade, 1550–1850* (Cambridge, Mass., 1938), pp. 24 *et* 27.

19 'Report on accidents in coal mines' (*P.P.*, 1849, VII; Wharncliffe muniments in Sheffield City Library, by courtesy of the Earl of Wharncliffe.

20 R. V. Taylor, *Biographia Leodiensis* (London and Leeds, 1865), p. 490. I am indebted to the Earl of Mexborough and Sir William Lowther, Bt., for information.

21 See D. Spring, 'The English landed estate in the age of coal and iron, 1830–80', *Journal of Economic History*, XI, 1 (winter 1951); Wray, *op. cit.*, p. 23; *Fleet Papers*, 13 January 1844. I am indebted to Mrs H. M. Beaumont, Mrs Mary Ward, the hon. E. L. Jackson, Mr J. R. R. Fullerton, Miss C. E. Leeke, Sir Everard Radcliffe, Bt., Capt. J. E. B. Radcliffe, M.C., and Mr J. Towneley Taylor for information; 'Return', *loc. cit., passim*.

22 Crewe-Milnes muniments in Sheffield City Library, by courtesy of the Marchioness of Crewe; Bateman (1883), *op. cit.*, p. 228; 1919 Report, II, pp. 672 *et* 674 *et* 690.

23 Bateman (1883), *op. cit.*, pp. 76 *et* 213 *et* 148. I am indebted to the Marquess of Ailesbury, D.S.O., T.D., the Earl of Cardigan, the Earl of Rosse, Mr G. N. Shackleford and Major R. H. Pardoe for information.

24 'Return', *loc. cit.*, p. 107; G. E. Wentworth, 'History of the Wentworths of Woolley', *Yorks. Archæological Jour.*, XII (1893); J. W. Walker, *Wakefield* (Wakefield, 1934), p. 457; J. Wilkinson, *Worthies . . . of Barnsley* (London and Derby, 1883), p. 19.

25 J. Hunter, *South Yorkshire* (London, 1831), II, p. 281 *et seq.*; Wilkinson, *Worsborough, op. cit.*, p. 245 *et seq.*; 1919 Report, II, pp. 672 *et* 674; Vernon-Wentworth muniments in Sheffield City Library, by courtesy of Major C. J. Vernon-Wentworth and Messrs Lancaster & Sons.

26 Bateman (1883), *op. cit.*, p. 315; Leeds MSS in Yorkshire Archæological Society collection, by courtesy of the Duke of Leeds; Wilkinson, *Worsborough, op. cit.*, p. 253; 'Mining royalties, third report' (*P.P.*, 1890–91, XLI), pp. 126–8; Wray, *op. cit.*, p. 23. I am indebted to Major H. Meynell, M.C., the Earl of Yarborough, Mr W. D. Danwell and the Lord Savile for information; 'Return', *loc. cit., passim*.

27 'Return', *loc. cit.*, 114; Bateman (1883), *op. cit.*, p. 493; Bolton Abbey MSS, by courtesy of the Duke of Devonshire, M.C., and Mr E. E. Hay. I am indebted to Mrs E. E. Yorke for information. See A. Raistrick, 'The lead mines of upper Wharfedale', *Yorkshire Bulletin*, V, 1 (February 1953).

28 Nostell MSS, by courtesy of the Lord St Oswald, M.C., and Major T. L. Ingram; Galloway, *Annals*, *op. cit.*, I, p. 320; Ashton and Sykes, *op. cit.*, p. 8; Wray, *op. cit.*, p. 23; Bateman (1883), *op. cit.*, p. 119; 'Midland Mining Commission, first report' (*P.P.*, 1843, XIII), pp. cxlv *et* 11–12; 1871 Report, III, appendix 27; 1919 Report, II, p. 689.

29 Bateman (1883), *op. cit.*, p. 85; Ashton and Sykes, *op. cit.*, *passim*; Walker, *op. cit.*, pp. 524–5; Machin, I, *op. cit.*, *passim;* 1871 Report, III, appendix 27.

30 Wray, *op. cit.*, p. 16; 'Return', *loc. cit.*, p. 57; Wharncliffe and Bretton MSS; 1871 Report, III, appendix 27.

31 Galloway, *Annals*, *passim*; Taylor, *op. cit.*, pp. 302–3; *Leeds Mercury*, 27 June 1812; Ashton and Sykes, *op. cit.*, *passim*; 1830 second report, p. 224; W. G. Rimmer, 'Middleton Colliery, near Leeds, 1770–1830', *Yorks. Bulletin*, VII, 1 (March 1957); E. K. Scott, 'Memorials to pioneer Leeds engineers', *Trans. Newcomen Soc.*, XI (1930–31).

32 'Return', *loc. cit.*, p. 21; Biram correspondence in Wentworth Woodhouse muniments.

33 'Return', *loc. cit.*, pp. 27 *et* 36 *et* 94; 1871 Report, III, appendix 27; I am indebted to Mr E. P. Stocks for information.

34 'Return', *loc. cit.*, p. 41; W. Grainge, *History and Topography of Harrogate* (London and York, 1882), pp. 429–30. I am indebted to Mrs M. Greenwood and Mr B. C. Greenwood for information.

35 Harewood MSS, by courtesy of the Earl of Harewood and Mr N. A. Ussher; Lane-Fox MSS in Leeds City Library, by courtesy of Col. F. G. W. Lane-Fox.

36 A. M. W. Stirling, *Annals of a Yorkshire House* (London, 1911), II, pp. 79–80 *et* 82–3; P. Slater, *History of the Ancient Parish of Guiseley* (London, 1880), p. 284; Spencer–Stanhope muniments in Sheffield City Library, by courtesy of Mrs M. E. I. Fraser–Spencer–Stanhope.

37 Ferrand MSS in Yorkshire Archæological Society collection and the Cartwright Memorial Museum, Bradford, by courtesy of the late Colonel G. W. Ferrand, O.B.E., to whom I am indebted for much further information; *Keighley News*, 17 August 1872.

38 Frickley Hall MSS, by courtesy of Colonel R. J. P. Warde-Aldam, T.D.; see my article, 'The squire as businessman: William Aldam of Frickley Hall, 1813–90', *Trans. Hunter Archæological Soc.*, VIII, 4 (1962); *cf.* A. G. Ruston, D. Whitney, *Hooton Pagnell* . . . (London, 1934), pp. 118–22 *et* 231.

39 See my article, 'West Riding landowners and the railways', *Journal of Transport History*, IV, 4 (November 1960).

40 1843 Report, pp. ciii–civ; 1852 Report, p. 65 *et passim*; Machin, *op. cit.*, I, *passim*.

41 1890 Report, pp. 59 *et* 78.

42 *Digest* (1905), *op. cit.*, I, pp. 239–41 *et* 66; 1890 Report, pp. 55 *et* 59 *et*

61 *et* 72; 'Final Report' (1893), pp. 13–14 *et* 37 *et seq. et* 79; 1871 Report, appendix 61; 1919 Report, ii, pp. 672 *et* 674.

43 I am indebted to the librarians of Queen's College, Dundee, Kilmarnock, Lanark, Leeds University, Nottingham University, Stoke on Trent, Leeds, Sheffield, Glasgow University, the Scottish Central Library, Wigan Mining and Technical College, Birmingham University, the Tolson Memorial Museum, Huddersfield, the Yorkshire Archæological Society and the Cartwright Memorial Museum, Bradford, for assistance; to Mr Frank Beckwith for helpful advice and to Professor D. F. Macdonald of Queen's College, Dundee, for valuable comments on this paper.

BARON F. DUCKHAM

# 4 The Oaks disaster, 1866

Despite the richness of the contemporary sources—notably the Inspectors of Mines' reports, special government inquiries, the minutes of Royal Commissions on mine safety and even the gruesomely detailed accounts of local journalists or pamphleteers—little has subsequently been written on Yorkshire's major colliery disasters.[1] There is assuredly room for comparative regional studies of mine safety, especially for the years of rapid physical growth which the coal industry experienced in the latter half of the nineteenth and early years of the twentieth centuries.[2] Here the intention is more modest: to look at the scale and impact of Yorkshire's most serious mining catastrophe: the explosions at the Oaks Colliery, Barnsley, in December 1866. What follows is, then, an attempt to reconstruct the events and the atmosphere of the disaster. The justification for the narrative approach adopted must be simply that the story of the Oaks remains comparatively unknown—but worth telling.

Until 1847 the Yorkshire coalfield had been spared the really serious mass disasters which had occurred elsewhere. Until then the limited area of the coalfield and the generally small scale of the productive units had provided some insurance against the type of explosions which periodically wrought such human destruction in Durham and Northumberland. In fact, of the thirty-three known British mine disasters which before 1847 had claimed twenty-five or more lives, all but five had taken place in the north-east of England.[3] With the gradual exploitation of the 'fiery' Barnsley bed, however, and the emergence of larger collieries, the scene was being set for accidents comparable to the worst in other coalfields. On 5 March 1847 the Oaks Colliery exploded, a calamity which carried away the lives of seventy-three men and boys.[4] It was to be grimly ironical that the county's worst disaster was also to be at the self-same mine. Meanwhile between the two disasters other devastating blasts occurred at a number of Yorkshire pits:[5]

| Date | Colliery | Death roll |
|------|----------|------------|
| 24 January 1849 | Darley Main | 75 |
| 20 December 1851 | Warren Vale, Rawmarsh | 52 |
| 19 February 1857 | Lundhill | 189 |
| 8 December 1862 | St Edmund's Main | 59 |

By 1866, then, the developing Yorkshire coalfield was no longer a stranger to the large-scale underground catastrophe.[6] Until the explosion at Senghenydd in 1913 the Oaks disaster remained for nearly half a century Britain's worst mining accident; and until national memory faded the colliery's monosyllabic name was synonymous with sudden death and incalculable grief.

Owned by Messrs Firth Barber & Co., the Oaks Colliery was situated on the Manchester, Sheffield & Lincolnshire Railway about a mile south of Barnsley. It was then one of the largest mining units in Yorkshire, and beneath its three shafts 285 yards deep lay a maze of some fifty miles of galleries—not counting the numerous 'goaves' or wastes from which coal had already been taken.[7] By 1866 the coal to the rise had been mainly extracted; consequently operations were concentrated to the dip, in workings reached by an inclined plane near the bottom of the pits and running approximately east by south.[8] From the technical viewpoint it was considered a well appointed mine, efficiently managed. The consultative viewer, John Thomas Woodhouse, was an eminent mining engineer of the day,[9] while John Edward Mammatt, the resident viewer, was undoubtedly a rising star of a then rapidly developing profession.[10]

Assuredly the colliery was fiery, but no ingenuity had been spared in securing adequate ventilation. Two furnaces, side by side and fed with fresh air, sent the return air into the upcast shaft some seventy yards from the fires.[11] The total air current descending the downcast pits was 152,000 cu. ft per minute, of which the 'working' 135,000 cu. ft (17,000 cu. ft of air was required to feed the furnaces) was divided into nine main splits.[12] A serious issue of firedamp from a fault at the end of the dip north level was piped to the bottom of the downcast shafts and used for lighting the lamps there (in fresh, not return, air, of course). Elsewhere, and certainly on the coal faces or in return airways, safety lamps only were the rule. Having said this, it remains true that a number of men had made a complaint about a weak point in the ventilation only twelve days before the accident.[13] This had apparently been corrected by the management, and a proposal by some of the hewers to invite the inspector (C. Morton) to examine it was accordingly dropped.[14] Later there were inevitably some who held that the explosion would not have occurred if Morton had been called in. But there is no evidence to suggest that there is any truth in this.[15]

In the wider sphere of relations between capital and labour the immediate past in the Yorkshire coalfield was none too happy.[16] The Oaks miners had taken part in the long campaign by colliers to be paid by weight of coal produced rather than by measure and to have their own checkweighmen to ensure fair play. Clause 29 of the Act of 1860 had at long last introduced the right of the men to choose their 'justice man',[17] but in practice it had to be done at their own expense and in the teeth of a generally obstructive attitude on the part of the owners. Checkweighmen could all too easily be victimised, and it is estimated by Machin that despite the enabling legislation only eight of them existed in the whole of south and west Yorkshire in December 1864.[18]

The Oaks men had been on strike in 1858 and had been locked out in 1860, when they at first refused to sacrifice a justice man to whom their employers objected.[19] The year 1864 witnessed an effort by the more determined miners of the district to push through wage increases. The cycle of business activity was on the upward trend, and the men claimed a fairer share of the profits. Their recent experience had not made them more tractable. During the third week of February the Oaks miners came out; after five weeks they won union support, and a singularly bitter struggle developed. The Coal Owners' Association was intransigent, and it may well be that its actions were such as to make the dispute technically a lock-out. In May the employers toughened further and began to evict colliers from the tied cottages, with the result that the men and their families were compelled to borrow tents and camp in the surrounding fields. In June the union members were keeping body and soul together on strike pay of 5s weekly per man and 8d per dependent child, while the owners endeavoured—with police protection, it might be noted—to work the colliery with blackleg labour from Staffordshire and elsewhere.

Dreadful privations were undoubtedly suffered by man, woman and child—the *Sheffield Independent* spoke of 'partial famine'[20]— and with the onset of winter the men scoured the countryside for empty barns or any more substantial shelter they could find. From the third week in November the South Yorkshire Miners' Association raised support to 10s for men and 1s 6d for children per week.[21] Only on 17 December 1864 was a reasonably fair compromise reached, but feelings had run high and much of the men's bitterness and resentment was stilled only by the fearful explosion which ended their struggles for ever almost exactly two years later. The strike of 1864, like the accidents of 1847 and 1866, forms an important part of the unfortunate yet formidable legend of the Oaks.

One point of union activity is more directly relevant. The South Yorkshire Miners' Association decided in April 1866 to support widows at the rate of 5s weekly whose husbands died in mining accidents and to allow 1s a week for each orphaned child.[22] For 113 married women, thirteen other (old) parents and 330 children of the vicinity of the Oaks this decision was to prove timely indeed. In fact the union met its commitments after the great disaster in the spirit as well as to the letter, giving immediate help to the dependants of several non-members. A special levy and a public appeal proved to be necessary to pay for all the funeral grants and other aid; but we may be sure that the pitmen of south Yorkshire begrudged not a penny.

## The first explosion

The first and most deadly explosion of a series of no fewer than seventeen ignitions took place at about 1.20 p.m. on Wednesday 12 December 1866.[23] A loud report was heard throughout the surrounding area to a distance of three miles. According to the *Barnsley Chronicle*, 'The convulsion shook the whole neighbourhood as if the earth had been rent by an earthquake'.[24] Volumes of dense black smoke and clouds of black dust rose from the mouths of the pits 'like that from a suddenly agitated volcano'.[25] On a farm at Cudworth, almost five miles away, men engaged in winter ploughing found the ground around them being covered with a sprinkling of fine coal dust and soot.

At the pit head the shaken officials hastily examined the headgear. They discovered that the cage in No. 2 shaft had been quite blown away and that the one in No. 1 pit was broken and disconnected from the rope. The winding engine had also suffered some slight damage. But as the smoke continued for several minutes to pour ominously from the downcast shafts it was principally of human life and not of machinery that the horror-stricken surface workers thought.

The explosion, they knew, could not possibly have come at a worse time. Wednesday at the Oaks was 'making-up day', when the miners made up their week's work.[26] Normally 147 sets of tools were employed in the pit, which accounted for almost 300 men.[27] On top of these would be some seventy or more day labourers or officials. The management had no complete record of exactly which men were in the mine, and it was the union and not the employers who were best able subsequently to compile a list of the missing. The approach of Christmas, too, as the *Chronicle* commented, was 'an additional inducement for the unfortunate victims of this sad accident to have been more than usually regular at their work in order to supply their humble boards with a bountiful supply of Christmas cheer.'[28] No one was sure on that first afternoon how many might have been killed. The *Yorkshire Post* thought 'about three hundred and fifty lives lost'[29]—an estimate which was to be slightly too high for the first explosion, but eleven too few for the total disaster.

On the pit bank fevered activity had quickly replaced the inertia of the stunned minutes following the blast. The ropes were wound up the shafts and a new cage was fitted for use in No. 1 pit.[30] As luck would have it, the rope was badly chafed. It was an old one, and arrangements had been put in hand a day or two earlier to have it replaced. From the very outset Thomas Dymond, the managing partner, and David Tewart, the under-viewer, were faced with the dilemma of losing precious time changing the rope or risking the damaged old one. Courageously they decided to chance the existing rope. If anyone below had survived the blast, the heat and the afterdamp, speed was absolutely essential before more of the pernicious gases returned to snuff the last sparks of life. (In coal-mine explosions the toll of life exacted by afterdamp has almost always been significantly greater than that caused by the blast *per se*.)[31] By about 2 p.m. Dymond, Tewart and a deputy, Charlie Siddons, were ready to begin the descent. They had not yet been able to prepare for an extended exploration of the work-ings—if such were indeed possible—but their slender hope was that a few men might have been able to pick and stumble their way through the smoke and suffocating atmosphere to pit bottom.

Meanwhile the roads leading to the colliery from Barnsley, Hoyle

Mill, Ardsley, Stairfoot, Worsborough Common and even Dodworth were crowded with relatives and friends of the Oaks workers. The scene was such, said the *Chronicle,* that language was powerless to describe it with justice.

From all directions men, women and children—the most frantic terror and anxiety depicted on the countenances of those whose husbands, fathers, sons, or brothers had that morning descended the fatal shaft— were all hurrying breathlessly to the Oaks . . . To endeavour to describe the streams of human beings as they rushed along to the one common centre would be a task of some difficulty. Here was a wife and mother who had been arranging her toilet against the anticipated return for the day of the loved ones who had left home at five in the morning so unsuspicious of danger—alas for the mutability of human anticipations!—half running, half walking, in dishabillé, with a babe in her arms and dragging a young one by the hand; while another who had no children, or who had left them in the care of a neighbour, rushed wildly along, heedless of obstructions, not staying to pick her way along the muddy roads, and thinking only of those in whom her hopes and happiness were centred.[32]

It is not to be supposed that the crowds were composed solely of those likely to suffer bereavement. A fact natural to such closely knit communities was that almost anyone who heard an explosion immediately made for the wrecked colliery. Many Barnsley shopkeepers and other small tradesmen were among the first to gather. The local police under Superintendent Greenhalgh, and eventually several of the district's magistrates, arrived to maintain the necessary order; and within a short time of the disaster at least six doctors had offered their services at the pit bank.[33] And along, too, came the newspaper reporters, conscious enough of their inability to convey fully to middle-class readers the horror and stark reality of the suffering they witnessed. 'The pen of Dickens', noted one of them, 'would come short of adequately describing the wild excitement which prevailed'.[34]

Some of the reporters were in time to witness a few of the survivors, fearfully burnt, being raised to the bank. They hastily drew what word pictures their inspirations gave them, inevitably perhaps concentrating on the dreadful injuries of the men and boys recovered or on the emotional outbursts of the crowds of distracted wives, mothers, sisters and sweethearts, now beside themselves with anxiety. Such a pitiful crowd of near desperate women was not easy to handle with tact and firmness, and it must have been a considerable relief to Greenhalgh when Colonel Cobb, Chief Constable of the West Riding, brought much needed reinforcements later in the day.[35]

Each time the cage came to the bank onlookers, particularly women, surged forward. If the victim had already been recognised, his name was called out until some unfortunate being claimed the injured man as a husband, son or brother. Only too ofter the rescued miner or boy was burnt beyond recovery. 'It would almost seem', the *Chronicle*'s reporter was compelled to write, 'that the complete extinction of life would have been a merciful consummation'.[36] Details given at the inquest about the last few hours of some of these poor men, taken home to die in excruciating pain, provide a sad gloss on the observation.[37]

Toiling through the scenes of death and injury underground, or waiting their turn to relieve the parties of explorers, were very soon no fewer than seventy to eighty volunteers. Viewers and men alike came from many neighbouring collieries; some of the former from much farther afield. There was never any lack of willing rescuers at the Oaks. Throughout the disaster the selfless efforts of those who not only risked their lives for their fellow men, but in some cases actually sacrificed themselves, were beyond praise. The catastrophe of the Oaks Colliery, like other great mine disasters, is a story of unspeakable human waste; but it is also one of shining human courage.

Thomas Dymond was undoubtedly one of the heroes. He represented in this connection one of the best qualities of British mine ownership: the almost invariable personal bravery of a very high order in the face of any accident to its employees. (And if the coal owners can historically not infrequently be indicted for a laxity that contributed to accidents, the proprietors of the Oaks can almost certainly be exonerated in this particular case). Dymond's rescue party had, as we have seen, descended the pit shortly after 2 p.m. They can have had little faith that they would find anybody alive, for 'rapping' on the rope just before the descent had elicited no response from the bottom.[38] To their genuine surprise, then, they found twenty to thirty survivors, all more or less badly scorched or affected by afterdamp but still alive, huddled together near the foot of the shaft. These were the men who were first sent out of the pit and whose arrival at the surface was alluded to a moment ago. Only six of them were to recover from their burns. None could tell the explorers anything of real consequence save what was already known: that there had been a violent and devastating explosion. But as to the possible cause there was little clue these poor remnants of human beings could give.[39]

Dense and quite deadly afterdamp hung between the rescuers and most of the remaining workmen in the mine. But the worst forebodings seemed confirmed by what the volunteers found in the small portion of the workings they *were* able to penetrate. Thirty-eight charred victims—the almost unidentifiable corpses of what only a little earlier had been vital men and boys—were almost immediately discovered. The rescue party made arrangements to have the bodies removed and also called up more help to make temporary repairs in the air courses so that a better ventilation could be restored.[40]

As exploration penetrated a little farther, the full and appalling extent of the disaster became apparent to all—not as an intellectual proposition merely, but as grim reality. The long inclined engine plane resembled a battlefield. There they lay, the once lusty workers of the Oaks: colliers who had fallen in their tracks as they hurried in alarm from their 'benks'; boys on duty who had died at their posts; youthful drivers next to their dead horses. Fathers and sons were locked in their last embrace; brother was stretched out side by side with brother, overcome in all probability within minutes or seconds of each other; some had obviously stumbled for the last time over obstructions in their path or over uneven parts of the ground; others had simply slumped into death as noxious gases overwhelmed them. Few of these bodies on the plane were burnt or injured in any way; their end had been one of suffocation, so often a more remorseless killer than blast or flame. The picture can scarcely be recreated without the risk of sinking into either sentimentality or conventional description.[41]

Requests for additional explorers always met an instant response. As the watchers noted, 'had treble the number of volunteers been required who actually descended, they might have been had'.[42] The very danger of the situation, with the ever present possibility of further explosions, seemed to increase the men's wish to help rather than to deter them. They knew that where assistance was required it was required urgently. Calculations of personal hazard were scarcely made at all in mine rescue work. (At St Edmund's Main in December 1862 ugly scenes had in fact followed the inspector's order to prevent foolhardy attempts at descending the shaft.)[43] Some men, of course, had immediate relatives to work for: a volunteer named Cartwright who struggled on until he collapsed had three brothers in the mine.[44] But others from neighbouring collieries, who hardly knew more than a handful of Oaks miners by name, also gave nothing less than their best.

Throughout all the operations the fact that grave perils still threatened was concealed from nobody. Barometric pressure remained low, the ventilation was not wholly repaired and the coal was infamously gassy.[45] No one doubted that a second ignition could easily take place, though the very magnitude of the first perhaps made rescuers feel that the gods had now finished with the mine. Afterdamp was known to be present in large concentrations, while no man who descended the shaft during the earlier stages was unaware that the rope was damaged and might break. Only when hope of finding any more men alive had ebbed away was Dymond willing temporarily to suspend operations to fit a new rope and secure the cage.[46] Already the *Barnsley Chronicle* was finding what solace there was in the valour of the explorers:

There are other scenes in which true heroism is displayed than the field of battle—there are gallant men who have promptly responded to other sounds than the boom of the cannon, the dash of arms, or the strains of martial music. Napoleon and Wellington never commanded braver or more willing soldiers—men more fearless of danger—than those who rushed to the Oaks Pit to render their assistance on the first alarm of the awful calamity being given on Wednesday afternoon.[47]

Time and again during the next few weeks or months—in funeral sermons, commemoration services, public meetings for the relief of sufferers, at the inquest and in the inspector's report—reference was made to the bravery of these rescue parties.

By 5 p.m., then, some thirty men and lads had been removed from the mine and work was proceeding on the dismal task of raising what dead had so far been discovered. Characteristically some of the sadder stories or ironic incidents were already being recounted among the bystanders.[48] One man had descended the pit only a few minutes before the explosion; a trifling delay—a few more words with one of the surface workers, perhaps—and he would have been spared. Another collier, Charles Thorley of Dodworth Bottom, had but recently left his previous colliery and had begun at the Oaks that very morning. Luck had served others better. George Cotton and George Ibbartson had lain too long in bed that morning and had not gone down; William Wards had fortunately had to go to Chesterfield on that black Wednesday; William Hutchinson and John Ouram had come out of the mine ten minutes before it exploded because their work had been ended for the day when a portion of a tramway fell in. One survivor, Smith Bates, had stopped work early to attend a funeral. The blast hit him while he was dressing, hurled missiles against his body and almost knocked him unconscious. Somehow he had none the less managed to battle his way through the chokedamp and debris to safety. His own brother, who had worked on, was among the victims.

None of these events was unique in its nature to this explosion. Such varied anecdotes formed one of the principal ingredients of the legend which evolved around every great colliery accident. Many were taken and few were spared; but to the bereaved was left the strictly unanswerable question, why *him*? 'Providential escapes', 'melancholy cases' and 'remarkable incidents' (as the contemporary press called them) might be carefully retold by any number of tongues, yet they were for ever beyond any human scrutiny. Religion no doubt helped some of the bereaved; but one suspects that for many the only support was a deep-seated stoicism or fatalism.

## A second tragedy

During the evening and night the bleak and gaunt pit head was lighted by the colliery's own gas lights. They burned untiringly within their plain metal shades, a controlled combustion of the very elements which had slaughtered the manhood of the district. Colonel Cobb cleared the immediate vicinity of bystanders, who now kept vigil by the carpenter's shop, where an adjacent hut had been pressed into service as a temporary repository for some of the dead.[49] Identified bodies had been removed by their kin. At the pit mouth the rope had at last been renewed and the work of bringing out corpses went slowly forward. Every so often the cage would ascend with another dead man or boy and the grim business of recognition would begin again.[50]. Another six volunteers would have their names entered and descend to look for further dead. It was a chill and comfortless routine. And all the time in mean cottages mothers, sisters and wives tended the last cold needs of their loved ones.

In the evening another of the heroes of the Oaks disaster arrived at the pit: Parkin Jeffcock, a partner of John Thomas Woodhouse, who was, as we have noted, the colliery's consultant viewer.[51] A man who had already won the widest respect both professionally and also for his evangelical zeal and kindly paternalism, Jeffcock was determined to spare no personal effort whatsoever in his search for the bodies of victims or the possible miraculous survivor. After receiving a brief report he descended the mine with two other officials, Minto of Mount Osborne and Agnes Main collieries, and John Smith, underground steward of Lundhill (itself scene of a devastating explosion in 1857).[52] Below the surface they conferred with several of the viewers or engineers, some of whom they formally relieved. Then a dauntless party of Jeffcock, David Tewart, two under-deputies and two firemen from the Oaks, and several others, began a tireless exploration of the workings. Most of them toiled throughout the night.

As the ventilation was slowly restored by the renewal of brattices or the temporary rebuilding of stoppings, so the explorers pushed on deeper into the mine. Apart from the dangers mentioned, the men had to contend with the additional hazard of an insecure roof —another feature of an exploded colliery. Indeed, there had already been considerable falls over the length of nearly a mile, while at many points large quatities of coal or stone blown down by the explosion completely blocked the way.[53] All this exploration was accompanied without the modern aids of telecommunication and breathing apparatus.

By breakfast time on Thursday most of the night's volunteers had been relieved, six at a time, by their comrades. But Jeffcock was still underground when, between 8 a.m. and 9 a.m., Dymond and others sent word down to him that they were more than prepared to take his place. Jeffcock's answer was simply a request that the temperature in the shaft should be ascertained, in case the mine was (as some suspected) growing hotter and therefore more likely to re-ignite.[54] On the surface the grey dawn was beginning to give way to what the *Chronicle*'s reporter described as 'a moist, mild morning'. The roads to the pit were starting to fill once more with 'eager pedestrians' or with miners coming to volunteer for work in what was being called a cavern of slaughter.

A warning that something serious might indeed be amiss came to a number of the explorers at about 8.30 a.m. A party of about sixteen under William Sugden, one of the Oaks under-deputies, was some 750 yards from the pit bottom at the time. Suddenly the men perceived an unmistakable disturbance to the air current. 'She's sucked', cried some. Sugden, anticipating an explosion, despairingly exclaimed, 'Oh! lads; we are all done', whereupon a rush developed to reach the cage.[55] All the men save Sugden were drawn to safety;

as an official he clearly considered it his duty to remain behind. Another deputy, Mathew Haigh, had also noticed the 'suck'— which he, no doubt correctly, attributed to a slight ignition of gas— and had too given the alarm. Six cages full of men were saved in this way, with apparently as many as fifteen in some of the loads.[56]

On the bank the fugitives met some mild derision from six relief volunteers who were still ready to proceed below. These six none the less checked that the ventilation was still flowing normally at the upcast shaft before descending. It was a few minutes later, at about 9 a.m. and just as a thermometer was being lowered into the shaft, that the pit fired with great violence for the second time.[57]

The men around the pit mouth were tumbled back 'one over the other', as T. W. Embleton later described it to the North of England Institute of Mining Engineers.[58] In No. 1 shaft the cage was blasted up into the headgear and for the second occasion within twenty-four hours the muffled boom and black pall of smoke announced to the men and women of Barnsley that sudden death was in their midst once more. It is impossible, all the sources assure one, to recapture the sense of utter hopelessness which then engulfed everyone. 'The heart sickens', wrote the *Yorkshire Post,* 'in contemplating such a frightful addition to the deplorable record of this unparallel catastrophe.'[59] In attempting at this later date to assess the mood of abandonment and anguish which must have swept through the remnants of the brave rescuers on the cold grey surface, those terrible, desolate words spoken by Gloucester in *King Lear* come readily to mind:

> As flies to wanton boys are we to the gods;
> They kill us for their sport.

'Strong men cried like children', reported the *Barnsley Chronicle;*[60] and it was some minutes before the need to go through at least the motions of action impressed itself on the stunned, almost stupefied ring of miners and viewers on the bank. Just in case someone might have survived—though hardly a soul believed it conceivable —the cage was lowered to the bottom and, after a few minutes, slowly raised. It was empty.[61]

Yet all that was needful had to be seen to be done. Two men came forward and lay down with their heads over the shaft. The other occupants at the pit mouth remained perfectly still while their comrades together shouted into the depths below. Not one answer was returned; the silence was complete. Again they shouted;

and again no sound issued from the bit bottom. The fate of the twenty-seven explorers known to be below was now considered as sealed. All the experts agreed that not a living thing could have held on to life in the hell-like atmosphere of the Oaks.[62] The intrepid and earnest Jeffcock was undoubtedly dead; and with him had gone Smith, Tewart and the others.

Nothing remained that could be immediately attempted. The platform was cleared of rescuers and guards were posted to keep back the immense crowd which grew throughout the day. Not a train arrived in Barnsley without its throng of passengers, enquiring the way to the Oaks.[63] Rain fell; and the trample of sad or curious feet reduced the approach roads to a sea of almost impassable mud. Distinguished visitors too—like Viscount Halifax, the Lord Lieutenant of the West Riding, or Major Waterhouse, MP for Pontefract—came to view the scene of the tragedy. A telegram from Windsor was received which asked in the Queen's name whether the loss of life had in fact been as serious as reported. J. T. Woodhouse arrived to find his worst fears for the safety of his partner, Parkin Jeffcock, confirmed. Clergymen of all denominations were in constant attendance.

The whole district had in truth been reduced to a vale of weeping.[64] Men compared the total slaughter with biblical or classical scourges; they compared it with Culloden, with the breach of Bradfield reservoir near Sheffield—with any great loss of life from antiquity onwards within their knowledge. As all now realised too well, there had certainly never been a mining disaster to equal it. And with recovery operations suspended, speculation mounted about the cause of the catastrophe. Many believed that the initial firing had resulted from the colliery's having suddenly become overpowered by an unexpected and perhaps enormous issue of gas. (Such occurrences were by no means unknown at the Oaks.) Where or how the ignition had actually happened was indeed a question never to be answered with absolute finality. One popular theory was that some blasting operations in a new stone drift must have been responsible. It remains a likely hypothesis.

The new drift's purpose was to provide a more effective channel of ventilation than the top end of the inclined plane between the dip levels and the downcast shafts (see fig. 4.1).[65] The man in charge of the operations, William Wilson, survived long enough to state that the explosion had come only a split second after the last shot of powder was fired which pierced the drift's final barrier of rock.

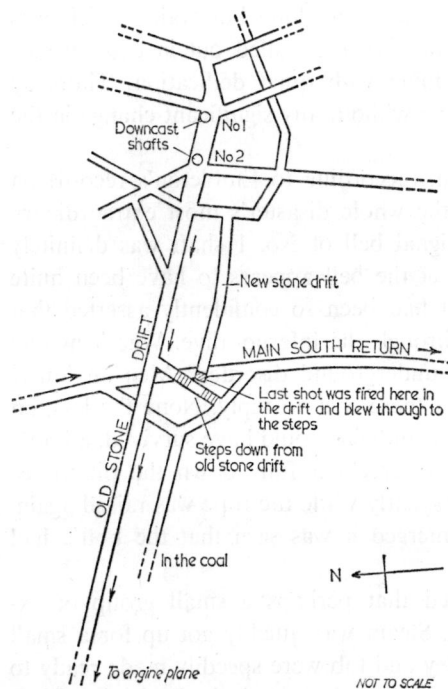

Downcast shafts
No 1
No 2
New stone drift
DRIFT
MAIN SOUTH RETURN →
Last shot was fired here in the drift and blew through to the steps
Steps down from old stone drift
OLD STONE
In the coal
N ←
To engine plane
NOT TO SCALE

FIG. 4.1

Had the flame from this shot met with some unsuspected pocket of gas? (The drift had earlier been found gas-free.) There was endless discussion of this as well as of more high-flown theories. The question will be reconsidered shortly.

*Closure and enquiry*

At 7.40 p.m. a third explosion occurred: dense black smoke billowed forth from No. 2 pit after 'a violent blast of wind' had been felt.[66] Flames and sparks later discharged freely at the surface, and it was clear that the mine was well and truly on fire. One of the effects of the explosion was to derange the ventilation hopelessly, the air current now being sucked *down* No. 1 shaft and the furnace pit. Smoke and sparks continued to be emitted by No. 2 throughout the night. Men were appointed to watch and report any significant alteration of circumstances, though nothing had really been hoped for since the second ignition. The principal viewers and the colliery's owners had discussed tactics at length, but had not yet come to any firm decision. There was little to be done but wait—which was exactly what the Barnsley fire brigade, called out in case surface buildings took fire, were doing with quiet dedication. Thursday night became Friday morning without any significant change in the total position.

It was at about 4.30 a.m. (according to Embleton's record) on Friday 14 December that the whole disaster's most extraordinary incident took place. The signal bell of No. 1 shaft was definitely heard to ring.[67] The effect of the bell appears to have been quite uncanny, especially since it had been so confidently asserted that no one could have come through the inferno alive. Was it merely some strange result of the underground disorder? Men anxiously shouted down the shaft, but there was no reply. None the less, on the remote chance that a human being could have survived, a bottle of brandy and water was lowered carefully down the pit to see what happened. All waited silently while the rope was raised again. When the end at last re-emerged it was seen that the bottle had gone.

Immediately hope revived that perhaps a small group of explorers might still be alive. Steam was quickly got up for a small saw-mill engine, and a pulley and tub were speedily made ready to serve as temporary headgear and cage respectively. In the meantime some of the mining engineers had been summoned. Despite the obvious danger of further explosions T. W. Embleton and J. E. Mammatt insisted not simply on sending the makeshift 'cage' down but on descending in it themselves. Years later, when Mammatt was giving evidence before the Royal Commission on Accidents in Mines, Sir George Elliot recalled the occasion:

I believe you were at the Oaks when I was there with Mr Woodhouse. I remember you performed a very daring deed in going down with young Mr Embleton, for which I thought you ought to have been rewarded with the Victoria Cross.[68]

Their descent was perilous in the extreme, for, as Embleton later described, the explosion had blocked the pump dams and huge feeders of water poured down the shaft as uncontrolled as waterfalls. Only with the very greatest difficulty could they keep a light burning at all.

At the bottom they found a solitary survivor, Samuel Brown. No one else could be seen or heard and there was no further hint of life. The mine was now quite impenetrable. At the top of the incline wrecked timber and corves of coal were burning fiercely. Of Parkin Jeffcock there was not the slightest sign.

Samuel Brown, whose escape must be reckoned one of the luckiest in mining history,[69] had been a member of an exploration party which had descended on Thursday morning at 7 a.m. With others he had gone down the incline, where two more bodies had been found. After visiting the shaft bottom once more they turned back into the mine and met several men hurrying towards the cage (presumably those with Sugden who had been alarmed by the 'sucking' of the air). Jeffcock and his party had been seen to go deeper into the workings, though in a different direction.

With three companions. Barker, Hoyland and Young, Brown had gone to what was known as the 'lamp hole' and rested there. It was while they were at this point that the second explosion erupted. Brown remembered little of what happened and his comrades were silenced for good by the blast, 'I remained there [at the lamp office] until I lost my faculties', he explained later;

and remained in that position for some time, after which I began to recover. I then made my way to the bell wire, and received an answer from above. I have to state that two persons which I felt with my hands were all that I came across during my stay in the pit, and I supposed them to be dead.[70]

Actually he had first gone to No. 2 shaft, where he had found a large fire and resignedly sat down. Fortunately he fought off the apathy with traditional Yorkshire composure. 'This will not do; I must seek summat', he had told himself.[71] Eventually he struggled through the darkness to No. 1 shaft in the way described.

Later that day a further meeting of colliery viewers, attended by C. Morton, the government inspector, was held at the King's Head in Barnsley. It was unanimously accepted that the mine probably now contained serious standing fires and that any attempts even to try to examine the underground workings were futile and dangerous in the extreme.[72] At this and subsequent meetings a plan emerged for putting out the conflagration. This was essentially to stop up the shafts so as to exclude all air, yet to revive the pumps to prevent the whole colliery from flooding.[73]

From 4.45 a.m. on Saturday 15 December to 3.20 a.m. on Tuesday 18 December no fewer than fourteen fresh explosions shook the Oaks Colliery.[74] Some were very slight or at only one of the shafts; others were violent and issued from two or all three pits. Filling operations could clearly not be delayed. On 17 December the first load of soil and stone was tipped into the furnace shaft and on the following afternoon the filling of No. 1 was also commenced. A specially constructed scaffold or platform was slowly lowered on the shaft guides down No. 2 on 7–9 January 1867 as far as just below the Melton coal. Here it was suspended and loads of clay were cast down upon it. Piercing the platform's centre and extending up to the bank was a 10 in. malleable iron pipe from which gas could escape and which permitted measurements of pressure, temperature and so on to be periodically made. In fact readings of the barometer and pressure gauge were recorded hourly from 30 January to 5 November 1867, on which latter date the clearing of spoil from the pits began.

In the meantime there had been the inquest, which extended over a period of thirteen days, a succession of meetings to promote subscriptions for the bereaved, consultations by mining engineers and a report from one of Her Majesty's inspectors. C. Morton, the district inspector, was not, however, the author of this last-mentioned document. As an official statement in March 1867 remarked, Morton had resigned his appointment shortly after the disaster 'and has been totally unable to make a Report'.[75] In a sense he too was a victim of the Oaks;[76] and the report which was eventually filed was drawn up by his colleague, Joseph Dickinson. All these events in their several ways throw light upon the catastrophe and on public attitudes to it.

Evidence given at the inquest is highly informative about the detail surrounding the accident, but not absolutely conclusive.[77] Much of the questioning was done by Morton—which perhaps helps to explain how the strain finally told on a man already a chronic sufferer from rheumatism—and naturally a great deal of interest centred on operations in the stone drift. Neither Tewart nor Mammatt had ever found gas in the drift, but the men contracting for the work had been warned to test for it and report any ominous signs.[78] The drift ran parallel to the beginning of the engine plane and in essence connected the downcast shafts with some steps leading from the plane down a travelling road which then ran in the same direction as the plane (see fig. 4.1). Just below the plane, or incline, and the drift, almost at the point where the drift entered the steps, the main south air return passed underneath. Naturally there was no open communication between the incline or steps and the air return, but it is just conceivable that the last shot fired in the drift had indirectly acted on the return air. However, we need for a moment to consider the wider background of colliery conditions.

In his report Dickinson showed that enough firedamp *could* theoretically have been present in the mine to produce an explosive mixture, even if no unusual outburst had occurred.[79] The disaster came at a time of day when the coal faces had been worked for several hours and would naturally have given off some firedamp; it happened after 1 p.m., which, as the warmest part of the day, meant that the air was more greatly expanded and thus possessed of less diluting force relative to the gas; it occurred, moreover, when barometric pressure was falling; and it was after one of the furnaces had been 'slackened for cleaning', which must have temporarily weakened the velocity of the ventilating current. Dickinson calculated that the rise in temperature and fall in barometric pressure between 1 a.m. and 1 p.m. could have resulted in a 4 per cent air–gas expansion. (It might be noted that during this period of low pressure in mid-December 1866 there were several mine explosions, including a serious one at Talk o' the Hill Colliery, Staffordshire, which killed ninety-one persons on the same day as the second Oaks explosion.) In other words, one did not need to postulate any *abnormal* issue of gas.[80]

As to the point and mode of ignition, Dickinson confessed that he could assert nothing with total conviction. Yet he believed firmly that evidence at the inquest was sufficient to put forward what is certainly an extremely plausible hypothesis. He argued that one could virtually rule out faulty or unlocked safety lamps at this well managed mine; and he regarded the possibility of a lamp being illegally opened as slight, for the men were well aware of the dangers.[81] Of course there was always a chance that a lamp might have broken accidentally, but that was something again which no one would ever know. In the absence of hard facts about any misuse of safety lamps there remained only two other possible sources of danger: open lights and the blasting operations.[82]

Open gas lights existed in two places: 'from the bottom of the downcast shafts for 150 yards along the old south level, and also for 400 yards down the engine plane'.[83] Both were, of course, ventilated by fresh air. The only other open light permitted was at 'Thompson's box hole', a wooden office used for relighting safety lamps, and again in a position ventilated by fresh air. Blasting was prohibited in general in the mine, but was allowed, as we have seen, in the new stone drift that was being made. Dickinson's theory elegantly combined the two factors of open lights and blasting.

The near simultaneity of the final shot in the drift and the great explosion naturally persuaded almost everyone that the two were intimately connected. Evidence was moreover forthcoming to suggest that the last charge (which was meant to complete the drift) had been bigger than the earlier ones.[84] It blew through on to the steps and not simply back into the drift as the previous shots had done. The concussion of this larger charge was clearly considerable —and, significantly, would reach a portion of the mine not affected by earlier work in the drift.[85]

The flame from the shot might well have ignited some odd pocket of firedamp in an old 'slit' or 'cut-through' in the south side. In any case the concussion could theoretically have been powerful enough to disturb gas from the goaves,[86] which could also have made its way into the main south air return through a near-by opening sealed by two doors, or through a slit not tightly enough stopped up. The hypothesis naturally rests on the concussion being as large as supposed and on either the doors or stopped slits being less than airtight. However, if the flame from the luckless blast did penetrate into a danger area the possibility of a kind of chain reaction undoubtedly existed in theory. As the report suggested,

The firedamp might there have been lighted, and it would run back in a train to the goaves. I consider this not unlikely, as it would give us a centre from which the main blast had apparently radiated such as would reconcile the effects which appear to have been produced. The blast, as it was found to have done, would thus drive out along all the south levels, and the opposing force would become neutralised by one part of it coming against the other at the upper part of the engine plane, as it appears to have done.[87]

This at least remained the official theory and it has, as observed, clear merits. Mammatt later stated that he considered the notion of the explosion being precipitated by shot-firing in the stone drift 'utterly impossible'. He believed the simultaneity of the shot and the general ignition 'an unfortunate coincidence, but nothing more', and preferred to suppose that the mine had been overwhelmed by a sudden and immense gas outburst which fired at Thompson's box hole, at a defective lamp, or at some illegal source of light.[88] His difficulty was in accepting that concussion from the blown-through drift could move gas from goaves half a mile away. We shall never know the truth. Without being unfair to Mammatt, it bears remarking that explanations of explosions which were totally unlinked with any kind of management oversight were sometimes attractive (if only unconsciously) to local officials.

There was never any official suggestion of laxity on the part of management. Yet Dickinson disliked the way in which the fiery Barnsley bed was worked and said so in no uncertain terms. 'To what then is the cause of the explosion to be attributed [?] In my opinion clearly to the system upon which the colliery was worked'.[89] He disapproved of long-wall working faces at the rise side of the goaves, where firedamp from these wastes tended to drift upon the men; and he did not really favour the taking of long roads through increasing numbers of goaves as the work advanced farther from the pit bottom. Instead he preferred methods where levels were first driven out to the far ends of a royalty and where the men gradually worked their way 'homewards'. In this manner the goaves would be left behind without there being a need to keep the outer roads open—and the 'reservoirs' of gas would be left in largely unused areas of the mine.

Whether the 'Barnsley method' contributed directly or indirectly to the Oaks explosion must remain somewhat obscure, but it could be argued that in principle advancing long-wall extraction *was* more dangerous than the retreating method, given the technology of the day. In any case, Dickinson developed his point in May 1866 and 1867 in his evidence to the Select Committees on Mines.[90] Mammatt, who was later himself a witness before at least two government inquiries, agreed in May 1869 in evidence taken before the Coal Commission (1871) that goaves lying in the middle of workings were 'a great element of danger, no doubt'. But in response to a question about other methods, he foresaw enormous practical difficulties in driving straight out to royalty boundaries at the winning of a typical Yorkshire colliery:

I do not think it could be universally practised in South Yorkshire; for this reason, that when a colliery is started the proprietors often do not know how much coal they may require; they may lease 500 acres to begin with, and when that is almost worked out they may take another 500 acres, so it is impossible to drive out to the ultimate boundary in the first instance.[91]

Whatever the merits of the systems and the possible clash between economics and safety, the Oaks explosion alone had little effect on their subsequent choice by mining engineers. Yet, however slack one may believe owners to have been in maintaining safe collieries (and surely the Oaks proprietors were better than most), they would have had to be mentally deficient to countenance serious explosions at anything other than an exhausted colliery. Even if we assume that they were sometimes indifferent to roof falls, we can hardly suppose that they lightly permitted methods calculated to blow up their mainly uninsurable assets.

The disaster took the lives of 361 men and boys. Of the 340 persons in the pit on Wednesday 12 December only six ultimately survived. Twenty-seven were killed on the following morning, twenty-three of them volunteers from other collieries. Public sympathy was immediate, widespread and generous.

The men's union anticipated an overnight claim of some £2,500 on their funds—funeral grants of £8 were payable—and they appealed on 14 December for public contributions.[92] Private subscriptions, too, were being opened almost everywhere. Queen Victoria offered £200, the Lord Mayor of London began a fund which within a fortnight had reached £10,000, members of the Bar in Leeds collected among themselves, Hull merchants and ship owners sent contributions—and the story was similar in Sheffield and countless other places. Among various meetings, one chaired by Earl Fitzwilliam in Barnsley's court house on Monday 17 December caused the greatest local interest. It was attended by many notables (not a few being mine owners or lessors) including Lord Wharncliffe, Viscount Halifax, the Archbishop of York and several local landowners and clergymen. The expressions of sorrow were genuine and the wish to help real. But the sentiments expressed, even on an occasion such as this, could not mask the deep social divisions between men and owners, labour and capital. It was thus entirely natural for Lord Wharncliffe not merely to deplore the loss of those who lived 'by sweat of their brow, and supported their wives and families by the labour of their bodies', but also to mourn, almost separately as it were, 'others who occupied a higher station in society'.[93] Similarly only one person at the meeting raised objections to the somewhat curious wording of the second resolution:

That this meeting further expresses its cordial sympathy with the proprietors of the Oaks Colliery, not simply for the great loss of property entailed but by the crushing sorrow endured by the terrible loss of lives of their workmen, and the bereavement of those connected with them.[94]

Unlike the Hartley Colliery disaster of 1862,[95] the widows and orphans of the Oaks did not have the slight satisfaction of knowing that the deaths of their loved ones contributed directly to new mining legislation. The toll of life underlined the need for more State intervention and wider powers of inspection, but they were tardy in coming. A select committee, set up in 1865, worked through to 1867, and a miners' deputation to the Home Secretary after the accident failed to hurry the government into action. Because of a number of false starts and wider political considerations which cannot be followed here, a new Act was not passed until 1872.[96] Its chief provision, largely based on the select committee's proposals, included the certification of managers and a host of regulations for greater underground safety. But it would have come when it did and in the form it did without the appalling sacrifice at the Oaks. Indeed, by the time the measure reached the statute book there had been another dozen or so very serious explosions to add to that of the Oaks, including a huge loss of life at Ferndale, Pontypridd, in November 1867.

And what of the ill fated colliery itself? New labour was recruited to replace the old, fresh shafts were sunk and additional workings commenced. Wherein lay the sense of abandoning good coal? Asked about the colliery when he was giving evidence before the Royal Commission of 1881, John Edward Mammatt, hero of the Oaks, remarked that some eighty bodies were still unaccounted for:

7425   Are the men quite reconciled to it?—Oh, yes, we never hear anything of it now.

7426   And all these men are entombed in the pit?—We have a different set of men at the colliery now.

7427   Have you been there very often, and have you found whether there was much difficulty in overcoming that sentimental feeling?—For a few months there was that feeling, but it has quite died out. We sometimes come across some bones, we did the other day, and we sent them up to the top, but nobody claimed them, and they were buried; there was only a skull and a piece of leg bone.[97]

Sentiment, then, had taken second place to bread and butter, as it must. There would have been no benefit to the Barnsley area if the mine had been permanently closed. There could be no fitting monument, certainly not that of an abandoned colliery, to the men and boys of the Oaks.

## Notes

1 A popular account which contains several references to Yorkshire mine accidents is Helen and Baron F. Duckham, *Great Pit Disasters: Great Britain, 1700, to the Present Day* (Newton Abbot, 1973). The present study, with minor revisions, is taken from chapter 6 of that book.

2 Most regional histories of the miners' unions have, of course, some reference to accidents, but the general treatment of mine safety has remained rare outside the technical literature. See, however, R. N. Boyd, *Coal Mines Inspection: its History and Results* (1898), and more recently, P. E. H. Hair, 'Mortality from violence in British coal mines, 1800–50', *Economic History Review*, XXI, 3 (second series, 1968), pp. 545–61.

3 See the table given in H. and B. F. Duckham, *op. cit.*, pp. 201–9. Three of the disasters were the result of inundations; the remainder were all caused by explosions.

4 Sir Henry de la Beche *et al.*, *Reports on the Gases and Explosions in Collieries* (HMSO, 1847), pp. 59–68.

5 Here again accidents involving only death rolls of twenty-five and over are given. (Reports of the Inspectors of Mines, 1851–62.)

6 It should, however, be borne in mind that the coalfield which bore the brunt of the larger-scale explosions was South Wales. See H. and B. F. Duckham, *op. cit.*, pp. 158–61.

7 Reports of the Inspectors of Mines for the Year 1866: Report on the Inspection of Mines in the North and East Lancashire or Manchester District for the year ended 31 December 1866, by Joseph Dickinson. The report on the Oaks disaster, appended by Dickinson to his report on his own district, covers pp. 42–7 of the 1866 volume. It will hereafter be referred to as 'Report, the Oaks Colliery explosion'.

8 Report, the Oaks Colliery explosion, 'plan showing ventilation at the time of the explosion', between pp. 42–3.

9 Woodhouse, who had a wide consultative practice, was described by Dickinson as 'one of the most eminent mining engineers of this kingdom'. (*Ibid.*, p. 44.)

10 Mammatt, who was twenty-seven at the time of the disaster, eventually became 'either the consulting viewer or manager' of several Yorkshire collieries. (Minutes of Evidence of the Royal Commission on Accidents in Mines, 1881, paras. 7343–4.)

11 Thus there was little danger of the gas-laden return air coming into contact with the furnaces themselves.

12 Report, the Oaks Colliery explosion, p. 44.

13 *Ibid.*, p. 47; transcript of the inquest, *Barnsley Chronicle*, 22 December 1866.

14 Report, the Oaks Colliery explosion, p. 47.

15 Dickinson unequivocally declared, 'So far as I am aware no duty has been omitted. Until his illness set in he [Morton] was one of the most energetic of inspectors . . .', (Report, the Oaks Colliery explosion, p. 47.)

16 F. Machin, *The Yorkshire Miners: a History*, I (Barnsley, 1958), pp. 328–39.

17 23 and 24 Vict., c. 151, the Mines Regulation Act.

18 Machin, *op. cit.*, p. 317.

19 *Ibid.*, 81–100, 328–9. The following is largely based on pp. 330–9.
20 *Sheffield Independent*, 13 June 1864.
21 Machin, *op. cit.*, p. 339.
22 *Ibid.*, p. 348.
23 T. W. Embleton, 'Notes on the Oaks Colliery explosion . . .', *Transactions of the North of England Institute of Mining and Mechanical Engineers*, xxv (1875–6), pp. 29–38.
24 *Barnsley Chronicle*, 15 December 1866.
25 *Ibid.*
26 *Ibid.*
27 *Ibid.*
28 *Ibid.*
29 *Yorkshire Post*, 13 December, 1866.
30 *Barnsley Chronicle*, 15 December 1866.
31 See H. and B. F. Duckham, *op. cit.*, *passim.*
32 *Barnsley Chronicle*, 15 December 1866.
33 *Ibid.*; *Yorkshire Post,* 13 December 1866; *Sheffield Telegraph*, 13 December 1866. An exception must be made in the case of William Wilson's evidence, noted later in this essay.
34 *Barnsley Chronicle*, 15 December 1866.
35 *Yorkshire Post*, 13 and 14 December 1866; *Barnsley Chronicle*, 15 December 1866.
36 *Barnsley Chronicle*, 15 December 1866.
37 *Ibid.*, 15 and 22 December 1866.
38 This was a common means of quick communication between bank and pit bottom after an explosion.
39 *Sheffield Telegraph*, 14 December 1866; *Yorkshire Post*, 14 December 1866; *Barnsley Chronicle*, 15 December, 1866.
40 Embleton, *loc. cit.*, pp. 29–30; *Barnsley Chronicle*, 15 December 1866.
41 The details are based on descriptions given by volunteer rescuers and are taken from the press sources already noted, especially the *Barnsley Chronicle*, 15 December 1886.
42 *Yorkshire Post*, 13 December 1866.
43 H. and B. F. Duckham, *op. cit.*, p. 29.
44 *Barnsley Chronicle*, 15 December 1866.
45 Embleton, *loc. cit.*, pp. 29-30.
46 *Barnsley Chronicle*, 15 December 1866.
47 *Ibid.*
48 The following list of incidents, so typical of all the larger mine disasters, was pieced together from the press accounts. It is not intended to be of intrinsic historical interest; its significance is to illustrate the way in which the scale and impact of the disaster could be comprehended only by individualising or personalising events.
49 *Barnsley Chronicle*, 15 and 29 December 1866; *Yorkshire Post*, 14 December, 1866.
50 *Barnsley Chronicle*, 15 December 1866.
51 For Jeffcock see the memoir written by his brother: J. T. Jeffcock, *Parkin Jeffcock, Civil and Mining Engineer: a Memoir* (London and Derby, 1867).

52 *Barnsley Chronicle*, 15 December 1866; Embleton, *loc. cit.*, pp. 29–31.
53 Embleton, *loc. cit.*, p. 31; *Barnsley Chronicle*, 15 December 1866; *Shef-field Telegraph*, 13 and 14 December 1866.
54 *Barnsley Chronicle*, 15 December 1866.
55 *Ibid.*
56 *Ibid.*
57 Embleton, *loc. cit.*, p. 30.
58 *Ibid.*
59 *Yorkshire Post*, 14 December 1866.
60 *Barnsley Chronicle*, 15 December 1866.
61 *Ibid.*
62 *Ibid.*, 15 and 29 December 1866; *Yorkshire Post*, 14 and 15 December 1866.
63 *Barnsley Chronicle*, 15 December 1866.
64 The following is based on the various press reports already cited.
65 Report, the Oaks Colliery explosion, p. 43.
66 This and the technical details which follow are (unless otherwise stated) taken from Embleton's account, *loc. cit.*, pp. 30–2.
67 The account in the *Barnsley Chronicle* of 15 December 1866 states that some individuals had claimed to have heard sounds from the pit bottom before this—i.e. between 3 a.m. and 4 a.m.—though they were not believed. Embleton, *loc. cit.*, is silent about this.
68 Minutes of Evidence of the Royal Commission on Accidents in Mines (1881), para. 7424.
69 There have, not unnaturally, been some very fortunate escapes, but Brown's survival in a gas-filled mine with standing fires bordered on the miraculous. It is a pity that his evidence could contribute little to what we know of the disaster in its wider sphere.
70 *Barnsley Chronicle*, 22 December 1866.
71 *Ibid.*
72 *Ibid.*, 15 and 22 December 1866; Embleton, *loc. cit.*, p. 31.
73 Embleton, *loc. cit.*, *passim*; *Barnsley Chronicle*, 29 December 1866.
74 The following details are again from Embleton, *loc. cit.*, pp. 32–8.
75 Home Office statement of 20 March 1867.
76 It might be noted that local criticism of a district inspector (or sometimes the whole inspectorate) was by no means uncommon after a great mine disaster, the grievance usually being the long gaps between an inspector's visit to the colliery. Commenting on 29 December 1866 on Morton's resignation, the *Barnsley Chronicle*, for example, declared that 'the present system of inspection [was] at best a farce', and went on to hope that 'the question will be asked during the inquiry when *he* [Morton] was last down the Oaks pit'.
77 In very many mine disasters the exact occasion and location of explosion was, of course, impossible to identify because of the death of vital witnesses. Inferences could often be made from observations of the effect and supposed direction of the blast, but in such cases little more than the balance of probabilities could be considered.
78 Mammatt later claimed that when he had examined the drift a day or two before the disaster he had found 'nothing but fresh air in it',

(Minutes of Evidence of the Royal Commission on Accidents in Mines, 1881, para. 7399.)

79 The concentrations of firedamp and the circumstances most easily conducive to mine explosions are discussed in D. and J. S. Penman, *The Principles and Practice of Mine Ventilation* (second edn., 1947), pp. 24–7, 75–96; and W. Payman and I. C. F. Statham, *Firedamp Explosions and their Prevention* (1931), pp. 1–11.

80 Report, the Oaks Colliery explosion, 42–3.

81 Possibly Dickinson was somewhat dogmatic on this particular point and did not sufficiently allow for either human error or cupidity. However, it does not affect the theoretical validity of this main argument, which was to find a possible *rationale* of the explosion that fitted the known facts.

82 This again assumes that the mine's management was too alert and general discipline too high for any of the men to have risked smoking below ground.

83 Report, the Oaks Colliery explosion, p. 43.

84 *Ibid.*, p. 43.

85 *Ibid.*, p. 43.

86 Goaves were waste areas from which coal had previously been extracted. In a fiery mine they often acted as reservoirs of firedamp, and there is ample testimony of the gassy nature of the Oaks Colliery.

87 Report, the Oaks Colliery explosion, p. 44.

88 Minutes of Evidence of the Royal Commission on Accidents in Mines (1881), paras. 7397–402.

89 Report, the Oaks Colliery explosion, p. 44.

90 Minutes of Evidence of the Select Committee on Mines (1866), paras. 7519–31; Minutes (1867), paras. 545–8.

91 Report of the Commissioners appointed to inquire into Several Matters relating to Coal in the United Kingdom (1871), I, Proceedings of the Committee C 'on waste in working', para. 1067. See also paras. 1066–71.

92 These representative examples of fund raising are taken from the press sources already noted.

93 *Barnsley Chronicle*, 22 December 1866.

94 *Ibid.*

95 See J. E. McCutcheon, *The Hartley Colliery Disaster, 1862* (Seaham, 1963), *passim*. The legislative response to this accident was the Act of 1862 (25 and 26 Vict., c. 79), which made it compulsory for every mine to have at least two outlets.

96 35 and 36 Vict., c. 76, Coal Mines Regulation Act.

97 Minutes of Evidence of the Royal Commission on Accidents in mines (1881), paras. 7425–7.

JOHN BENSON

# 5 The establishment of the West Riding of Yorkshire Miners' Permanent Relief Fund [1]

## I

Coal mining has always been regarded as a dangerous occupation, although the true extent of the miners' liability to industrial injury during the nineteenth century has still to be recognised. 'Between 1800 and 1850 the joint efforts of professional mining engineers and a humanitarian "safety movement" brought about a marked reduction in mortality from explosions. But this success was not matched in other fields of accident prevention'.[2] The result was that in the Yorkshire coalfield, as elsewhere, the miner remained likely to suffer several industrial accidents during the course of his working life.

Fatal accidents alone claimed a prodigious toll. Of every thousand Yorkshire miners employed in the mid-nineteenth century, between three and four were killed every year.[3] Nor, with the sinking of deeper pits and the use of more complicated workings, had the county's safety record shown any improvement by the 1870s, for during that decade 1,174 men (3·4 per thousand per annum) died during the course of their employment.[4] Of these casualties, though, only 22 per cent were killed in those large-scale accidents[5] which aroused so much public concern.[6]

The great majority of fatalities were caused by isolated, and therefore almost entirely unpublicised, incidents. Even contemporaries who realised that comparatively few deaths in the industry resulted from major disasters tended to equate the problem of mining accidents exclusively with fatal occurrences. The failure to appreciate the extent of non-fatal accidents was not surprising, since, as the mine inspectorate itself recognised, the official returns were severely defective.[7]

Since no accurate statistics for non-fatal accidents are available, it is necessary to rely upon estimates based on limited known figures. This was the approach pursued by many trade union leaders during the second half of the nineteenth century. In 1864, for example, John Holmes of the West Yorkshire Miners' Association argued that there occurred approximately four non-fatal accidents for every death which resulted from an industrial injury.[8] Even such a calculation, however, grossly underestimated the number of non-fatal accidents. Between 1860 and 1897 the proportion of non-fatal accidents to fatalities (excluding those caused by accidents claiming more than four lives) remained constant in every English coalfield at almost exactly 100 : 1.[9] If this ratio is applied to Yorkshire it becomes clear that, at the most conservative estimate, more than 90,000 of the county's miners were injured during the 1870s.

The number of mining accidents occurring in the Yorkshire coalfield during the second half of the nineteenth century was therefore far greater than has generally been supposed. Of every thousand miners working in the county during the '70s 0·4 were killed each year in disasters and 1·7 in other fatal accidents, while a further 174 received injuries sufficiently severe to necessitate absence from work.

## II

It is against this background of a non-fatal accident rate greatly in excess of the known fatal accident rate that the provision of compensation for colliery accidents during the third quarter of the nineteenth century must be viewed. The relief of the dependants of those killed proved to be quite inadquate. Even after major disasters, when the greatest amount of aid was forthcoming, the families of the dead were but poorly assisted.[10] This becomes clear from events following the Oaks explosion. The Barnsley Board of Guardians at first received no applications for relief because the owners, Messrs Firth Barber & Co., were providing the widows with financial aid and allowing them to continue to reside, rent-free, in company houses.[11] When applications were made later, however, it was only after bitter controversy that the Board agreed to relieve the twenty-six widows (out of a total of 156) whose only means of support was the publicly subscribed colliery disaster fund[12] at the rate of 2s a week plus 1s a week for each child.[13]

The Oaks accident insurance club, to which many of the deceased had belonged, proved unable to meet the demands placed upon it,[14] but the Ancient Order of Foresters met all claims[15] and the Royal Liver Friendly Society paid thirty-four claims totalling £192 19s 0d.[16]

The public disaster fund allowed all widows 5s a week until remarriage and their children 1s 6d a week until they reached the age of twelve.[17] The South Yorkshire Miners' Association temporarily relieved the twenty-six widows whose husbands had not been union men[18] and, as Dr Duckham has shown, permanently relieved the dependants of all fully financial union members.[19] In other respects, though, the leaders of the association did little for the families of those killed. Although they recognised that they had a duty to take all the legal action open to them to protect the coal-mining community, they decided that, considering the generosity of the employers and the uncertainty of the law, combined with the certainty of ruinous costs, it would be unwise to begin proceedings for compensation.[20]

Thus a widow with two children, whose husband had been a member of the South Yorkshire Miners' Association, received £8 for funeral expenses, was permitted to live rent-free and might obtain benefit from a friendly society. She was also entitled to a total of 10s a week for the duration of her widowhood and 5s weekly until her children reached the age of twelve. But in November 1876, less than a month before the tenth anniversary of the disaster, the miners' union decided that its funds were insufficient to continue relief and it suspended the allowance of all widows who had been in receipt of benefit for a decade.[21]

Inadequate though relief was after major disasters, it was vastly superior to that offered to the dependants of men killed in single accidents or to the many miners injured during the course of their employment. In the absence of those sources of relief which became available only after large-scale accidents, the injured and bereaved were forced to rely upon the Poor Law, their employers or upon their own thrift.[22]

Following fatal colliery accidents it was usual for all Boards of Guardians to offer applicants outdoor relief. Payments, though, were uniformly low; even in the Barnsley Union, which according to some Guardians enjoyed the reputation of being the most liberal in the West Riding,[23] weekly payments did not exceed 3s for widows and half that sum for their children.[24] Numerous restrictions were also placed upon the payment of relief. Thus while the Barnsley Guardians were prepared to support small children, they expected widows to work;[25] nobody, it was confidently asserted, believed that assistance should be offered to a widow who was able to earn her own living.[26] Help was also refused when it was believed that the dependants of a dead man had failed to use a friendly society funeral grant in a responsible manner. As late as 1882, when a miner was killed at the Featherstone Manor Colliery, leaving a widow, two children and one adopted child, the Pontefract Board of Guardians refused to grant outdoor relief, and the chairman

pealed forth and severely animadverted on the widow's profusion in spending her money in funeral cards, biscuits and wine, in order that her husband might be put away respectably.[27]

By the mid-nineteenth century it was established practice for Yorkshire coal owners to provide coffins for the victims of fatal accidents,[28] while both Lord St Oswald and Earl Fitzwilliam, continuing to perform the traditional charitable activity of the landed aristocracy, assisted the families of those who died in their pits.[29] Otherwise the only relief offered by the proprietors was that made available by their pit clubs, membership of which constituted a condition of employment.[30] To the employer a compulsory pit club offered solid advantages; but to the employee it rarely offered a satisfactory source of compensation. Few owners published accounts,[31] and it was commonly suspected that they used the men's subscriptions to create substantial bodies of capital for their own use.[32] It was claimed in 1863, for example, that at Messrs Charlesworth's pits 'the rates of contribution . . . leaves [sic] a good profit to the employer, who pockets the same and gives no account'.[33] Many funds were actuarily unsound[34] and even the allowances nominally paid rarely proved adequate. Funeral grants of £2–£4 were made by South Yorkshire pit clubs, and although payments were higher in the west of the county, nowhere was permanent provision made for those bereaved by colliery accidents.[35]

Enforced membership of pit clubs, however unpopular, did little to encourage Yorkshire coal miners to join other friendly societies insuring against fatal accidents. Support was given, though, to both the West and the South Yorkshire Miners' Associations, to which, during the prosperous early '70s, more than half the county's miners belonged.[36] Both unions organised widow and orphan and funeral benefits, although the provision of relief was far from satisfactory.[37]

However large the family of a miner killed on his own in, say, south Yorkshire during the early 1870s, its members received only a free coffin from the employer, a grant of under £6 from the pit

club and a small allowance from the parish. Additional benefits
were provided, it is true, if the deceased had been a member of a
friendly society or of the South Yorkshire Miners' Association,
although in these circumstances the Poor Law allowance was
automatically reduced.[38]

Compensation was no better for the many miners injured in non-
fatal accidents. Lord St Oswald and Earl Fitzwilliam assisted their
own employees,[39] and the destitute could always obtain small allowances from the parish. Otherwise relief was to be had only from the
pit clubs or from the non-fatal accident funds of the two major
Yorkshire mining unions. Pit clubs occasionally provided free
medical attention[40] but their weekly allowances were always
temporary and never exceeded 8s a week.[41] Club rules frequently
forbade the payment of relief to any member who left the pit for
any reason,[42] a restriction which both discouraged mobility of labour
and which was easily exploited by the employer during industrial
disputes. Thus disabled miners at Tinsley Park were informed
during the course of a strike in 1869 that, as they had left their
employment, they were no longer eligible for relief from the pit
club.[43] Payment was sometimes completely refused. William Gibson
claimed to have worked for Messrs Charlesworth for more or less
sixty years and to have subscribed to their sick and accident fund
for nearly a third of that time; but he received no relief when
forced to stop work in 1884 after being blinded in the pit.[44]

There were then, striking inconsistencies in the distribution of
compensation, with the families of men killed in major disasters
receiving a disproportionate amount of aid. But after no industrial
accident during the third quarter of the nineteenth century did
Yorkshire miners and their dependants ever obtain adequate assistance.

### III

The liability of Yorkshire miners to industrial injury and the
inadequacy of existing sources of compensation, particularly for
those not involved in major catastrophes, stimulated two attempts
to establish mutual insurance funds[45] during this period. These
efforts floundered, however, on the failure of the promoters, drawn
exclusively from the employers' side of the industry, to secure the
support of the men.[46]

In 1862 the West Yorkshire coal owners, reacting against the activities of the London-based and aristrocatically led National Association for the Relief of British Miners,[47] tried to form their own society. The West Yorkshire Northern Association for Promoting a Miners' Widows and Orphans Fund was aimed at all miners working north of the Lancashire & Yorkshire Railway[48] and was intended to cater for those small accidents where no public subscription was raised.[49] Management, it was proposed, should be shared between the owners, the men and members of the public. In return for a weekly subscription of 1d by underground workers (½d by boys) substantial benefits were offered; the widow of any member killed in the pit would receive 6s a week for herself and 2s a week for each child under the age of twelve, while the dependants of an unmarried man would be relieved as the circumstances were felt to justify.[50]

Despite the addition of a permanent injury benefit and the interest of several large owners,[51] the employers organising the association failed to gain general support even from their own side of the industry. Most owners remained wedded to the advantages to be derived from their individual pit clubs[52] and were reluctant to support any regional scheme.[53]

The second attempt to form a mutual insurance fund covering a large part of the county followed the Oaks disaster. Despite the financial success of the public Colliery Explosion Fund, its management committee perceived the weaknesses of the existing system of compensation and urged the establishment of a fund for south-west Yorkshire on the model of the Northumberland and Durham Miners' Permanent Relief Fund, which had been formed in 1862.[54] A general committee of 'noblemen and gentlemen'[55] emerged to manage the new society, and a sub-committee[56] was appointed to prepare a draft set of rules which was to be circulated among members of the general committee.[57] Early in 1867 the committee obtained the sum of £2,284 17s 4d, which had been allocated to Yorkshire from the surplus of the Hartley Colliery relief fund[58] with the earnest recommendation to all regional recipients of the 'desirability of encouraging, with the means thus placed at their disposal, the establishment of permanent relief funds in their respective localities, and of aiding those already in operation'.[59] The money was deposited with the Wakefield and Barnsley Union Banking Company in the names of three trustees, Earl Fitzwilliam, Lord Wharncliffe and Viscount Halifax.[60]

Although launched in a climate of public opinion which, following

the Oaks explosions, was receptive to such a scheme, the South
West Yorkshire Miners' Permanent Relief Fund never materialised
because the organisers failed to publicise the proposed society.
'Certainly', as the *Barnsley Chronicle* commented a decade later,
'nothing was ever done in the way of eliciting the opinions of the
men working at the pits in the district'.[61]

## IV

Not until 143 miners were killed in an explosion at the Swaithe
Main Colliery in December 1875 did it prove possible to mobilise
both the owners and the men in support of a regional mutual
insurance society. The inefficiency of the existing range of compensation became fully exposed after the Swaithe explosion. It was
apparent that not even the dependants of those killed in major
disasters could always be reasonably assisted, for it proved possible
to raise only £10,003 of the £15,000–£20,000 needed to relieve the
families of the deceased.[62] Many felt it unreasonable to seek subscriptions to the Swaithe Main Colliery Fund while large surpluses
remained from the Oaks and Hartley disaster funds.[63] Others
believed with the mayor of Bradford that, following the prosperity
of the coal industry during the early '70s, it was the employers,
rather than members of the public, who should bear the burden of
relieving the bereaved.[64]

The employers themselves were coming to the view that it would
be advantageous, both financially and in terms of public relations,
to substitute a fixed liability for their existing open-ended com-
mitment after colliery accidents. The owners of the Swaithe Main
Colliery, Messrs Mitchell & Co., for example, found the provision
of assistance, particularly the payment of fourteen weekly allowances to the seventy-two widows and 168 children, a considerable
financial burden.[65] Yet they deemed it advisable also to subscribe
£1,000 to the public disaster fund lest feeling against them should
become intensified. 'I am convinced,' one admitted, 'that if we do
not subscribe, the whole burden will fall upon us, whereas if we do
subscribe, I think our efforts will be supplemented by the liberality
of the public.'[66]

The miners, of course, needed little convincing of the inadequacies
of the relief available following industrial accidents. It was becoming
increasingly clear, though, that even the benefit funds of the West
and South Yorkshire Miners' Associations, to which many looked

for assistance, did not constitute a reliable source of compensation. During the '70s lodge accident funds were used to support labour activities, liabilities were recklessly increased and retrospective alterations to the rules were introduced to deprive widows of benefit.[67]

It was the apparent breakdown of two major sources of compensation, the trade union accident scheme and the colliery disaster fund, which finally created a climate of opinion favourable to a new system of relief. The employers, the miners, and indeed the general public, all came to appreciate the potential advantages of any scheme based upon the fixed financial support of both sides of the Yorkshire coal industry.

Realising that the movement of public feeling towards such a scheme provided a propitious moment, the rector of St Mary's, Barnsley, the Rev. H. J. Day, wrote to the *Barnsley Chronicle* in December 1876. He urged upon his readers the example of the Northumberland and Durham Miners' Permanent Relief Fund and listed the advantages of such a society:

First, to the masters, who, for the trifling payment of (say) 20 per cent on the amount of men's contributions, make themselves secure against pecuniary liability in case of accidents, at the same time establishing a bond of sympathy and goodwill between themselves and those whom they employ; and, second, to the men, who in return for the very moderate subscription of threepence a week become entitled to such benefits, which cannot possibly be procured to the same extent by their own unaided subscriptions . . .[68]

It was an attractive argument which helped to break down the suspicions of the unions. The members of the Pindar Oaks lodge of the South Yorkshire Miners' Association, who under their secretary William Watson[69] had already declined to support any more colliery disaster funds, now resolved to offer the Rev. Day their 'most hearty support'.[70] Watson accordingly held a series of conversations with the rector, and on 10 January 1877 they together organised a preliminary meeting to which Watson invited representatives from other pits. The rules and annual reports of the Northumberland and Durham society were discussed and it was decided that those present should form a committee (with power to add to their number) to confer with other lodges about the establishment of a permanent relief fund for Yorkshire.[71] A further meeting, under the chairmanship of the Rev. Day, was held on 22 January and was 'addressed . . . at considerable length' by Alexander Blyth, the secretary of the Northumberland and Durham fund.[72] It was resolved

That the Rev. H. J. Day be requested to inform the Permanent Fund Committee [of the Swaithe Main colliery fund] that the miners generally, working at the several pits in the district are favourably disposed towards the establishment of a Miners' Permanent Relief Fund, on the same principles as the Northumberland and Durham Fund.[73]

The Rev. Day's arguments appeared equally attractive to many owners. The permanent fund committee (of the Swaithe Main fund) decided to support the establishment of a West Riding Miners' Permanent Relief Fund and asked the trustees of the Yorkshire portion of the Hartley surplus for a grant of £250 to meet preliminary expenses. With unaccustomed vigour the trustees immediately agreed.[74]

The provisional leaders of the nascent society mounted a vigorous campaign throughout south Yorkshire and in parts of Derbyshire and west Yorkshire.[75] Determined efforts were made to persuade both employers and employees of the advantages which they would derive from the new organisation. Local owners were circularised,[76] and, although many remained suspicious,[77] a number did actively campaign in favour of the fund. Thus R. Hartley, one of the directors of the Silkstone and Dodworth collieries, offered his support at a meeting held at Dodworth church school in February 1877.[78] More concrete encouragement was given by those owners who agreed to pay 20 per cent of their employees' subscriptions,[79] and by the end of 1877 sixteen proprietors had paid £175. Payments of over £10 were made by the Wombwell Main, Wharncliffe Silkstone, Swaithe Main, Monk Bretton, Darley Main, Strafford Main, Mitchell Main and Edmunds' Main colliery companies.[80]

The success of the permanent relief fund also depended upon the support of the Yorkshire and Derbyshire miners' trade unions, whose sympathy was eagerly sought. John Catchpole, the Derbyshire miners' leader, worked for the fund from its inception[81] and helped 'Miners and others employed about the Pits . . . [around Chesterfield] willing to assist in forming branches of this Society, . . .'.[82] Initially, though, the leaders of both Yorkshire unions were hostile, for they were inclined to regard the new society as a rival to their own ailing accident schemes.[83] On 22 January 1877, for example, the leaders of the South Yorkshire miners confessed that 'our thoughts respecting this fund are not favourable at present . . .';[84] but a fortnight later a sub-committee was appointed 'to ascertain if there be any possibility of our liabilities being taken over by the Permanent Relief Committee, and if so, upon what terms, . . .'.[85] With this in mind the representatives of the union and the permanent fund met, and according to the *Barnsley Chronicle* this produced 'a tacit understanding' between the two sides.[86] The instability of the benefit funds of the two major Yorkshire unions had thus brought even the most fervent trade unionists to accept that the miners' permanent relief fund had a complementary role to play in the field of accident compensation.[87]

The withdrawal of active union hostility ensured the successful establishment of the West Riding of Yorkshire Miners' Permanent Relief Fund. The first collection of subscriptions was made on 10 March 1877,[88] when there were between 1,500 and 2,000 members.[89] Of the twenty-two branches five had more than a hundred adult subscribers: Wombell Main (281), New Oaks (215), Woolley (190), Swaithe Main (166) and Pindar Oaks (122).[90] By the end of June there were 3,249 members in twenty-nine branches.[91] At the first delegate meeting, which was held in the town hall, Barnsley, on 18 September 1877,[92] the officers of the permanent relief fund were appointed. Earl Fitzwilliam was made president, four 'noblemen and gentlemen' (the Earl of Wharncliffe, Viscount Halifax, W. S. Stanhope, F. W. T. V. Wentworth and the Rev. H. J. Day) were chosen to be vice-presidents and William Watson was elected secretary. Also elected were trustees,[93] arbitrators,[94] a treasurer[95] and a committee of management which consisted of three honorary and twelve ordinary members.[96] By the end of the year the society numbered 3,941 members (equivalent to 6·4 per cent of the miners working in Yorkshire) in thirty-nine branches throughout south Yorkshire and north Derbyshire.[97]

## V

Despite criticism by both owners and men of some of the society's management practices,[98] support for the West Riding Miners' Permanent Relief Fund grew steadily. The society proved itself to be manifestly superior to other forms of compensation.[99] This was not so much because the amount of relief granted was greater than that offered elsewhere but because the benefits promised were invariably provided. Unlike the benefit funds of the trade unions, the resources of the permanent relief fund were never used for other than their original purpose. The society's payments, in contrast to those of the pit clubs, could not be manipulated by the owners, and whereas every colliery disaster produced its crop of failed friendly societies the West Riding fund always honoured its commitments.

Recognising the superiority of the West Riding Miners' Permanent Relief Fund over other sources of assistance, most Yorkshire colliery proprietors agreed to deduct the men's subscriptions at source, thus diminishing the likelihood of a member accidentally or casually falling into arears. William Watson confirmed

that whilst only the few companies subscribed [20 per cent on their employees' contributions], the vast majority of them helped in managing the Society at much less cost than it could be managed if they were kept outside the colliery offices.[100]

With such encouragement the membership of the fund increased from 3,941 (6·5 per cent of those employed in the Yorkshire coalfield) in December 1877 to 9,725 (16 per cent) in 1880 and to 16,138 (25 per cent) by the end of 1883.[101] In spite of the extension of the owners' liability for accidents by the Workmen's Compensation Act of 1897,[102] support for the permanent relief fund continued to grow until 1908, when the membership stood at 35,643, a figure which, as a quarter of a century before, represented a quarter of those working in Yorkshire collieries.[103] Membership declined after 1908, however, as the Yorkshire Coal Owners' Mutual Indemnity Company Ltd, with which the employers insured their liability under the 1897 Act, forbade the making of 'any deductions in respect of the Miners' Permanent Relief Fund or any accident club who pays benefit to men who draw compensation'.[104]

The membership figures alone, though, do not fully reveal the leading compensatory role assumed by the West Riding fund after colliery accidents of every type. By 1883, when the society's membership was equivalent to a quarter of all Yorkshire miners, its funds were relieving the equivalent of a third of all Yorkshire colliers injured during the course of their employment, the dependants of more than 60 per cent of those killed and, at a cost of £3,725, all those bereaved by major disasters.[105] During its first twenty years' activities the society relieved seventy-seven aged and infirm members at a cost of £5,880, 386 widows and 786 children at a cost of £51,990 and 54,686 members injured in the pit at a cost of £106,601.[106]

After its establishment in 1877 the West Riding fund quickly came to assume, and to maintain until the beginning of the twentieth century, a dominant role in the provision of relief to those injured and bereaved by accidents in the Yorkshire coal industry. It was this development more than any other which accounted for the improvement in the compensation for industrial accidents offered to Yorkshire miners and their dependants during the final twenty years of the nineteenth century. The sound basis on which the society was founded and the steady progress it subsequently made enabled it to fulfil that early promise which had led to the *Barnsley Chronicle* to comment in September 1877

That goodly and well proportioned ship, the West Riding of Yorkshire Miners' Permanent Relief Fund, the keel of which was laid early in January last, has now started on its voyage, fully manned and well equipped with stores, and, though it will doubtless, before reaching smooth water, encounter not a few adverse gales, and may have to ride on the crest of many a boisterous wave, yet we trust that it will weather all the storms that may beat against its timbers and prove a sound sea-going craft for many a long year to come.[107]

*Appendix 5.1. Accidents in Yorkshire collieries entailing the loss of five or more lives, 1860–76*

| Date | Colliery | Lives lost | Cause |
|------|----------|------------|-------|
| 15 February 1860 | Higham | 13 | Explosion |
| 4 April 1862 | Westwood | 6 | Explosion |
| 8 December 1862 | Edmunds Main | 59 | Explosion |
| 13 November 1863 | Thrybergh Hall | 6 | Fall down shaft |
| 12 December 1866 | Oaks | 334 | Explosion |
| 13 December 1866 | Oaks | 27 | Explosion |
| 12 April 1867 | Brightside | 5 | Breaking rope |
| 7 October 1872 | Morley | 34 | Explosion |
| 20 November 1874 | Rawmarsh | 23 | Explosion |
| 5 January 1875 | Aldwarke | 7 | Explosion |
| 6 December 1875 | Swaithe Main | 143 | Explosion |
| 9 December 1875 | Methley | 6 | Explosion |

*Source.* Reports of HM Inspectors of Mines and Quarries, 1860–76.

*Appendix 5.2 West Riding of Yorkshire Miners' Permanent Relief
Fund: contributions and benefits*

### Contributions

Entrance fees

| | |
|---|---|
| Under sixteen years of age | 9*d* |
| Above sixteen years of age | 1*s* 6*d* |

Fortnightly contributions

| | |
|---|---|
| Under sixteen years of age | 3*d* |
| Above sixteen years of age | 6*d* |

### Benefits

| | |
|---|---|
| Accidental death of unmarried member under sixteen years of age | £12 |
| Permanent disablement of ditto | 4*s* per week |
| Temporary disablement of ditto | 3*s* per week |
| Accidental death of members above sixteen years of age leaving no dependent relative | £23 |
| Accidental death of members above sixteen years of age leaving dependent relatives | £5 |
| Widows or other dependent relatives | 5*s* per week |
| Each child (if under age) of members accidentally killed | 2*s* per week |
| Permanent disablement of members above sixteen years of age | 8*s* per week |
| Temporary disablement of members above sixteen years of age | 6*s* per week |
| Aged and infirm members' benefit | 6*s* per week |

*Source.* WR, first delegate meeting, minutes, p. 19.

### Notes

1 I wish to thank Dr R. G. Neville and Dr C. H. Thompson for their help in the preparation of this paper.
2 P. E. H. Hair, 'Mortality from violence in British coal mines, 1800–50', *Economic History Review,* second ser., XXI (1968), 560.
3 *Ibid.*, 546.
4 Based upon J. Benson, 'The compensation of English coal miners and their dependants for industrial accidents, 1860–97' (unpublished Ph.D. thesis, University of Leeds, 1974), tables I, IV.
5 Defined as accidents claiming five or more lives. See appendix 5.1.

6 For other English coalfields see J. Benson, 'Colliery disaster funds, 1860–97', *International Review of Social History*, XIX (1974), part I.

7 *Reports of HM Inspectors of Mines and Quarries*, J. J. Atkinson, 1864, p. 30. A non-fatal accident is defined as any injury resulting in one or more days' absence from work.

8 *Transactions and Results of the National Association of Coal, Lime and Ironstone Miners of Great Britain, held at Leeds, November 9, 10, 11, 12, 13 and 14, 1864* (1864), p. iii.

9 This conclusion is based upon the evidence of organisations with direct knowledge of mining accidents: see Benson, 'Compensation', pp. 27–30.

10 Benson, 'Compensation', pp. 472–81.

11 Public Record Office, M.H. 12/14682/5610, R. B. Cane to Poor Law Board, 18 December 1866.

12 See below, p. 94.

13 *Barnsley Chronicle*, 9 February 1867; *Yorkshire Post*, 6 February, 1867.

14 *Yorkshire Post*, 27 December 1866.

15 *Barnsley Chronicle*, 15 December 1866.

16 J. Payne to *ibid.*, 12 January 1867.

17 *Barnsley Chronicle*, 5 January 1867. For the inadequacy of the relief provided, see Benson, 'Colliery disaster funds', 76–84.

18 National Union of Mineworkers (Yorkshire Area), Barnsley; South Yorkshire Miners' Association, *Minutes*, 21 January 1867.

19 Above, p. 69. The provision of relief, though, was frequently unsatisfactory. See my 'English coal miners' trade union accident funds, 1850–1900', *Economic History Review*, second series, XXVII (1975).

20 South Yorkshire Miners' Association, *Minutes*, 25 November 1867.

21 *Ibid.*, 27 November 1876.

22 The common law, Lord Campbell's Act and the mines regulation Acts were in practice so weak that at no time before 1897 was a significant amount of compensation gained as the direct result of legal action. (Benson, 'Compensation', pp. 91–135.)

23 *Barnsley Chronicle*, 26 January 1867.

24 Benson, 'Compensation', p. 41.

25 *Barnsley Chronicle*, 26 January 1867.

26 *Ibid.*, 9 February 1867.

27 'A Sympathiser' to *Wakefield Express*, 24 June 1882.

28 *Ibid*, 1 February 1879; *Barnsley Chronicle*, 17 February 1872.

29 West Riding Miners' Permanent Relief Fund (hereafter WR), *Twelfth Annual Report*, p. 8.

30 *Leeds Intelligencer*, 17 May 1862; *Trans. Nat. Ass.*, pp. 8, 44; *Select Committee on Acts for the Regulation and Inspection of Mines*, 1866, J. Normansell, qq. 3692–3.

31 *Trans. Nat. Ass.*, p. 44; *S.C. Regulation and Inspection of Mines*, J. Normansell, q. 3698.

32 *Trans. Nat. Ass.*, p. 44.

33 *Ibid.*, p. xi.

34 Benson, 'Compensation', pp. 285–9.

35 *Trans. Nat. Ass.*, pp. 44–9; *Colliery Guardian*, 13 December 1862; *Barnsley Chronicle*, 17 February 1872; *Yorkshire Post*, 13 December

1875; *Rules of the Simon Wood Colliery Accident Fund* (Elsecar, n.d.), No. 8.

36 *Yorkshire Post*, 20 November 1873.

37 See above, n. 19.

38 J. Frith to *Barnsley Chronicle*, 8 July 1876.

39 WR, *Twelfth Annual Report*, p. 8.

40 *Trans. Nat. Ass.*, pp. 44–9; Barnsley Public Library, WR, Records, Letters, 1882, No. 28, D. Conaurou to W. Watson, 2 January 1882.

41 *Colliery Guardian*, 13 December 1862; *Trans. Nat. Ass.*, pp. 44–9; *Simon Wood*, No. 8.

42 WR, Records, Letters, 1879, No. 64, T. Wild to W. Watson, 1 July 1879.

43 *Barnsley Chronicle*, 15 May 1869.

44 *S.C. Employers' Liability Act*, p. 555, appendix 18, letter from W. Gibson, 3 June 1886.

45 Funds financed by both employers and employees.

46 *Barnsley Chronicle*, 26 February 1876.

47 Benson, 'Compensation', pp. 392–9.

48 *Colliery Guardian*, 10 May 1862.

49 *Leeds Intelligencer*, 17 May 1862.

50 *Ibid.*, 3 May 1862.

51 *Ibid.*, 10 June 1862.

52 See above, p. 95.

53 *Leeds Intelligencer*, 17 May, 10 June 1862; *Colliery Guardian*, 1 November 1862.

54 *Yorkshire Post*, 29 December 1866. By 1866 the fund had 7,500 members (12.2 per cent of the miners employed in Northumberland and Durham). See Benson, 'Compensation', table XIV.

55 Characterised more colourfully by Reginald Bury as 'masters and what are commonly called swells'. (R. Bury to *Barnsley Chronicle*, 25 December 1875.)

56 R. Craik, W. P. Maddison, W. A. Potter and W. Stewart.

57 *Yorkshire Post*, 26 January 1867; *Barnsley Chronicle*, 27 January 1877.

58 £20,374 7s 3d of the £81,839 raised after the entombment of 204 men at the Hartley Colliery, Northumberland, in 1862.

59 *The Tragedy of the Coalfields: West Riding Miners' Permanent Relief Fund Friendly Society, 1877–1927* (Barnsley, 1927), p. 6.

60 *Barnsley Chronicle*, 8 January 1876. The money continued to earn interest until the question of a mutual insurance fund was taken up again after the Swaithe Main explosion of 1875.

61 *Barnsley Chronicle*, 27 January 1877. Lord Wharncliffe, indeed, denied even being aware of his appointment as a trustee: *Mining Journal*, cited by *Barnsley Chronicle*, 9 May 1874; *ibid.*, 11 December 1875.

62 On 25 February 1876 the disaster fund resolved to form a permanent fund committee, but 'nothing of a practical nature was done'. (WR, First Delegate Meeting, *Minutes*, pp. 6–7.)

63 *Yorkshire Post*, 13 December 1875; *Barnsley Chronicle*, 18 December 1875.

64 WR, Records, bundle on Swaithe Main explosion fund, *Circular to Colliery Proprietors*, 28 March 1876; 'A Believer in Retributive Justice'

to *Barnsley Chronicle*, 25 December 1875; *ibid.*, 18 December 1875, 25 March 1876; *Yorkshire Post*, 18 December 1875.

65  Barnsley Public Library, Swaithe Main Colliery Explosion Relief Fund, minute book, 9 March 1876; *Barnsley Chronicle*, 18 March 1876. See also *Yorkshire Post*, 11 December 1875.

66  Cusworth Hall Museum, Doncaster, 'Swaithe explosion, 1875 and 6', J. Tyas to C. Bartholomew, 21 December 1875.

67  Benson, 'Trade union accident funds'.

68  *Barnsley Chronicle*, 10 December 1876.

69  In 1877 Watson was also president of the South Yorkshire Miners' Association.

70  *Barnsley Chronicle*, 27 January 1877.

71  *Ibid.*, 13 January 1877.

72  *Ibid.*, 27 January 1877. For Blyth see *Dictionary of Labour Biography*, vol. 3 (forthcoming).

73  WR, First Delegate Meeting, *Minutes*, p. 7.

74  *Ibid.*

75  *Barnsley Chronicle*, 7, 12 February 1877.

76  WR, Records, cuttings, '1887. Aug.', Rev. Day's circular to owners, 31 January 1877.

77  *Ibid.*, Letters, 1877–8, No. 53, D. Holford to W. Watson, 24 September 1877.

78  *Barnsley Chronicle*, 7 February 1877. See also *ibid.*, 12, 19 February 1877.

79  *Ibid.*, 19 February 1877.

80  WR, *First Annual Report*, pp. 9, 18.

81  J. E. Williams, *The Derbyshire Miners: a Study in Industrial and Social History* (1962), p. 458.

82  WR, First Delegate Meeting, *Minutes*, p. 19.

83  *Barnsley Chronicle*, 19 February, 27 November 1877; 31 January 1880; 29 January 1881; 'Nemesis' to *id.*, 21 September 1878; *Mexboro' and Swinton Times*, 26 September 1879.

84  South Yorkshire Miners' Association, *Minutes*, 22 January 1877.

85  *Ibid.*, 5 February 1877.

86  *Barnsley Chronicle*, 19 February 1877.

87  In January 1878 Ben Pickard of the West Yorkshire Miners' Association privately informed William Watson that 'although we cannot give any active assistance to your system, I don't know that we are desirous of putting anything in the way . . .' (WR, Records, Letters, 1877–78, No. 115, B. Pickard to W. Watson, 13 January 1878.) Eighteen months later Pickard felt able to announce publicly that 'The only widows' and orphans' fund which can be successful is that of the Permanent Relief Fund . . .' (*Barnsley Chronicle*, 14 June 1879.)

88  For subscriptions and benefits see appendix 5.2. The complete rule book of the West Riding of Yorkshire Miners' Permanent Relief Fund is reproduced in Benson, 'Compensation', pp. 444–65.

89  WR, First Delegate Meeting, *Minutes*, p. 7; *Barnsley Chronicle*, 26 March 1877.

90 *Barnsley Chronicle*, 26 March 1877. Two of the pits (New Oaks and Swaithe Main) were, of course, the scene of recent disasters.

91 The membership represented 5 per cent of the miners employed in the Yorkshire coalfield. (WR, First Delegate Meeting, *Minutes*, p. 8; Benson, 'Compensation', table I.) The first fatal accident to a member took place on 1 June 1877, when John Dunk was injured at the Wheatley Wood Colliery. He died on 4 August, leaving a wife and six dependent children. (WR, First Delegate Meeting, *Minutes*, p. 8.)

92 See *Barnsley Chronicle*, 22 September 1877.

93 Honorary: S. J. Cooper, J. Tyas, R. Inns; ordinary: W. Fearn, E. Jones, J. Quarmby.

94 J. Blackburn, G. Guest, H. Canter, A. Paterson, J. Wood.

95 Joseph Wilkinson.

96 Honorary: Alderman Carter, Alderman Newman, C. J. Dibb; ordinary: S. Lambert, W. Jackson, J. Bostock, C. Tipping, J. Fairhurst, C. Wroe, H. Cooper, J. Wilcock, G. Gomersall, H. Neville, G. Clarke.

97 WR, *First Annual Report*, p. 8; Benson, 'Compensation', table I.

98 Benson, 'Compensation', pp. 318–22, 411–24.

99 This section is based upon *ibid.*, pp. 418–19, 425–6.

100 WR, *Eighteenth Annual Report*, p. 7.

101 Benson, 'Compensation', table XIV.

102 60 and 61 Vict., c. 37.

103 *Tragedy of the Coalfields*, p. 12; *Potts' Mining Register and Directory for the Coal and Ironstone Trades of Great Britain and Ireland* (North Shields, 1910), p. 198.

104 *Tragedy of the Coalfields*, p. 12. Membership fell to 18,159 by 1910 and to half that figure by 1915: WR, *Thirty-ninth Annual Report*, p. 16.

105 *Tragedy of the Coalfields*, p. 11; Benson, 'Compensation', tables IV, V, XV.

106 WR, *Twenty-first Annual Report*, pp. 53, 55.

107 *Barnsley Chronicle*, 22 September 1877.

JAMES MACFARLANE

# 6 Denaby Main: a South Yorkshire mining village

## Background

Denaby Main is a South Yorkshire coal-mining village. It is situated between the townships of Conisbrough and Mexborough, and the main Sheffield–Doncaster railway marks its northern boundary. The origins of the village came in 1868, when the Denaby Main Colliery Company was registered. Shaft-sinking operations had started on the Denaby estates in 1863, and the Barnsley seam of coal was finally proved at Denaby four years later, when coal was reached in September 1867.

At the time when the exploration and sinking was taking place Denaby Colliery was the farthest east in the Yorkshire coalfield and there was some doubt about the success of the venture. When coal was reached the *Colliery Guardian* commented:[1]

### Opening of a new and extensive coalfield

The Barnsley seam of coal has just been reached in an entirely new district, at a place called Denaby, about seven miles from Doncaster, the shaft, which is the deepest in Yorkshire, is rather more than 422 yards deep, and the coal, which averages nine feet in thickness and is of excellent quality, underlies the magnesian limestone. In reaching the coal a bed of fine cannel, rather more than a foot thick, as well as other seams, were passed. The work of reaching the Barnsley bed occupied rather more than four years, as a great deal of water had to be encountered, and more than sixty yards of tubbing had to be placed in the shaft. This involved a very large outlay, and took about twelve months to accomplish. It may be stated that, not a great many years since, persons engaged in mining operations were of the opinion that the coalfields terminated where the line of the magnesian limestone commenced; but geologists contended that the coal existed under the formation dipping into the east to an extent unexplored. This has been proved to be correct . . . and further verified in the present instance. The Denaby Colliery is the property of Messrs Pope and Pearson (West Yorkshire colliery owners), is well situated for carriage by canal and railway and will give employment, when opened out, to something like 500 persons.

This extract from the *Colliery Guardian* of 12 October 1867 gives a number of clues as to the nature of the coal owners at Denaby Colliery. They were obviously men who were willing to take risks —real risks. Men who were willing to sink capital in an area which had not been 'proved' must have had commercial toughness. This quality of toughness is further emphasised in the way they over-came the problem of flooding in the shaft (at a very early stage in the sinking process) and did not 'jack up' the operation. In addi-tion to their commercial toughness the Denaby Colliery owners must also have been men of substance, able to risk capital on such a high-risk venture, with possible loss of capital and a certainty of no profit over the first four or five years of mining operations. These same owners are an important ingredient in the Denaby story; with few changes they retained control of Denaby Colliery until the 1920s.

In 1893 the Denaby company opened out Cadeby Main Colliery, about one mile to the east of the older colliery, and changed the company name to the Denaby & Cadeby Main Collieries Ltd. These two collieries remained in the control of this company until November 1923, when the virtual ownership and control passed to Messrs William France Fenwick & Co., ship owners, of London. In March 1927 the Denaby & Cadeby company amalgamated with other South Yorkshire colliery companies to form the Yorkshire Amalgamated Collieries Ltd (with a total capital of £3·2 million). In May, 1936, after various further changes, the Amalgamated Denaby Collieries was incorporated and the seven collieries in the Yorkshire group were transferred to this company. The Amalga-mated Denaby Collieries remained the controlling company until nationalisation of the coal mines and the end of private ownership in 1947.

Denaby Main Colliery was finally closed in 1968, one hundred years after the foundation of the original company and the opening of the Barnsley seam of coal. This seam was still worked up to the very end, and worked with pick and shovel—'hand-got into tubs'. No conveyor belt, coal-cutting machine or shot-firing was employed in the coal-getting process. The getting method remained the basic traditional collier skill—and sweat. Haulage was in tubs or 'corves', with hand 'tramming', pit horses and endless rope. Two additional seams were also being worked on more modern mining methods—

the Parkgate or Deep and the Haig Moor seams. The reason for the Denaby closure was said to be the amalgamation of the pits with Cadeby Main Colliery.

The year 1869 was the first year that a fully opened out Denaby Main Colliery could be worked. On 3 March of that year a lockout commenced at the pit; it continued for over six months, until September 1869. The point at issue between workpeople and the coal owners was the right of the workers to join a trade union. The owners were intent upon working the colliery on the 'free labour' principle, but some Denaby miners had joined the South Yorkshire Miners' Association early in 1869 following a dispute over the size of corves and payment for coal filled. The masters reacted and in February gave the union men twenty-eight days' notice, with an option of being re-engaged on the owners' terms—terms which included a declaration on the part of each miner that he did not belong to a trade union. Few men accepted the offer; the lock-out began as intended, and 350 miners terminated their contract with the company and brought out their tools.

Those miners who lived in company houses at Denaby Main were evicted from their homes, and by the end of March the owners had begun importing non-union colliers—mostly from Staffordshire. At first the strikers gave only peaceful opposition to the new men and amused themselves by 'baaing' the black sheep lustily. As the lock-out developed reactions became more violent and fines or prison sentences became commonplace. A number of attempts were made to end the dispute, by the mayor of Sheffield and A. J. Mundella, the Sheffield MP. One such attempt, in May 1869, brought the following response from Richard Pope, the managing partner at Denaby:

Sir,
We beg to acknowledge the receipt of your circular, enclosing another signed by several noblemen and members of Parliament . . . As regards ourselves we state that we have no dispute with our workpeople . . . and therefore . . . we have nothing to arbitrate on. The only question at issue between us and our late workpeople—who are now legally and permanently discharged, and have therefore no claims upon us more than they have upon yourselves—was as to the question of the Miners' Union: but, as we have determined that this colliery shall be worked on the free labour principle, we must . . . decline any arbitration or conciliation which shall seek to interfere with principles we may deem right to adopt for the management of our own capital and the conducting of our own business.   R. Pope, Managing Director[2]

This statement by the managing director at Denaby suggested a quite uncompromising attitude towards the dispute, but in September, after six months of conflict, a compromise was reached. A meeting was held at the Victoria Hotel, Sheffield, with the mayor of Sheffield in the chair and attended by A. J. Mundella, MP, Mr E. Baines and G. Huntriss representing the Denaby Colliery Company and J. Normansell of the South Yorkshire Miners' Association. It was agreed at this meeting that 'Denaby Main Colliery workmen should be employed indifferently, whether Union or Non-Union men, without inquiry' and the first victory of the Denaby miners was won. Work resumed at the colliery for the union miners on Thursday morning, 16 September 1869, after a six-month struggle assisted by the material help of the Glass Bottle Makers' Union. This dispute was the forcing ground of the new Denaby Main lodge, and the experience, no doubt, was important in moulding the character of this branch of the miners' union.

In the 100 years of its existence the Denaby Main branch of the miners' union won a reputation for militancy, with a record of industrial conflict that included many major strikes and lock-outs. On at least three occasions after 1869 the miners of Denaby were evicted from their cottages. Evictions took place in 1877, 1885 and during the great 'bag-muck' strike of 1902-03. This latter strike resulted in important legal actions by the colliery company against the Yorkshire Mineworkers' Association, seeking damages for losses caused by strike activity. (This legal case is still used as a precedent, and it was cited recently in the National Industrial Relations Court and the Court of Appeal in reaching judgements about trade unions' responsibility for the actions of their shop stewards.) This case, the Denaby and Cadeby Colliery Company v. the Yorkshire Mineworkers' Association, was finally resolved in the House of Lords in 1906. (There was also another case arising from the same dispute: Howden v. the Yorkshire Mineworkers' Association.) If the case had gone against the YMA it would have bankrupted the union. As it was, R. Page Arnot suggested in his history of *The Miners*,[3] the worry of the Denaby case helped to cause the premature death of at least one Yorkshire miners' leader.

The village of Denaby Main was almost entirely made up of colliery-owned houses—two-up, two-down miners' cottages with no bath and only outside water closets. In 1885 the Denaby lodge secretary, in a letter to the Home Secretary, claimed that 'the Denaby Colliery Company own the whole of the property in the village with the exception of two houses'.[4] These miners' houses were 'tied', and if a workman left the employment of the company, or during industrial disputes, the family could be evicted from their home. Denaby Main was a 'company town' in other respects besides jobs and housing. The village schools were originally Denaby Main Colliery schools. The parish church was built by the company and the trustees controlling the patronage of the 'living' were appointed by the company. The original company store was converted to the Denaby Main Industrial Co-operative Society on the initiative of the colliery manager, and the Denaby Main Hotel (mentioned by Fred Bramley) was built by the company and the licensed victualler was a company servant appointed and dismissed by the board of directors. The octopus-like tentacles of company power even spread to village sport, as illustrated in the interview with Bob Shephard. In short, the colliery company controlled most of the important institutions within the community other than the Denaby Main lodge of the Yorkshire Mineworkers' Association.

The interviews contained in the present paper are an attempt to obtain a limited comparative perspective of life within the Denaby community from the viewpoint of two retired Denaby workmen and a Denaby housewife. It is hoped that the present introductory essay might also prove helpful in giving the interviews themselves some historical perspective.

*An interview with Robert Henry Shephard*

Robert Henry Shephard—'Bob' to the men and women of the Yorkshire mining village of Denaby Main—worked for most of his life as a collier at Denaby Main Colliery. He started work in 1901, 'on the first working day of the year', when he was thirteen years of age, and retired fifty-six years later in 1957. He was then seventy years of age. Apart from a break of a few years earning his living as a part-time professional footballer, he lived and worked in Denaby and in addition to earning his living in the pit he also became president of the local branch of the Yorkshire Mineworkers' Association (later the National Union of Mineworkers) and a local authority councillor, five times chairman of Conisborough Urban District Council. His life story and his record of service to coal miners and to the people of Denaby Main covers a long life span and contains some fascinating insights into a working life. Bob's personal memory of the 'bag-muck' strike of 1902 is itself of sufficient interest to justify the present record of interviews, which took place in July–August 1971: Bob was then eighty-three years of age. These interviews also demonstrate the importance of sport in working-class relationships and as a link with the Church and churchmen in the early part of the present century.

*Where were you born, Bob?*

I was born on 24 December 1887 at No. 7 Clay Lane, Mexborough, on the same night as the screens at Denaby pit caught fire. Two weeks after I was born my mother and father moved house to No. 11 Doncaster Road, Denaby Main.

*Did your father and mother come from Mexborough originally?*

No. My mother originally came from Bentley. My father came to Yorkshire as a boy after his father had been killed in a pit accident. The bottom dropped out of the chair and they had to pick him up from the shaft bottom in a sack. I think my grandmother must have come up to some relatives in this district; she came up to Yorkshire from Maidensbrook, Salop—Shropshire—after she was widowed by my grandfather's death.

*What do you remember of your childhood and schooldays?*

I started primary school when I was three years old, it was at the back of Doncaster Road, near the railway line, and we had to pay twopence a week in advance—every Monday. At five years of age I was transferred to Rossington Street School, and then, when I was nine, I moved across to the Large Hall School, built by the colliery company in 1894 and one of the best schools in south Yorkshire. This school had a very large hall which had classrooms going off it: the hall was used for a variety of social functions and dancing—the end room at the head of the hall was semi-circular in shape and was used as the vestry, and the school was used as a Protestant church before the present Denaby church was built. I stayed at this school until I was thirteen, when I left to work in the pit.

*What date was that, Bob?*

I started work at Denaby on the first working day of the year 1901.

*What job did you do?*

My first job was in the pit bottom, coupling tubs, then I went trapping the air doors open and shut for the drivers; these had to be used for ventilation. After that I went lamp carrying. When I was seventeen I went pony driving; my pony was called Prince and we worked on the haulage, pulling slack on the tail rope of a main-and-tail engine, as Prince refused to pull tubs.

Lane end of the village and the other at the back of the second block

In the 1890s there were only two taps in Denaby, one at the Denaby of houses in Cliff View. Some women of the village got together and

*What was Denaby Main like when you were a boy?*

went to see the pit manager about having water laid on to their homes
and a copper boiler so that they could wash their husbands' clothes
more easily. Mrs Frogatt, Mrs Cartwright, Mrs Ball and my mother
were the women who went to see the manager, Mr W. H. Chambers.
A reservoir was built on top of the Crags by the company and water
pumped from the No. 2 shaft at Cadeby Main Colliery. The same
women went to see the manager about having gas lighting in their
homes, and a gas works was built. With this new lighting it was like
a new world to be home at night or in school. Before the gas came we
only had candles or paraffin lamps. The village was originally a pleas-
ant parish to live in, and we used to play opposite the Institute on
what we called The Green, but it did not last long. As the pits developed the company built more houses at a density of forty-nine to the
acre, and this took away the open fields of the older village. People
from the other places round about looked down on you if you came
from Denaby Main. The houses were lacking in many amenities, the
streets were very close together and the sanitation was poor, the houses
had middens for ashes and rubbish and a closet, but these had no
water to flush them. Then the company laid water on to the toilets
and as the years rolled by a sewerage works. Some of the older houses,
those in Cliff View, Annerley Street and Thryburgh Terrace, had gardens, and you could keep pigs or grow vegetables, but the new houses
didn't have gardens, and some of the new building took up the old
gardens.

*What was it like during the bag-muck strike, Bob—you must have
been working at Denaby when it took place?*

As I said earlier, I commenced work at Denaby Colliery in January
1901, and after fifteen months the bag-muck strike began over payment for filling bag dirt. The Barnsley Bed coal seam was over six foot
thick and in layers: two feet eight inches, which was called Day Beds,
then there was bag dirt over the Day Beds, which ranged from six to
eighteen inches thick. Above the bag dirt was a further layer of coal
two foot six inches thick and the best seam of coal in the country, both
house coal and hards, or should I say steam coal. A top layer of the
seam was not worked because it was kept up to bind the roof to
strengthen the rock above, for safety reasons. The men had to move
the bag-muck to get the coal, but the company made no payment for
this work. The strike lasted more than six months and during the
early days of the strike (or lock-out, as the men stated) there was a
lot of trouble. The miners who were tenants of colliery houses had
been turned out of their houses and the company boarded up the
windows. Families had to find anywhere to live: in the churches,
chapels, with relatives or friends who resided outside colliery houses,
in tents, in the open fields. It was a terrifying time for our people in
the fields or anywhere they could go; then they (the company) intro-

duced blacklegs, and brought in the Metropolitan Police to look after the blacklegs. This did not stop the women and children from throwing stones or anything they could find to pelt the blacklegs. The miners' families howled at the blacklegs and they were militant, telling them to leave the pit and go home. There was a great number of tussles with the men as they proceeded to the houses which the company had provided. These were all in one block, to keep them under the protection of the police. After about ten or twelve weeks there was a fire down the East Plane district of the pit, in the '70s stall, and the company asked the union for men to go to work to put the fire out, but they told them to use blacklegs to do the work, as in the men's mind they (the company) wanted to break the Yorkshire Miners' Federation, but eventually the branch relented and allowed so many men to help put the fire out. The owners took the union to the law courts for damages, and the union engaged Mr Rufus Isaacs as their barrister— he later became Lord Reading. When the strike was over the men drifted back, but some had got work at other places, as their strike pay was negligible. It was surprising how the people had carried it— it was the courage which the women displayed in the damned hard times. They had to put up with soup kitchens and bread given by tradesmen. They made potato butter, mixing butter and potatoes to make it go further, and most of the food there was went to the children.

*Apart from work and industrial troubles, what was life like when you had left school and started work in the pit—what kind of spare-time activities did you have?*

During the strike of 1902 Denaby United joined the Midland Counties Football League, and that was a big event in the life of the village. I played football myself, and in 1905 played with Denaby Church team in the Mexborough Sunday School League. I played three years with the church team, then I was given a trial with Denaby United in the last match of the season versus Rotherham County in the Midland League. Then I went back to play with the church team and in 1908–09 season I was playing with Denaby United reserves. We won the Sheffield Association League. In the season 1909–10 I got into Denaby United first team, and in 1910–11 I was asked by the club if I wanted to be transferred to Doncaster Rovers, but I had a good job at the pit and did not want to leave Denaby. The Doncaster Rovers officials waited around at the Reresby Arms (a local public house) to see my father when he came home from work. I was in bed at 8.45 p.m., as I had to go to work the following morning (Saturday) and play for the club in the afternoon. Then my father came home and he was persuaded to call me downstairs. The Denaby United representatives told me that my work at the pit would be all right (the Denaby Club wanted the transfer fees), but when I went to work on the Monday morning I was told to go where I was playing football. I kept going to the pit and was sent a mile and a half to the workplace but could not get more than one shift a week. On only one week out of seven did I manage two shifts, so I decided I had enough getting up at 4.30 a.m. to go and try to get work. I said if they were going to victimise me I would be better off staying in bed. I tried to get work all over the district, and I tried all the pits in the area, but by being so well known I was always told that I could have work if I played football for their team, but I was tied up with the Rovers. In 1912 I did find work at the Fitzwilliam Colliery at Hemsworth, and I was happy there. When war broke out I was still working in the pit, and in 1916 I removed back to Denaby for work. My wife was always wanting to come back home, as she called Denaby, so I agreed, and we were settled once again. After giving up playing football I took on refereeing and carried on with that until 1938, when I took over the manager's job at Denaby United.

There were also concerts and other musical items in the village, and the teachers' operatic society, held at the Large Hall, organised by Mr Moses Soar, with Mr Butler and Mr Taylor, choirmaster at the church, as conductor. We had Bible class on Sunday afternoons, with more than 100 members; the vicar was the Reverend F. S. Hawkes and the curate was the Reverend Kenneth Kirk. I still went to Bible class after I played for Denaby United; the vicar and the curate travelled home and away games with us, and we were delighted to have them with us, they gave a lot of enthusiasm and support and were very highly respected. It was a very sad day when the vicar, the Reverend F. T. Hawkes, left the church to go to South Africa, and the curate, the Reverend Ken Kirk, also left the Denaby church. He was that very kind that he became the Bishop of Oxford. Both of them looked after the welfare of the village and people, and they had very good congregations at the church services. I don't think the same has been as popular since.

*You have talked about football and other community activities. What about your own UDC and union activities?*

I was a staunch member of the Denaby and Conisborough Labour Party and in 1931 (I had joined in 1920) I was nominated to stand as candidate in the urban district council elections for the West Ward, which I won very comfortably. In 1935 I was chairman of the UDC, and while in office I had to read the proclamation of King George V Jubilee Year, which brought me the King George Jubilee Medal. I was also elected president of Denaby Main branch of the Yorkshire Miners' Association. We had occasion to have a breakdown: the big shaft broke in the winding engine house and the men refused to go down the pit, as there was no second way out. (If anything had gone wrong with the second shaft the men would have been stranded down the pit.) The colliery company summoned the men, and we had to appear at the West Riding court house; we won, but the company wasn't satisfied and they appealed to the Law Courts in London. Our solicitor was Mr Donald Dunn, and we asked him to get us a very good and able barrister. We asked if he could get Sir Stafford Cripps, and we had him for our defence. He played on the fact that the men were within their rights, and the Lord Chief Justice dismissed the appeal, but both sides had to pay their own costs. So we won again against a conviction and our men received their unemployment benefit out of it, which was a pleasure to the branch—I and Mr J. T. E. Collins, branch secretary, had attended the court on behalf of the workmen.

I was chairman of the local authority five times during my term as councillor: my first appointment in 1932 I was asked to raise funds for the bairns, and we gave the children something to wear during the depression. The men were only working three days a week, then the company brought in a four-day week and this prevented men from drawing unemployment benefit. We did what we could for the children in the circumstances and provided shoes for the worse off. Then I was asked by the headmistress, a Miss Williams, to try and run dances to raise funds for her nursery school. We helped her make a success of her school and provide beds and rocking horses, etc., and she was very thankful for our efforts.

One time I was appointed on the committee dealing with pensions for persons of seventy years of age. We had a lot of Irish-born men living in the district, and we had to get information about how long they had resided in our own area, as the registers in Ireland were all burned in 1871. It was an unthankful job to find the people who were entitled to the ten-shilling pension, but I am sure that the majority were satisfied with our efforts. I was president of the Denaby branch when we became the National Union of Mineworkers. It was around that time that the branch secretary and I met the agent of the colliery about changing the gas over to electric light in the houses. We brought in Cadeby branch of the NUM to help us, and it finished up at the Yorkshire Miners' offices at Barnsley. We invited the manager of the Yorkshire Electricity Board from Leeds and he eventually agreed. In all I was president of the Denaby branch of the union for nearly twenty years and a local authority councillor for thirty-eight years.

*We've talked about work and recreation and your public activities. What about your family life?*

I think the family is a very important part of a man's life. I was married in 1911 and my wife died ten years ago, in 1961, just six weeks short of fifty years of marriage. We had ten children, and seven of them are still alive, six sons and a daughter.

*Postscript.* At the time of this interview Bob lived alone and looked after himself in the large colliery house which had provided a home for his family. He did most of his own cooking and cleaning and remained a very active man.

## An interview with Fred Bramley

Fred Bramley was born at Denaby Main on 20 October 1896. His father worked at Denaby colliery, and the family were evicted from their home during the bag-muck strike in January 1903. From that time Fred lived in Mexborough, a neighbouring township. He never married and for many years he shared his sister's house. Fred started work at Denaby Main Colliery on his fourteenth birthday, worked there until 1914, when he went to work at Manvers colliery. He returned to work at Denaby Main in 1928 and continued to work there until he retired. More than forty-five years of work in the pits, thirty-six years at Denaby Main.

Fred Bramley was always a good union man but never a branch official; he was satisfied to serve for many years, nearly thirty years of unbroken service, as a lodge committee man. In my own view Fred Bramley was what trade unions are about. An honest, forthright, essentially simple man, who had his own views of what was fair, reasonable or desirable and was willing to stand his ground for his views. In the branch meetings at Denaby Fred Bramley would continue to pursue his point in his own peculiar way until satisfied with the answer given. 'I'm very sorry, Mr Chairman,' he would say. 'I know that I'm a bit slow but could you please explain again what so and so was about. I realise that everybody else might understand what it's about, and I'm sorry to appear so awkward, but I hope the branch will be able to go along with my point and give a little time to the question'. This way he not only got his information but he also kept branch officials on their toes and gave the younger branch members an education in tactics.

Fred Bramley was interviewed by J. M. and Mr H. Williams on 6 September 1971.

*When and where were you born?*
Sprotborough Street, Denaby Main, on 20 October 1896.
*Was your father a collier?*
No, he had been a pit worker but he took up as a sort of general labourer. Before the bag-muck strike he worked on the coal face as a filler, in spite of a bad arm from infancy he could do owt as anybody

else could do, they tried him on a number of different jobs in the pit. He worked with the ponies one bit and they got a disease among the ponies, pink eye they called it, and they used to get one pony drunk to go and get another pony out of the workings. They used to send beer down t'pit for 'em, for the ponies, as a sort of medicine.

*Was your father a union man?*

He never held office in the union but he was a regular attender at union meetings and very militant, very militant for a cripple, and there are devious ways—you know? Well, he got blackballed in t' bag-muck strike.

*Which school did you attend?*

We were turned out of the house during the bag-muck strike and came to Mexborough. I can't remember if I started the infant school at Denaby, I wouldn't be certain about that, but I wasn't old enough to go into the senior school then, you see . . . at the most I would only be six years old. I can't remember going to the infant school at Denaby but I remember going to the infant school in Mexborough.

*Can you remember being evicted from your home?*

No. I couldn't memorise the date at all, but I can just faintly remember, as you can imagine at that age, the mounted police in t' village. They turned you out, you see, for arrears of rent when you'd been on strike that long you couldn't pay . . . They were forced to leave you the bed, you know, but they didn't carry it downstairs, they threw it out of the top window into the street.

*Who did the evicting?*

The bailiffs. Well, they'd protection of police, you see.

*Did you get somewhere to live straight away?*

We found somewhere straight away but it were under pittance, you know; we went to live at my grandmother's house, my father's mother.

*Did you go back to live in Denaby after the strike was over?*

No. My father said that he'd never live in Denaby again—he wouldn't be turned out twice.

*Did your father work at the pit when the strike was over?*

No. He got blackballed.

*Where did he go and work then?*

Well, he was out of work, he couldn't get a job at no pit, you know, he was out of work for a long time, then he got a job general labouring. He never worked in t'pit again—he wouldn't have got a job in t'pit again, they were very strong then, you see—the coal owners. They sent for the Old Man after strike when he'd been out of work a long time and offered to sign him on, on the understanding that he went to live in his old house, but he wouldn't.

*Have you any idea how long it was before you got a house of your own?*

Well, I should say about four years.

*So you finished your school days in Mexborough?*

Yes, at Doncaster Road School, and I left school when I was fourteen and started at Denaby pit on my fourteenth birthday, 20 October 1910, the first bloody day possible. I worked at Denaby until 1914, when I left, or you may have termed it being sacked. Personally I think I was sacked as a backthrow to t'Old Man. Anyway I went to Manvers Main to work and stopped there until 1928, when I returned to Denaby.

*What was your first job in the pit?*

Lamp carrying, that was the first job, carrying oil lamps, but it didn't last long. When another lad was set on and you'd got a little bit of pit sense they sent you door trapping—opening the ventilation doors to let the ponies through when they were pulling tubs . . . After that I went pony driving. I didn't go to work in the coal until I went to work at Manvers Main. I enlisted from Manvers in 1915.

*Did you go overseas?*

Yes. I had nearly three years overseas.

*Can you remember in a more specific manner the kind of things that were causing trouble between you and the management before you left Denaby to go to Manvers?*

Well, when I look back, I was kind of militant and I wouldn't let nobody shove me round. There were a big feller come there, he was deputy on my district, he came from up north. You could feel his antagonism, and one day he set all the men off to work, leaving me and my two brothers stood at the boxhole. Anyway he addressed me and said, 'Thou go so and so.' My brothers had jobs to go to, but he didn't set them off. He said again, 'Thou go so and so.' Well, I never answered him. He was a big feller and he said, 'Ah've told thou to go so and so.' Well, I didn't use any insolence but ah still stood there and he moved to the boxhole door—I thought he was going to knock me through t'wall, he was that aggravated. He said, 'I've told thou to go so and so,' and I said, 'There's no "thous" at our house, we've all a name, Mr Phelps.' Well he went back to the boxhole and he was raving, he didn't know how to get out of it. He set the other two off then and I had to see the under-manager. Of course, the deputy was right.

*Was there any point in going to the union with that kind of problem?*

Well, no, there wasn't. It had been a very militant union at Denaby, you know, and a good union pit, strong in membership, but after the strike you could get no support for Denaby from the Yorkshire Miners' officials at Barnsley. I'll give you an instance of this, when the branch decided that no member would ride in the shaft with blacklegs or non-union men, and they were stood waiting for the chair and this chap wa' first, when the gaffer come and he got on the chair. The banksman directed the first man on to the chair but he refused, saying he wouldn't 'ride with a non-union man', but he got the sack and nowt could be done about it.

*Do you remember the names of any of the Denaby branch officials around this time?*

No. To be honest, I can't bring them to mind.

*Do you remember hearing of Nolan, the lodge delegate, during the bag-muck strike?*

Yes, I do. I think Nolan was blackballed, but I couldn't swear to that. I only met him once, and he was making enquiries on how to contact a man. There was no branch room in Denaby, you know: the branch declared Denaby 'black' so far as meeting rooms went, and the Mason's Arms at Mexborough was the headquarters.

*Why was the Reresby Arms in Denaby declared black? That wasn't owned by the colliery company.*

No. But the colliery company had control of it through the effects of trade. For example, the old militia club that's been up since the South African war, it used to have a licence, but the pit bobby used to stand at the top of that lane and them that went in there instead of the Drum (the Denaby Main hotel—owned by the colliery company) had no work at the pit the following day—just for the day, like. Well, that was the influence used, you see.

*What made you come back to Denaby from Manvers?*

Well, we hit some bad work at Manvers. I'll tell you this—I shouldn't have gone to Denaby if I'd known what I knew when I got there. As a matter of fact I was stood on principle at Manvers when I finished and that was as near to being blackballed as damn it. They had a principle fund at Manvers, you know, and the branch, through local funds, paid principle money out for not working contrary—if a man stuck up for his principles they paid him principle money. Well, I wouldn't stand to be pushed about and I knew the bad work shouldn't have been mine so I got my heckles up and came out on principle and they paid me principle money. The workmen at Manvers paid into a special principles money fund—it had nowt to do with the union at Barnsley.

*So you came back to Denaby in 1928?*

Yes, I started work in the deep seam, the Parkgate, in the stewpot. I never thought a bloody man could work in such conditions. By, talk about heat! It was steep, you see—self-ventilating, no gas. When I came home the first day my sister asked how I'd gone on. I said, 'I've finished,' but I'd burned my boats at the other end and you don't improve a job by leaving it, so I worked the first week and I thought to myself, 'I'll bloody master it.' When I looked in the glass on Saturday morning I looked like Marley's ghost—I honestly couldn't imagine a feller working in such conditions. Talk about hot! Me and my mate used to take six pints of water apiece and have another two gallons sent down. Neither of us were supposed to drink it, according to what we said, but it was always empty about three parts of the shift time. You got nowt extra, no allowances for this work. You got 10s 6d a day and that was it. The day as I started at Denaby there were five men left same job to go to another pit.

*Were you in the union when you came back to Denaby, Fred? Did you go to branch meetings?*

I did. A lot of people didn't know when I first went back to Denaby why it was so important that I—a freshman—attended every meeting, but I knew why. It was for my own protection. I could picture ahead that there could be some trouble, and I thought, 'There'll be somebody with me.'

*Who were the Denaby branch officials at this time?*

Well, Arthur Roberts was secretary, I think Ben Gethin was president and Eddie—Eddie Collins—was branch delegate.

*What was the attendance like at branch meetings then?*

Very poor, unless there was some trouble. Perhaps twenty-four or thirty men.

*How did this compare with Manvers?*

Manvers was poor, just the same. Denaby was a more militant pit than Manvers—conditions altered so much, you see—but Manvers were a more homely pit. Workmen were more social. At Denaby a man had all on to look after himself. You hadn't much trouble at any of the family pits, Fitzbilly's [Earl Fitzwilliam's], etc. There weren't much trouble, you know, at little pits. You see, there were a stronger set of owners at Denaby. They could rule the roost—I'd heard it quoted that in the bag-muck strike Buckingham Pope said that he had a square yard of gold and he'd sink it before the miners would win. He had other collieries going, you know, over in west Yorkshire, whereas Manvers was a family pit.

*Were there many rag-outs or strikes at Denaby then?*

When I went back? No, no, because, as I said, they were feared, you see, of incriminating themselves, see—that's where the danger was. I was disgusted when I worked there to know what they were getting, and I thought, 'We'll soon alter that, and it only needed somebody to have a go. As it were, if they hadn't had some militant members at the branch . . . After all, it's them who make a good branch secretary, isn't it?

*What about Eddie Collins?*

He'd have been a good man, mind you—but he wouldn't have been able to carry as much weight, you see, because they would know the men were evading him.

When I came back to Denaby from Manvers I told them that I'd never worked at Denaby before, because I thought they might not set me on if I told the truth. But I knew that you could be sacked immediately for being set on under false pretences, so I had to watch my p's and q's a bit.

*When did you first get on to the branch committee at Denaby, Fred?*

Well, I should only be guessing, but I think it was 1931 or 1932. But I was never satisfied with the constitution of the committee at that time.

*Why?*

Well, I'll quote one instance. There was an outside attack on Eddie Collins—from company men—and I thought, 'I'll test strength of committee,' and I took a feller down and said, 'Don't say nowt at meeting, but I want thee to witness what I say. Don't vote—I'm not going to persuade thee to vote or say owt. Just listen to what I say, then if anybody says owt in t'pit tha' can report what I've said.' So I asked president, 'When are you going to stop this outside attack on our delegate?' 'Oh,' he said, 'he can look after himself.' I thought, 'I know he can.' Well, I said, 'Mr Chairman, when are you going to stop this inside attack on him?' I was referring to some of the branch committee. The chairman declared the meeting closed and wouldn't allow any discussion. That shows there was inside attack on Collins, doesn't it?

*They were attacking Eddie because of what—because he was political?*

I think he was a different man altogether as regards his honesty and everything about past officials. I don't think anybody could doubt his honesty of purpose, if they disagreed with his political views.

*What made you so convinced of Eddie, Fred? Had you worked with him in the pit?*

No, I never worked with him, but when I met him in the branch and heard him talk I was convinced by him.

*Did you always admire Collins?*

Yes—but I've differed from him, but I admired him in several ways. I often think sometimes that he was much too rigid with his economy in terms of branch funds, and people didn't get paid for what they did on deputations and the like. Them who were mostly in the office were in because they were in bad jobs, weren't they? But they only got a bloody half-crown and you could be there with the manager an hour and half or more. They ought to have got a day off work with pay for the deputation but Collins was too rigid on that question.

When we came on strike in 1926 we mortgaged ourselves and we owed more than a million pounds. You know, we got ten bob a week for groceries, and we got a bit of Russian gold, but it weren't much. Those ten bobs for groceries wanted paying off afterwards and there was a half-crown levy put on—you paid your ordinary shilling a week to the union and then there was a half-crown levy while the mortgage was paid off. Then it came out about the miners' union pension scheme, and they had to have been a financial member of the union from 1 February 1927. Well, if they weren't [financial members] it proved they hadn't met their obligations, didn't it? Eventually the union lifted this rule, but I'd never have lifted it because that was the only time the union was in difficulties, you know, and they'd slid out of their obligations; left it to the other members to help the union out of its difficulties. I often said I'd paid more than twenty shillings to t'pound for union, and some said it was impossible, but it was possible when you had to pay off another mans' debt.

*Who was the union president at Barnsley then?*

Herbert Smith. I think he was the most practical pit man we had. It's different today.

*Who do you think was the best Yorkshire leader, Fred?*

I think, Joe Hall. I didn't allus agree with Joe Hall either, but I think he's best that there has ever been in my time.

*What about Collins when he was elected to the area office at Barnsley?*

Well, if it had been me I shouldn't have let weight of the platform get me down—I should have still been Collins—I should sooner resigned than let the platform get me down.

## An interview with Harriet Hallet

Harriet Hallet was born at Mexborough, Yorkshire, in 1902, the daughter of a coal miner at Denaby Main Colliery and one of a family of ten children. She left school at thirteen years of age and worked at various jobs: in domestic service, in a cotton mill, and as a general help in a public house. In 1924 she married James MacFarlane, a collier at Denaby Main Colliery. For a short time she lived in rooms in her father's house, moving to live in a pit cottage at Denaby Main in 1925—six months before the miners' lock-out of 1926. Her first child, Joan, was born in 1925, in 1928 another child was still-born, and in 1930 a son, James, the present writer, was born. In April 1936 her husband died, aged thirty-nine years; he had been an active trade unionist, delegate of the Denaby Main lodge of the Yorkshire Miners' Association, a Labour member of the Conisbrough Urban District Council and secretary of a working men's club. His death left his wife a widow with two young children with an income from public funds of 18s a week, plus rent, a sum increased by 'taking in washing' and having her brother as a lodger. She was married for a second time, in December 1937 to Benjamin Homer, a collier at Denaby, and in 1939 a son, Kenneth, was born. In 1943, with a husband working shifts at the pit, her teenage daughter working twelve-hour shifts in a munition factory, and two children of school age to care for, she took on a shift job in a factory, finishing up with a physical breakdown three years later. In 1948 she again started work outside the home, as a cleaner at a local school—a job she continued to do for eighteen years.

The present interview took place in August 1972 in the two-up, two-down miners' cottage which is still her home. The inclusion of such an interview should provide a useful comparative element to the contributions of the oral history of Denaby Main. The fact that the subject of the interview is my mother has obvious drawbacks, but it also has advantages.

*Where were you born and what date were you born?*
I was born 8 March 1902, at 27 New Street, Mexborough.
*What was your father's name?*
Robert William Hallet.
*What was your mother's name before she married?*
Florence Reaney.
*What did your father's family do?*
Well, my father's father was a blacksmith.
*Have you any idea of what your mother's parents did?*
No, because they were left orphans, so they wouldn't know, I suppose.
*What other family was there when you were born?*
I was the third, and born on my father's twenty-first birthday, and there were seven followed me. Ten in the family altogether, six girls and four boys. James died at three months old, and one died during the 1918 'flu epidemic.
*Where did your father come from, before he came to Mexborough?*
From Sheffield, but where in Sheffield I don't know.
*What had he been working as, in Sheffield?*
I've no idea. I mean, he were only twenty-one when I was born, so he wouldn't have done a lot of work, would he,
*How long had he lived in Mexborough then?*
I don't know, but our Mary were born in Mexborough. That would be 1900. There were only fifteen months between me and Mary.
*He started at Denaby pit about 1900?*
I should think so, but I think he worked with my grandad a bit in Mexborough, at Truelove's, the blacksmiths.
*Was he working at the pit when you were born?*
I think he was. I don't know, to tell you the truth.
*He was working at the pit during the bag-muck strike, wasnt' he?*
That I don't know for certain.
*He always talked about the bag-muck strike, didn't he?*
He would talk about it, because they [the evicted miners] were there in tents, in the field in front of the house, weren't they?

*Where did you go to school?*
Doncaster Road School [Mexborough]. We used to call it Brown's
School.
*Why?*
Because it were Gaffer Brown [the headmaster].
*What age did you leave school?*
Thirteen.
*Did you like school?*
No, not particularly. I wasn't very bright.
*Where did you start work?*
Well, I worked before I left school, because I did potato churning
before then, for a fish and chip shop. You used to do two peggy tubs
full of potatoes for threepence. Four churns to a tub, hand churned.
*What was that—to peel them?*
Yes. And I used to go on a Sunday and help to scrub out.
*How much did you get for that?*
About one and sixpence. My mother used to think it was wonderful.
I used to have my supper every night for nothing, of course. She were
a grand old lady where I worked, Mrs Venables. She was a Salvation
Army woman, and she was the first person to take me to the seaside,
to Cleethorpes, with the Salvation Army.
*How old were you then?*
Thirteen. No, I should be less than thirteen. The first job I had my
dad took me to Sheffield, to a pub. All I had was a little paper parcel
with just a change of clothes, and perhaps two pinnies. I can't remember, but I can remember it was just a little parcel. And it was one of
the roughest places in Sheffield, down Aire Street. The gas tank was in
front of the pub and they used to be pitch and tossing all day in front
of the pub—I never forgive him for taking me there, my dad. But he
took me because I had an aunt and uncle who lived near the pub.
*What were the houses like there?*
Terrible. Ours were bad enough, but theirs were worse, and they had
a house full of kids as well. I found out they weren't married, and that
didn't suit me. So I didn't stop there long. I went from there to my
mother's sister in Eccleshall. Her husband had a quarry. He owned the
quarry, and his two sons worked for him.
*How many worked at the Quarry altogether?*
I've no idea.
*How long did you stop there?*
I think I stopped there about four month. Well, I didn't know anybody and my aunt were a big church woman.
*What was wrong with your aunt being a 'big church woman'?*
Oh, she were very pious, and that didn't suit me. Well I hadn't been
brought up to that. We went to chapel as kids, but I mean, it were too
restricted. It weren't like our family anyway, free and easy. When the

old man was sat there you daren't muff. It was free and easy at our house, even though we were poor. We weren't kept under, if you know what I mean.

*When did you start work at home in Mexborough?*

I came back from there and went to work at the Miners [Miner's Arms Hotel, Mexborough, 100 yards from her family home] for five bob a week, I think my Aunt Mary had only been paying me about three and sixpence.

*What did you do at the Miners?*

I would get up at half past seven, and work till nine before we had our breakfast, before we had a cup of tea. But we had a good breakfast, we had some good food. After breakfast, we just cleaned t'pub, what we hadn't done. It was a pretty big place, Miners. There were others beside me. There were three daughters, and they helped. We had a routine, we knew what we had to do each day, and then at night time I used to help wash glasses.

*So you worked from half past seven until ten o'clock at night.*

Oh, we hadn't days off then. I was friendly with the daughter and we'd be allowed to go to the pictures p'aps twice a week, but if we come in late we had to come in the side door so we shouldn't see her mother, and we had no supper.

*How long did you work at the Miners?*

It were like a home from home. I'd have a tiff and leave and then, if I went somewhere else—I came back about four times in all. I left once and went to Huddersfield and worked at a pub there. And that's when I walked out, because I were waiting on, and a man said something I didn't like, and I said I wouldn't wait on him no more, and the landlady said I should, and it were Saturday night. But I had still to go in that room and wait on, but the next morning I packed up and walked out. And it took me all day to get home, because it were a bad train service Sunday.

*Can you remember what your father said when you got home?*

No, because it didn't matter.

*So you always thought whatever you did he was on your side, basically?*

Oh, aye. Oh, yes.

*Where else did you work?*

I was eighteen when I met your dad. I was working at the Miner's. Your aunt worked privately at the doctor's service in Shipley and your dad didn't like me working at the Miner's—in spite of the fact that he met me there—and I got a place in Shipley—domestic service—two pounds ten a month, and that was the best job I'd had, and I was there about two years.

*What year did you get married?*

1924. I worked in domestic service for a year in Mexborough, and

I got married at Mexborough parish church.
*Where did you spend your honeymoon?*
We went to Shipley for the day.
*Where did you live when you got married?*
14 Doncaster Road, in the front room of my dad's house. There
were no houses available.

How I got one—or how your father got one, I should say—was that
my brother had to go into a santorium with suspected TB.
*How many lived at 14 Doncaster Road when you had the front
room?*
Nine or ten, including my mother, father and grandmother.
*What date did you come to live in Denaby?*
1925, at 40 Tickhill Street. We hadn't been in Denaby six months
when the strike started. The strike started in April, I think it was, and
my mother died in August. I hadn't any money, nobody had any
money. I think the funeral had to be paid for after the strike was over.
*How old was your mother when she died?*
Fifty-four and my grandmother lived to be eighty-seven.
*Your father's mother?*
Yes.
*You were saying earlier that you worked in the mill.*
That was one of the times I left the Miner's. Perhaps something had
gone wrong and this woman from the Barracks [Barracks='Sparrow
Barracks', the name given locally to the group of houses which included both New Street and Doncaster Road, Mexborough. These
houses were situated less than half a mile from Denaby Main Colliery
and are mentioned in various incidents surrounding strike activity at
the colliery in 1869 and 1885. A camp site existed in the fields in front
of the houses in 1903.] had taken her family and taken a house in Melton, and they made it sound so nice at mill so I thought I'd have a go.
We started work at half past seven while five half past seven while
twelve on Saturday. We got twenty-six shillings a fortnight. Coates'
cotton mill, it was. We paid eight shillings a week board, leaving five
bob a week for other things. There were still part-timers in the mills
when I worked there, you know—children working part-time and
schooling part-time.
*Did you like the mill?*
I didn't. I didn't like the smell, I didn't like the noise, and I didn't
like where we had to mash tea—there were no canteens you know.
You had to sit among your machines to eat. Where you had to mash
your tea were like a big boiler affair, and you had to ladle it out. I
didn't stop there long, then I came back to the Miner's again.
*Were you doing the same job each time at the Miner's?*
Yes, barmaid and helping out. It was the same landlady each time.
Mr Athron, the landlord, died in the 1918 'flu epidemic. It were just

after the war, you know, they were dying like flies all over then.

*So you came to Denaby as a young married woman in 1925? What was it like in Denaby?*

Well, I didn't want to come to Denaby (Why?) I didn't like Denaby. (Why?) I had been brought up in Mexborough. I wanted to live in Mexborough, but you couldn't get a house, so it was a case of having to come to Denaby. We lived forty yards away from my mother-in-law, and that were problems. We'd been buying furniture and putting it in my mother's room: a horsehair couch, a red mahogany sideboard. They were the furniture. I mean, they were good, but it were second-hand.

The houses in Denaby weren't like what they are now. 40 Tickhill Street were live with bugs when I took it, and it took me a long time to get rid of them. The walls were thick with distemper and I had to scrape it all off. I loved that little house. You could see green fields from it—you could see the crags.

*What did you think when the 1926 strike started? Can you remember what it was like?*

I remember what it were like, but at that time I weren't really interested in politics. But there wasn't the violence there is today. The majority passed the time picking coal from the tips. Aunt Mary always worked in the fields, you know, and she persuaded me to go potato picking, and I went, and left Joan with your dad. But I didn't get in t'door before I got a crack. (Why?) Because I'd gone. So I said, 'If he were too proud for me to go potato picking for three bob I shouldn't go for the money,' and I never did. Do you know what I took with me for my break? Bread and cold potatoes, and that's true. They don't know they're born. I think the most money we ever got were six shillings, then it dwindled down to three bob, then nothing. (How did you get by on that?) The milkman and the butcher—you had to have as little as possible—I paid every penny I owed. Mr Roberts was marvellous, the butcher. He used to come round with a van and a horse. And Mr Berry was the milkman, and he was all right. But milk would only be threepence a pint, you know, if that. There used to be a draper come round with a horse-drawn van, and I used to get bits from him. I think I owed him about eight shillings. I never got a lot, perhaps a dress for Joan or something like that, and I went and asked him if I could have a pair of black stockings for my mother's funeral, and he said no. Black stockings for my mother's funeral, and he refused, so after the strike I paid the eight shillings, and I never bought anything else off him. I never went in that shop again.

When the strike had been on three or four months I was wearing an old costume I had washed, and I met Granddad MacFarlane walking up Denaby. He didn't say anything to me but the message came back that he'd thought people would be wondering where I had got the money for my clothes—they'd be thinking he'd been getting money out of the union. [He was a member of the Denaby branch committee.]

*What was it like in the inter-war years, after the strike?*

Well, I mean, we were only just building up house. We'd only been in the house five months, and we hadn't a lot, only what we'd had before the strike. We'd a bed and what they go mad for now—a dressing table with a marble slab, and another one with two drawers and a glass above, and that were all the furniture I had upstairs. They were second-hand, but it was from a place I knew was all right.

There were never a lot of money. I mean, as far as I can remember, if I got two pounds for a weeks' wage I was well off. I never had no 'tick' shops. I paid for what I got. But on a Monday morning if you had perhaps half a crown in your purse you were lucky. And then the miners went on three days' work and three days' dole, but they had to go to the pit them days they weren't working and come back. I've put snap in your dad's tin that day that he should have gone to t'pit, and it was left in till the next day. They waste more now than we had to eat. I had a baby in 1928, he was still-born, a little boy, and then you were born in 1930. But I don't think I'd have had any more if your dad had lived, because he didn't want a big family. A very clean man, your dad, that were one thing about him. For all there were no baths, he never had a meal in his pit muck. He used to come in the back door, take his pit boots off on the stairs just as you come in, I had a paper on the chair and a cloth on the table, a pot of tea, cigarettes and matches on the table and the paper, and then he'd get washed. There weren't many miners did that.

*What do you know about his union activities, and things like that?*

I joined the Labour Party more for him, but I didn't like it. Well, I wasn't interested. It didn't appeal to me—I didn't like the women, for one thing. I were only a young woman and they were all older than me. They weren't my type. Well, I weren't a mixer at that time. Your dad took the Miners' Permanent Relief job, and I had to take that when he were on different shifts. And when I were having you I'd got to go and sit in Denaby Pit union box [office] one week and Cadeby another week. Cadeby I hated because there were a feller there and his language was filthy. On Thursday afternoon I had to wait for your dad to come in to sign for a cheque for the 'Lloyd George', as they called it then, and then go up the Crags to the bank to cash it, so there were money to pay out on the Friday. I think we got three pounds fifteen a quarter for that job. We bought furniture with that money.

*My father died in 1936 and left you a widow with two kids. What was that like?*

He died sudden. He were at a meeting at Barnsley on the Monday and went to a council meeting that night. He went to the doctor on the Tuesday and didn't go out that day. We went to bed and we used to read in bed, and we both read, and he got up and come downstairs, and I didn't come down then, I thought he were going to t'back. Anyway, I did come downstairs, but as I was trying to help him he stood up in the chair and collapsed. That were at five o'clock in the morning.

*So you were left a widow with two kids?*

Yes. There was eighteen shillings a week from the post office—ten shillings for me, five shillings for Joan, and three shillings for Jim. I had to go to Conisbro, to t'parish, as they called it, and they allowed me rent, eight-and threepence it was. You got diptheria about a month after your dad died. You were very poorly, in fact you nearly lost your life, and they knocked me that three shillings off because you were in hospital. There were no houses up by the hospital then, and I was a bit afraid to go on my own. Mrs Bennett used to come with me, and I had to pay her fare, because I daren't go by myself.

My brother came to live with me and I reported it to t'doings—parish—and they said he hadn't to pay me more than a pound week and they knocked me three shillings off the rent allowance.

*So your total income was eighteen shillings plus six shillings for rent allowance and one pound board and lodgings from your brother?*

Yes. And somebody reported me because I had been seen in the Comrades' Club. The man came to see me and said that I'd been reported, and I said, 'What for?' He said, 'You've been seen in "Comrades"', and I said yes, I have. I was with Mr and Mrs Bennett, and my brother gave me a shilling to go with. It were the old lady in the end house who had reported me, he told me it were. She used to go up [to the parish relief] and she said if there weren't so many young 'uns on this, old 'uns would have more.

*When did you get married again?*

18 December 1937, and Kenneth were born in the October 1939. I'd been married nearly two years when Kenneth were born.

*So you'd got a new baby at the beginning of the war. What were conditions like?*

Joan had gone in service at a convalescent home near Leeds.

*How old was she then?*

Fourteen. One or two of the girls round about had gone, and she wanted to go, so she went. She didn't get very much, but she used to send a few shillings home. Joan were very annoyed about Kenneth coming along. She was very put out when I were having him, but when he were born I wrote to her and told her we'd got a baby boy and what would she like him to be called, and it were her that christened Kenneth.

*That was a diplomatic move on your part, wasn't it?*

Well it was, that's what I thought. But when Kenneth come she wasn't happy to be away. She wanted to be home, and got a job at

Gallon's shop, sixteen bob a week. She used to go at half past eight in the morning, and it was sometimes seven o'clock at night when she come home—for sixteen shillings. She'd perhaps be seventeen when she went to Brigg's munitions works, working twelve-hour shifts. Ben weren't getting a lot of money, and Joan were keeping herself, and they were all going out to work, the women. Kenneth were about three. There were a nursery at school, so I thought, to make things a bit easier, I'd get a job, and I went to the powder works, but they wouldn't accept me there—why, I don't know. Anyway, I went to work at Maltby, three-quarters of an hour away by bus. It were shift work, all three shifts. Joan were working twelve-hour shifts. Ben were on shifts, but we always managed to get it so that one would be in when the other were out.

*What wage did you get at Maltby, on shift work?*

Three to four pounds a week. I were never on machines, they were too heavy for me. I did what they called a viewing job. That was five days a week on afternoons, six on other shifts. We worked Saturday morning on days, and on nights we worked Sunday nights. But I enjoyed working there—it were a change, it were a bit more company. But it were the blackout, and they weren't many pleasures sort of thing, and there were rationing and things to contend with. I finished up at Maltby with a heart attack. They said I just faded out, and when I went to Dr MacArthur he said, 'I think your time for work is finished. It's time you packed it in.' Well, Joan was working twelve hours, she couldn't do anything in the house.

*So doing a job and keeping a house going and looking after a husband and children was too much for you?*

Yes. I worked at Maltby ordnance factory about three years, all told.

*So you finished at the ordnance factory in 1945. That was the year the Labour government was elected. Can you remember anything about it?*

No, I can't.

*You'd vote Labour, wouldn't you?*

Course I should. Things improved a bit then. Money got a bit better in the pits, but I never had a lot of money. Even when Ben finished there, my wages [housekeeping money] were only seven pounds ten a week.

*How much housekeeping did you get in 1945?*

Two pounds ten a week, and that rose gradually to seven pounds ten a week housekeeping in 1965, but I never knew my husband's earnings.

I started as a cleaner at the school in 1948, and my wages when I started there for twenty-one hours a week was four pounds six shillings a month. The twenty-one hours was made up of working from seven while half past eight in the morning, and four while six at night, and

eight o'clock Saturday morning while half past eleven.
*How long did you work on that job?*
I worked at school about eighteen year altogether, but my wages gradually worked up, and they were paid weekly. When I finished it were nearly four pounds a week, I think. I worked two years after Ben retired, until 1967, when I was sixty-five. But I took in washing in between, and went out wallpapering. Took in washing, and if they met you in the street they didn't know you.

## Mr J. T. E. (Eddie) Collins

In one important sense the foregoing interviews are lacking a vital link in the Denaby chain. When the idea of having a number of discussions with Denaby people was originally conceived it was intended to include an interview/discussion with Mr J. T. E. (Eddie) Collins, the lodge secretary at Denaby for a period of twenty years. A preliminary discussion did take place during a country walk on 6 May 1972—the local government election day at Conisbrough, an event which Eddie Collins had rarely missed in fifty years of public life. Eddie had been present at his usual polling station before we set off for our discussion. (The Labour councillor elected on that day ensured a 100 per cent Labour council for Conisbrough Urban District—with the exception of one ex-Labour member who had had the whip withdrawn because, as a colliery official, he went to work, *under police guard*, during the recent miners' official strike.) At the time of our discussion it was intended to follow up the preliminary talk with another at a later date, but, at the time of writing, Eddie is confined to bed after a heart attack. It is still intended to have the proposed interview when he is well enough to stand the strain, but, in an attempt to give a more rounded comparative picture of the Denaby branch of the miners' union, and so that the comments about Eddie Collins in the present interviews are given context, the following short note might be of some assistance.

Mr J. T. E. (Eddie) Collins was born in Wombwell, a mining village near Barnsley. His father was a pit sinker and the family moved to Denaby Main when he obtained a job extending the sinking at Cadeby Colliery in the early 1900s. (Eddie told me that shortly after the arrival of the family in Denaby the RC priest called at the house 'because Collins was an Irish name'.) As a boy Eddie wanted to be a schoolteacher, and his parents allowed him to stay on at school in order to take the trainee teacher's examination, but, along with all the other candidates in his group, Eddie failed to pass the examination and he started work at Cadeby Colliery, moving to Denaby Main Colliery when he was seventeen years of age.

In his 'teens Eddie attended WEA classes in economics—the class tutor at the time was Mr Arnold Freeman of Sheffield University, sometime lecturer at LSE and a member of the well known Freeman family. In addition to these evening classes Eddie also went to summer schools at University College, Bangor. It was at Bangor that he met a number of South Wales coal miners, members of the radical left like A. J. Cook and Noah Ablett, and their influence helped to give him a greater interest in political issues. Eddie Collins was a founder member of the Communist Party of Great Britain and joined the Miners' Minority Movement in the early days of its existence. He ceased to be a member of the party after one year because 'he couldn't get to any meetings' but he continued with his membership of the Minority Movement.

Eddie's first representative job at Denaby colliery was as workman's inspector under the Coalmines Act. Later he was elected as delegate of the Denaby Main branch of the Yorkshire Mineworkers' Association, a position he held through the 1926 strike. In the early 1930s he was elected branch secretary, a position he held unopposed for twenty years before being elected as compensation agent, a full-time post at the Barnsley offices of the NUM (Yorkshire Area) in 1953, a post he held until his retirement. In addition to the offices already mentioned, Eddie Collins was for many years the checkweighman for the workmen of Denaby Main. He was first elected to the Conisbrough UDC in 1926 on a Labour Party ticket, and later to the West Riding County Council. When the Labour whip was withdrawn from him, Eddie stood as a 'workers' candidate' and as such won election to both the UDC and the WRCC against Labour opposition. On one occasion in his time on the WRCC Eddie challenged the chairman's ruling on the right to raise an issue and the police were called to evict him from the council chamber. Though at the time he did not have the Labour whip, the whole Labour opposition left the chamber in support. He withdrew from county council affairs on his election to branch secretary but remained a workers' candidate on Conisbrough UDC until 1945, when he rejoined the Labour Party.

Eddie Collins is a quietly spoken, scholarly man, shy and diffident, a rarely drinking, self-disciplined sort of character without flamboyant airs and with a precise, careful, almost pedantic manner, a gentle man. If the labour movement had to be divided into cavaliers and puritans, Eddie would be in the puritan camp. Two examples serve to illustrate this point. In the days of private owners at Denaby Eddie would never drink with the colliery management in the pit offices, and no drink passed his lips in that situation until the nationalisation of the mines in 1947. The second example is of Eddie refusing a lift in the car of a colliery official, preferring to walk or use public transport. Eddie Collins was and is admired and respected by the workmen at Denaby Main, though, as Fred Bramley demonstrates, not uncritically so. When I last spoke to Eddie, at the side of his sickbed, and we were quietly chatting about the past, he said that he thought the workmen at Denaby had been very kind to him. I asked him then what he thought of the nationalisation of the mines, and he replied, quite simply, that it had been 'nationalisation, not socialisation'. Eddie Collins was an important influence on Denaby and the Denaby Main branch of the NUM, an influence perhaps best symbolised in the slogans of the branch banner —no 'From obscurity to respect' or semi-religious scenes for Denaby Main, but 'Workers of the world, unite', 'Forward to socialism and world peace' and 'Retirement for all at 60'.

After his illness Mr Collins was interviewed as follows.

I was born in 1894 at Wombwell, near Barnsley, the eldest of a family of eight children—seven sons and one sister. My father was a coal miner working at Darfield Main Colliery when I was born. He was a Wombwell man, but my mother came from Romtickell, near Thurgoland, not far from Penistone. My father moved from Darfield to work at the New Oaks Colliery until it closed down in 1905, then he went to Hickleton Main. He didn't stop at Hickleton because they had a 'butty' system; he left to work at Houghton Main. He was at Houghton Main about three years, working as a ripper, before he left to come to Cadeby Colliery in 1908. At Cadeby he helped to sink the No. 2 shaft to the deep.

I went to school at Stairfoot, Honingley Lane School, and at Thurnscoe, Houghton Road School. I never went to school at Denaby because I was fourteen gone when we came here. I liked school. One of my teachers at Thurnscoe was Jack Wilkinson, he used to play centre-half for Barnsley at football. He was teaching me from standard VI to standard VII—that's when I left. He was a grand feller. I used to think so, anyway. Two of my brothers, our Arnold and our Karl, both went to the pit before I started in the pit. My father and mother let me go to school until I were fourteen (though I could have left before I was thirteen) because I wanted to be a schoolmaster. I sat at an examination at Mexborough. There were two boys—I was one—and two girls sitting the examination. We all four failed to get the examination successful. I left school the last week in July 1908. Neither my mother nor my father wanted me to go to the pit if I could get another sort of job. I went to Skellow: there was a job vacant, I've forgot what it was now, but anyway I saw it in the paper, asking for a youngster about fourteen, but it had been fixed up when I got there. I went to Pontefract too, for a job, but it was too late to get the position.

It were three months after I had reached the age of fourteen before I started work. I started at Cadeby Colliery, then my father was transferred from Cadeby to Denaby Colliery. They were sinking the deep electric shaft at Denaby, a pit down a pit, from the Barnsley seam down to the Parkgate. My father asked for me to be transferred from

Cadeby to Denaby, and I was employed taking muck away from the sinkers. The muck was being lowered down the west jinny into the Barnsley pit bottom. I was first lad down the deep pit, the Parkgate seam. I was seventeen years old, and the deputy in charge asked me if I would go down and as they filled a tub put it on the cage and send it up. My father was heading-out one side, a feller called Corney was filling for him, and a feller called Mullaney was heading out at the other side. When they'd finished heading-out round the shaft they started having some stalls up in the West and South districts, and when I was nearly nineteen I went into the coal down the South district, filling in one of the headings. I think the collier I worked for was called Burgin; anyway, the family came from Elsecar to Denaby. Afterwards they introduced Sisco coal-cutting machines into the headings. I was asked to go on them, so I did, and I was employed on coal-cutting machines even though I was only a filler.

I joined the union when I started work at the pit. Young lads had only threepence to pay, then it went up to sixpence a week. My father paid a shilling. My father was always in the union. I used to go and pay the union for my father when he worked at New Oaks Colliery. They paid it at Saturday then, and I'd go and pay it. I was a young lad about nine or ten years old, and I paid it for him several times. He was never in arrears, he always paid every week or he asked me to go and pay it. Union membership at Denaby was not much over fifty per cent during the first world war and before the first world war. Mind you, at that time they weren't getting very good wages, and that may have been one of the reasons for some not joining the union. There might have been between 1,200 and 1,300 in the union and there were above 2,000 at the pit. Eventually, in 1934, when I became branch secretary at Denaby, there was just over 1,200 in the union, and we'd about 2,200 workmen, and I thought, 'That's got to be altered,' so I used to be standing at the pit gates and asking them to join the union. I got men to join, and we had above 2,000 members before 1936. They used to hold Denaby branch meetings at the New Mason Arms, Mexborough, and then the following meeting was at the Reresby Arms, Denaby. The meetings were held fortnightly, and it was on a Thursday night usually—then it went to Sunday mornings, but I remember going to a meeting in 1916 on the Thursday night. The branch officials were elected in the branch room in those days: they didn't have the ballot vote at the pit head like they do now. I never missed a meeting of Denaby union branch from 1916, I attended every meeting from 1916 to 1953.

I became a Workmen's Inspector (under the Coal Mines Act) in 1919. Once when I came out of the pit after being on inspection down the pit I refused to have a drink, a whisky, with the manager. It was reported that I had refused, and they said that they were not trying to bribe me. I replied that I didn't believe in it, I felt it was entirely wrong to be drinking with the employers' representative, because our interests conflicted with theirs. I thought to myself that the best thing I can do is to get the Workmen's Inspector elected by pit-head ballot instead of in the branch room. During the first world war period I moved for a workmen's pit inspection on time after time but couldn't get the support of the local branch officials. There might have been twelve or even eighteen months between inspections. Eventually I got a hundred signatures demanding that Workmen's Inspectors be elected by pit-head ballot. They were, after that, and things improved at Denaby. It was an honour to be able to serve them (the Denaby men), you know, that's how I felt. The first inspector I went down the pit with was a feller who lived in Maltby Street. He was all right but when we came out of the pit, you see, they offered us a glass of whisky. Well, I wouldn't have any. Anyway, it was Watson-Smith, the manager. He said, 'I'm not trying to bribe you.' Later, when I used to be going on deputations, they wanted me to have cups of tea, but I would not have that, it was only after nationalisation that I did. A feller called Halford was the manager, and I asked him—seeing that I felt that we should eventually have miners' control of the pit, not the management —I asked him, I said, 'Would you have a cup of tea with me?' and that was the first time.

When I was seventeen or eighteen my father had me going to evening classes in mining, learning mining science and mathematics. Anyway, it was mining science I was mostly interested in. When I sat my examination I passed with distinction in mining science but failed miserably in mathematics. The mining science classes proved useful on pit inspections. The other workmen's inspectors used to ask me if I would test for gas in the stall or heading. I was the one that used to do the testing for gas. I started WEA classes at Denaby after a man— I'm trying to remember his name—came and spoke to us at the Large Hall, and they decided to have a WEA class then. Arnold Freeman became the class lecturer but the man who came first, I'm nearly sure, became somebody high up down in the London area. He might have become the Archbishop of Canterbury or something, I can't just remember the name now. There were scores of us there in the meeting, and above a dozen joined the class. I was the youngest lad to join. I also went to Bangor University in 1914, for three weeks, and I came across the South Wales Revolutionary Socialists. It was them that caused me to start to think differently. I went back to Bangor the following year, in 1915, but I could only have one week there because the war was on.

Later on I invited various people to come and speak at Denaby, Tom Mann and Harry Pollitt, just after the first world war. You see, I was chairman of the Minority Movement in Yorkshire, and we had meetings every month. There weren't many of us. I arranged for Tom Mann to come, and took the chair for him at Denaby and at Womb- well. The meetings in Denaby were on the Crags, in the open air. We had A. J. Cook, Secretary of the Miners' Federation of Great Britain, and he came to the Denaby branch meeting afterwards. Noah Ablett came, but he only stayed for the meeting. I think he spoke against The Drum, the Big Drum, the Denaby Main Hotel. I was chairman, of course. I can't remember whether there were any other members of Denaby branch who were members of the Minority Movement. I think there were one or two, but I can't remember their names.

The National Labour College movement was going, and I became a member, in fact I was the secretary in Denaby of the Labour College class. We had quite a number coming along, and I was secretary for it whilst it lasted. We had lectures for between two and three years, and then it faded away. You see, I was a member of the Socialist Labour Party then and a member of the Industrial Workers of the World, and the Labour College, that was the educational side, well, I felt that that was more linked up with the Socialist Labour Party and the Industrial Workers of the World. More linked up than, say, the WEA. We had Wally Hannington of the Unemployed Workers over to speak once; I think he was one of the main leaders of the Unemployed Movement.

I was a founder member of the Communist Party because I was in the Socialist Labour Party when it amalgamated, but I left the Com- munist Party after about six or seven months after it had been formed. My wife was having our second boy and she was having a bad time, and I didn't like to leave her to go to a meeting, and I felt, if I can't attend the meetings I don't want to be a member. I must be at each meeting when it was held, you know. So I resigned from the Com- munist Party but I told them that they'd no need to worry: that they could always rely on me supporting anything that was in the workers' interest. I joined the Labour Party in 1922 and the Minority Movement when it was formed, and I was expelled from the Labour Party in 1929 for refusing to leave the Miners' Minority Movement. After 1929 I usually had a Labour man put up against me in urban district and county council elections. A feller called Saxton, the Labour Party put him up against me, but he was defeated easy. I was a representative of the North Ward in Denaby on the Conisbrough Urban District Council for twenty-nine years, from 1926 to 1955, then I left the district, you see, and went to Barnsley. When I came back they wanted me to stand again, but I was between sixty-six and sixty-seven years old and I said, 'No, I think I'm too old to run.'

When nationalisation came I thought we should develop to workers' control of the industry, but unfortunately it hasn't worked out like that. The management, they're the people who control the industry instead of the workers. I used to repeatedly mention that we should be having workers' control of the industry: the miners should be running the industry, not these people that are in these high positions, because they've not had the experience underground that we've had. The miners should control the pit manager and elect the deputy—providing he was qualified. I am somewhat disappointed by the way things are now. I thought we should be developing more towards getting the idea that we should be having workers' control of the industry, and that the agricultural workers, they should be controlling the agricultural industry. It would be in the interests of the workers, because the workers should be the whole community, because anyone who is either physically or mentally capable should do some kind of work. There should be reduced hours of work—per shift. Six hours is plenty long enough for anyone. In the pit it should be only five. Why should a man be having to have food down the pit?

When I went to work as Compensation Agent in the Miners' offices at Barnsley the staff were very kind. I told them the first day I was there, 'I don't want you to look on me as your boss, I'm only a worker same as you are. I know that I've been elected Compensation Agent but I am a worker and you're workers, so don't look on me as your boss.' They were always so very good, right away till I finished. The first day that I was Compensation Agent I was down Kilnhurst Colliery and the last day I was Compensation Agent I was down Edlington or Yorkshire Main Colliery. I was Compensation Agent for the Yorkshire Area NUM for six years and six weeks, and I retired the day I was sixty-five, the day that I was down Edlington. I went and said goodbye to the staff at Barnsley and thanked them for all they'd done for me. At that time the other officials included Alwyne Machen. He was a good president and I got on very well with him. I didn't get on too well with Fred Colingridge because he had different views from mine. You see, I felt that we should always be prepared to go down the pit to see what the troubles of the miners were, and the safety conditions and so on. I went down forty-nine pits in Yorkshire during that period. I went to sixty-two pits because of the troubles that they had, but I hadn't to go down the pit in the other thirteen pits because they weren't having trouble like that. When they had any trouble I was going down the pit to see what the troubles were, and safety particularly. I felt that Rossington was a similar place to Denaby when I visited there. I went down their pit and I went to the meeting—that was similar in some respect to Denaby, but I liked Denaby best. After all, I was delegate of Denaby for ten years, from 1924 to 1934, and branch secretary from 1934 to 1953.

I was on the Miners' Parliamentary Panel for some years. I was top of the panel list, you know. It might have been Normanton constituency, at any rate I was one that had to go, and I put my point of view across to the selection meeting, and in the Barnsley area too, but each time they selected the other feller. Scholfield was the man at Barnsley. Scholfield and me were the last two. He got thirty-four and I got twenty-eight votes, so he was the man to stand as the candidate. W. E. Jones was the chairman of the meeting. He was a Yorkshire Area official. I didn't get on very well with him, because he regarded me as a Communist, you see. In February 1954 W. E. Jones called a meeting of the officials at Barnsley and he said that he'd called the meeting because I had been doing something that was against the custom of the full-time NUM officials. I had been going to different branches and speaking to the meetings when they were on strike, and he said I shouldn't go because it was understood that the officials should wait until the men went back. Well, he said that when they come for me, as they used to come, I agreed to go along to address their meetings. He said I'd been at eighteen strike meetings up to then—that were in 1954, and I only been at Barnsley for less than a year. Machen, he was president, said he could quite understand how I felt about it. I said, 'When they come to the offices and ask me to go and see what I can do for them I'm going, because I'm a servant for the miners.'

I didn't want to leave Denaby, you know. I told the Denaby men that when I'd been nominated to be an official of the Yorkshire area by ten union branches. Anyway, two men came from the other side of Barnsley and saw me—I lived at the top of Conan Road, in Conisbrough, then—and they said they wanted me to run to be an official. I said I didn't want to leave Denaby, I'd been at Denaby above forty years and I'd only seven years to go. They said, now look here, what you've done for Denaby miners we want you to do for all Yorkshire. Well, that's what they did. So I thought, 'That's done it. I must stand now.' So I ran to become an official. They convinced me that I should allow myself to be put up, and I was on the list. I got fifteen thousand votes more than the second candidate, and he was supported by West Yorkshire. I didn't want to leave Denaby, it was a good branch, they'd listen to what you had to say. We didn't have any difficulties in running the meetings, they were very good, very friendly towards each other.

## A concluding commentary on Denaby Main

It might perhaps be useful, as a concluding commentary on Denaby Main, to put forward some hypotheses attempting to explain the reasons for the apparently militant attitudes of the people and miners of that village and colliery. In one of his replies Fred Bramley suggested a number of reasons for the attitudes at Denaby Main. 'You hadn't much trouble at the family pits, Fitzbillies, etc. There weren't much trouble, you know, at little pits. You see, there were a stronger set of owners at Denaby, they could rule the roost—I'd heard it quoted that in the bag-muck strike Buckingham Pope said that he had a square yard of gold and he'd sink it before the miners would win. He had other collieries, you know, over in West Yorkshire . . .'

The practical experience of a working miner would seem to suggest that the cause of industrial conflict lies, in part, in the greater size of the workplace and substance of the owners. The owners at Denaby Main colliery were men of substance and, in addition, had a fair degree of commercial toughness, a point demonstrated in the risk taken in sinking a new colliery on an unproven area five miles to the east of the nearest colliery and at the line of the magnesian limestone fault. The manner in which the partnership overcame a serious water problem during the sinking process and continued to sink the then deepest shaft in Yorkshire is further demonstration of these qualities. These twin qualities of commercial substance and tough-minded attitudes were turned against the Denaby workforce from the time the pit was opened. The first example of company policy was the imposition of the 'free labour' principle in 1869. When the men refused to accept company policy on the confiscation of corves and determined to join the union, the employers responded with a totally uncompromising policy and gave notice to most of their labour force unless they signed their intention to give up the union. When the Denaby men persisted in remaining in the union, they were locked out and blackleg labour was imported. The company compromised with the workmen only after a dispute of six months' duration—this in the first full year of commercial operations and after four years with no return on a heavy and high-risk capital outlay during the shaft-sinking process. The events of 1877, 1885 and 1903 are further examples of the attitude of the Denaby Main colliery owners and management. A workforce faced with such a ruthless and intransigent employer, capable of evicting them from their homes, importing an alternative strike-breaking labour supply, and willing to sink 'a square yard of gold' before the miners would win, is likely to create its own countervailing force. In such a conflict situation there is no 'middle ground'—it is 'fight or submit'. The slogan adopted by the Denaby branch of the YMA of 'In the union or out of the pit' would seem to provide some evidence of this polarisation of interests.

In the early days of Denaby Main Colliery it would seem likely that other factors would also have some influence on industrial attitudes. For example it would not be unimportant that all the miners at Denaby were migrants from other regions. This influx of industrial workers, without the restraints on behaviour of traditional home ties or establised social patterns and institutions, would seem likely to adopt a 'new frontier' or 'wild west' social norm, to be less well disciplined than workers in a more settled environment.

A further factor to be taken into account is that, unlike most other Yorkshire coal mining communities, Denaby Main was almost entirely made up of colliery-owned cottages. The colliery company also built the local school, church, hotel, co-operative store, miners' institute, and the Boy Scout, football, cricket and St John's Ambulance facilities—in short, Denaby Main was a 'company town'. This factor gave the Denaby owners a greater degree of control over the lives of their workpeople than was the case in the older mining areas of west Yorkshire. In the older west Yorkshire area the coal owners had to share the social infrastructure with well established industry such as wool and textiles, and coal owners in these areas had far less social power than the Denaby owners. The 'total institution' nature of Denaby Main was a further influence which would tend to polarise inhabitants into one of two camps—'company men' or 'union men'. For the former the patronage of the company could extend into many spheres, including better jobs and housing; the phrases 'in the team' (the colliery football team) and 'in the band' (the colliery band) were used as shorthand explanations of the reason for workmen having a good job. For the union man the fight was total, and sanctions could be brought against them in a number of ways—but the power situation was not entirely one-sided. The close-knit nature of the Denaby community, with its blocks of pit housing and communal backyards, also made union sanctions more effective. The method could range from physical intimidation to a wall of silence. In housing situations such as those which existed at Denaby Main the industrial 'jungle telegraph', by word of mouth through the village 'backs', was a very efficient means of communication. There were no socio-industrial barriers to the free flow of industrial information such as there would be in a more complex and widely spread township. In such a situation community sanction against any renegade could no doubt be very effective.

The points made above are not intended as an exhaustive list of factors to explain the Denaby situation, but rather as a useful aid to any analysis and to give context to the views of the people interviewed. Other factors might equally be important in any attempt to explain the Denaby scene—the place and influence of religion for example, or the fact that the major market for Denaby coal was the Hull export trade. To make a reasoned assessment of these various influences would require more study in depth of the Denaby situation; it is hoped to undertake such a study at some future time.

## Notes

1 *The Colliery Guardian*, 12 October 1867, p. 330.
2 The *Rotherham and Masbro' Advertiser*, 5 June 1869.
3 R. Page Arnot, *The Miners* (Allen and Unwin, 1949), pp. 346–7.
4 P.R.O., H.O. 45/9653/A.39312 5511.

ROBERT G. NEVILLE

# 7 In the wake of Taff Vale: the Denaby and Cadeby miners' strike and conspiracy case, 1902–06[1]

## I

At the outset the Denaby and Cadeby miners' strike, or 'bag-muck'[2] dispute as it was popularly known, was as parochial and unimportant as its name suggests. However, because of the legal proceedings instituted by the employers against the Yorkshire Miners' Association (hereafter YMA), together with the Taff Vale decision and the legal antipathy to trade unions at the turn of the century, this unofficial strike escalated into a judicial battle, the financial results of which[3] could have temporarily ruined the Association. The Denaby and Cadeby conspiracy case was the first and last major trial of strength which occurred during the period in which the Taff Vale decision was of practical significance, viz. 1901–06. Important in the legal history of British trade unionism, the Denaby and Cadeby case revealed the full implications of the Taff Vale decision to an already shaken labour movement. Initially the legal proceedings tempered the defiant mood of trade unionists,[4] but the final result, which presaged the Trades Disputes Act, 1906, left them exuberant. The events of the strike and the succeeding legal struggle captured the imagination of miners everywhere, and levies were raised throughout many of the coalfields. Between 1902 and 1906 the YMA and its leaders were preoccupied with this case, which forms one of the most notable chapters in the history of the Yorkshire miners.

## II

Poor industrial relations and disputes concerning 'bag dirt' had been in evidence for many years prior to 1902 at the Denaby and Cadeby collieries, which are situated between the townships of Mexborough and Conisbrough, in south Yorkshire. After a particularly bitter dispute in 1885[5] relations between the men and the company were strained, and the Denaby and Cadeby Colliery Company directors were reluctant even to recognise the existence of the YMA. It is significant that from the 1890s until the Great War the company had the worst record of all Yorkshire colliery companies for prosecuting miners for offences against the Coal Mines Acts of 1887 and 1911. During the 1890s the YMA frequently complained that while legal proceedings were rarely taken against employers, managers and deputies, miners were regularly prosecuted for trivial offences, and moreover that the Denaby and Cadeby company was notorious for summonsing miners on the flimsiest of pretexts. The company was completely justified in punishing miners who endangered the lives of others by contravening the mines Acts, but it was much easier for both employers and men if fines were imposed out of court, with the appropriate deductions being made from the men's wages. The Denaby and Cadeby company often preferred to prosecute, and their record for the years prior to and after the conspiracy case reveals their stern and uncompromising attitude on this subject (see table 7.1).

TABLE 7.1. *Prosecutions of Yorkshire miners for contraventions of the mines Acts of 1887 and 1911, from 1900 to 1912*

| Year | Total prosecutions | Company with most prosecutions | The second highest number of prosecutions |
|------|------|------|------|
| | | Denaby & Cadeby Co. | |
| 1900 | 137 | 38 | 29 |
| 1901 | 89 | 24 | 7 |
| 1906 | 186 | 60 | 21 |
| 1907 | 172 | 64 | 16 |
| 1908 | 167 | 21 | 20 |
| 1909 | 249 | 76 | 48 |
| 1910 | 210 | 43 | 38 |
| | | Carton Main Co. | Denaby & Cadeby Co. |
| 1911 | 334 | 60 | 53 |
| | | Denaby & Cadeby Co. | |
| 1912 | 285 | 50 | 29 |

*Source.* YMA, *Annual Reports*, 1900-01 and 1906-12 (1902-05 not available).

The employers had, it should be noted, attempted to improve

the welfare of their colliers in several respects; in June 1902, for example, the company had built a new miners' institute in Denaby at a cost of £2,000 to commemorate the coronation of Edward VII. For many years W. H. Chambers, the managing director of the firm, had

> brought to the attention of the Board every suggestion he could think of for increasing the comfort of the inhabitants of Denaby. Schools, co-operative stores, churches and chapels for all denominations, cricket and football clubs, ambulance, mining and other educational classes, rifle club, choral society, brass and orchestral bands and numerous other institutions have been largely supported by the company.[6]

Such philanthropic activities had not, however, produced cordial relations between owners and men, for Denaby had become a 'company town' in which the employers wielded a large degree of control over the lives of the miners and their families. The town consisted almost entirely of company-owned cottages, and the inhabitants were largely dependent on the company for employment, housing and leisure amenities. These circumstances encouraged a polarisation of the work force of the two pits into 'company' and 'union'[7] men, and between 1869 and 1901 the Denaby pit was plagued by numerous strikes and lock-outs.[8] By the end of the nineteenth century the Denaby and Cadeby miners had gained a reputation for dogged militancy, whilst the owners were recognised to be amongst the most uncompromising in the West Riding.

### III

Grievances concerning 'bag dirt' had come to the fore by the turn of the century. The basic problem was that the men wanted extra remuneration for removing the dirt in addition to the $\frac{1}{2}d$ per ton they were allowed under a price list agreement of 1890. Repeatedly the company refused to agree to this demand. When the firm employed contract labour to perform the task which the miners refused to carry out, heated arguments ensued, for the owners deducted the cost of employing the contract labour (which they paid at the rate of $\frac{1}{2}d$ per ton) from the men's wages. In September 1901 a strike was only narrowly averted, and shortly afterwards the men unsuccessfully took their grievances to the county court. Changing working conditions at Denaby pit gave a new emphasis to 'bag dirt' grievances, for the rock became thicker, and although previously it could be 'dropped' relatively easily it now had to be hewn in a similar manner to coal with pick and wedge.[9] Additional grievances of an entirely different character were also raised, and matters came to a head in June 1902 after a 10 per cent reduction in wage rates had been ordered by Lord James of Hereford, the independent chairman of the Conciliation Board which regulated miners' wage rates in England and north Wales.[10] How far the wage rate reduction was the cause of the stoppage is a matter for conjecture, but it may have been a contributory factor. On 30 June 1902 4,000 men and boys stopped work without notice, with the full support of the executive committee of the Denaby and Cadeby lodges of the YMA, which had strongly recommended strike action.[11] In spite of this the strike was unofficial, for no ballot had been taken in accordance with the rules of the YMA, which also required that the men should give the proper notice to terminate their contracts, and indeed on the very day the strike began the council of the Association resolved that there should be an immediate return to work.[12]

The Denaby and Cadeby miners were in a vulnerable position. There were 100,000 tons of coal stockpiled at Denaby Main and 150,000 tons at Cadeby which the company could use for trading purposes.[13] The firm had a past history of mercilessly using every means at their disposal in order to apply the maximum pressure on striking miners to resume work. Moreover, because the men had been tortiously induced by their branch officials to strike without giving due notice in breach of their contracts, they could be brought to court for contravening the Employers and Workmen Act of 1875. In addition the strikers were not entitled to any money from the union. It was one of the rules of the YMA that strike action had to be endorsed by the Association's supreme governing body, the council, before strike pay could be disbursed,[14] and the Denaby and Cadeby branch committees had gone ahead with the stoppage against the express wishes of the council. Another rule stated that not only did a ballot vote have to be held before a strike could begin but there had to be a two-thirds majority in favour of a stoppage before the dispute could be officially recognised by the Association.[15] If the union had distributed strike money it would have contravened the rules which governed its very existence and operation. The situation was still more depressing for the Denaby miners, however. Even if a ballot had been held and the required majority secured making the strike official, because the stoppage had been tortiously induced, the Association would still not have been able to distribute strike pay. Two years previously it had been generally acknowledged that the Trade Union Acts of 1871 and 1876 had not affected the basically unincorporated status of trade unions, even those which had registered under those Acts, with the corollary that the corporate funds of trade unions were effectively beyond the reach of legal process. The situation that had existed between 1871 and 1901 had been an anomalous one, but one which everybody understood to have been conceded by the legislation of 1871 and 1876. In 1901, however, the Taff Vale judgement[16] subjected registered trade unions to a new, vicarious liability for the torts of their members, a liability which could be enforced against them because of their newly discovered 'quasi-corporate' status. In practice the Taff Vale decision meant that even the most carefully conducted legal strike could occasion costly litigation '. . . and probably the opportunity for getting the trade union cast in swingeing damages'.[17] Regardless of the conduct of labour, employers now had recourse to damage suits whenever they could show that a strike involved them in financial losses, and strike action had temporarily ceased to be a powerful union weapon. If the YMA had disbursed strike pay in early July 1902 it would have been supporting an illegal, unofficial strike and would have followed directly in the footsteps of the Amalgamated Society of Railway Servants. As one newspaper commented:

If the Miners' Association decided to grant pay to the men against the Law of the Masters and Workmen's Act, the Association would have something like £1,250 a week going out of the funds. Mr Buckingham Pope (a director of the company) would at once take Mr Pickard[18] into court and sue the Society through Mr Pickard and claim at least £1,000 a week . . . Was there a man amongst them who liked the idea of Mr Buckingham Pope being able to put his hands in their purse?[19]

It soon became apparent that the vast majority of the men supported their local leaders, and that the stoppage could not proceed unless the miners received strike pay from the YMA. Accordingly the strike had to be made both official and legal so as to facilitate the disbursement of strike pay without any immediate legal risk to the Association's general fund. In order to accomplish this the men would have to return to the pits and offer their services to the company. The employers would then either accept them back, in which case the men could tender fourteen days' notice, or they would offer them a new and presumably unacceptable contract, in which case the men could refuse to sign the document but would present themselves for work each day for the following thirteen working days. Eventually the Denaby and Cadeby colliers agreed to this plan of action, and on 17 July 1902 hundreds of miners trooped into the pit yards at the two collieries to take part in a charade. The company presented the men with new contracts, but only approximately forty of the Cadeby miners, and a handful of Denaby men, signed on.[20] The rest pitched their previously prepared notices into buckets outside the lamp rooms.[21] Farcically the miners went to the mines on the succeeding six working days, at the end of which time both branch secretaries wrote to Ben Pickard, concluding with the words: 'Seeing that our men have not had a pay day for one month, they are getting uneasy and will doubtless break away and sign the contract book.'[22] Threatened with the possible dissolution of the Denaby and Cadeby branches, a special YMA council meeting held on 24 July 1902 granted strike pay backdated to 17 July 1902.[23] By this time the necessary ballot had been held, producing an overwhelming majority in favour of tendering notices, thus making the payment accord with the Association's rules.

## IV

From the outset the Denaby and Cadeby Colliery Company and the South Yorkshire Coal Trade Association (SYCTA hereafter)[24] considered that the dispute had been organised by a small minority of militants who had exploited the dissatisfaction caused by the award of Lord James of Hereford.[25] The employers declared that the 'bag muck' question concerned none of the Cadeby miners, and only a small percentage of the Denaby men, and that there was no justification for the illegal strike. The owners refused to make an improved offer to the men for the removal of the waste rock, and all attempts to obtain a negotiated settlement failed. Initially the company managed to maintain the pits by using 'blacksheep' labour, for there was no organised molestation of blacklegs and the crowds merely stared in silence as the safety men trudged to work.[26] As the strike continued, however, the miners and their womenfolk became less tolerant. In early August bricks were thrown at safety workers, crowds of howling and booing women congregated at the collieries, and sheep's heads were carried.[27] On one occasion the mob threatened to blow up a 'blacksheep's' house, and on another fights broke out and two miners were arrested and charged with assault.[28] The number of blacklegs decreased, and after continued intimidation of safety workers the company distributed a proclamation in late August which ordered the withdrawal of all labour from the pits indefinitely.[29]

The company was determined to break the strike, and it was alleged that Buckingham Pope threatened that he had 'a square yard of gold' which he was willing to sink before the miners would gain a victory.[30] In a determined effort to win the struggle the company took legal action against some of their colliers for contravening the Employers and Workmen Act by failing to give fourteen days' notice to terminate their contracts. By early September 105 miners had been fined approximately £6 each,[31] and shortly afterwards a further 318 colliers were each fined £6 3s 0d.[32] The marked propensity to prosecute which the company had displayed before the dispute was now continued, these preliminary prosecutions being the opening shots of a four-year legal battle.

In January–February 1903 two important developments took place. Firstly, in an attempt to force the men back to work, the employers evicted 720 families from company-owned cottages. By 6 January 1903, when the first evictions occurred, conditions in and around Denaby were deplorable, and poverty and hunger had been prevalent for several weeks. Women and children were walking several miles to neighbouring towns and villages to beg for food, clothing, boots and money.[33] Before Christmas 1902 the Reverend Jesse Wilson, who became a popular local figure as leader of the relief campaign, fed 1,500 children each week. He commented later, in his garrulously biblical but interesting record of events:

My band of most willing workers were all impressed with the same fact, namely that the children were desperately hungry. They arrived at this conclusion through the eagerness of the little ones for plain bread. We thought that it being the festive season they would plunge into sweet cake, but the children asked for bread and butter.[34]

Over two hundred policemen, some mounted, moved into the district to conduct and supervise the evictions.[35] The constables cordoned off the streets, entered the houses, removed all the contents and locked the doors.[36] Pathetically men, women and children looked on in bewilderment. Carts provided largely by local traders carried chattels to barns, club rooms, schoolrooms and all available outbuildings in the district, and as far away as Barnsley, Rotherham and Doncaster.[37] Some families found shelter with relations and friends in the district, others were befriended by the local clergy, and the less fortunate were placed in marquees and bell tents. For those under canvas the bitterly cold winter conditions became a cruel endurance test. Wilson described what he saw in one of the encampments:

I went into a marquee . . . and saw a sight which saddened and sickened me. A few feet from the stove were a man and boy lying on a mattress with a thin covering over them. The boy was lying with his face to the man's back with his arm over the man, pulling himself as closely to the man as possible to create warmth, and yet he shivered with cold. His teeth rattled in his mouth.[38]

Throughout the winter the strike continued, and living conditions deteriorated rapidly. Two children died in the local chapels which formed their new homes; gifts of 'nipsey money'[39] and offers of help poured into Denaby and Cadeby from as far afield as Natal in South Africa,[40] collections of boots and clothes were made, soup kitchens played a vital role, some miners took casual employment to earn extra money, whilst others were reduced to singing, accompanied by accordions, in communal begging attempts.[41] Wedding rings and valuables were pawned, or sold, and Wilson gave away scores of valuable but inadequate food parcels every Tuesday. Hundreds of miners travelled from Kilnhurst, Swinton, Doncaster and other places where they had been billeted to receive these free hand-outs.[42]

The second development was that W. H. Howden successfully brought a legal action against the YMA restraining the union from distributing strike pay.[43] On 2 February 1903 the YMA executive announced that the Denaby and Cadeby men would have to return to work because the decision of the courts made it financially impossible for the union to support the strike any longer.[44] 'Nipsey money' was declining, street parades and demonstrations had been banned by the police, the miners and their families were enduring extreme hardship, and there was an increasing recognition that the dispute was inevitably drawing to a disastrous conclusion. Even before the YMA decided to end lock-out pay nearly 2,000 men and boys had returned to work, but in spite of these circumstances the strike continued for a further agonising seven weeks until 22 March 1903, when the men grudgingly took the decision to capitulate.[45]

## V

The principal reason why the strike ended in defeat for the Denaby and Cadeby miners was the cessation of strike money, brought

about by the legal action taken by William Henry Howden against
the YMA and its trustees.[46] Howden, a Cadeby branch member,
together with a dissident minority, claimed from the outset that the
strike was illegal and unofficial. He continued working at Cadeby
Colliery until 18 August 1902, when the company closed both pits.
From then onwards Howden received lock-out pay from the Association, although the police had advised him not to collect it personally from branch officials.[47] After he had successfully secured an
injunction preventing the YMA from disbursing strike pay, and
the injunction had been upheld in the King's Bench division, the
YMA took the case to the Appeal Court and the House of Lords.[48]
On both occasions the verdict was given against the union. In court
Howden denied that the Denaby and Cadeby Main company had
urged him to take legal action against the Yorkshire Miners' Association, or that the company was providing him with money to live
on.[49] However, it was revealed that the legal expenses were paid by
the employers, who in turn were financially supported by the
SYCTA.[50] Moreover Howden admitted that his solicitors were paying him a wage, but that he had no conception of who was financing them to provide these weekly hand-outs (sic). Later in their
official report of the Denaby and Cadeby case the Miners' Federation of Great Britain alleged that the company paid Howden £4 per
week.[51] Howden, it was repeatedly stated, was bringing the case on
his own account; although technically this was true, it was blatantly
obvious to all concerned that he was a tool manipulated by the
owners. Lord Beveridge commented that

. . . the colliery company, wishing to make the strike impossible, were
almost openly financing the nominal plaintiff and were really at the
bottom of the action. 'Why they don't get sued for maintenance of
another's suit I can't say.' So I wrote telling my father about the case.[52]

Howden's behaviour embittered the Yorkshire miners, and, presumably for his own safety, he left his home in New Conisborough and
moved to London.[53]

In the first trial in the King's Bench division the judge, Justice
Grantham, directed the jury to uphold the injunction taken out by
Howden. The judge supported the prosecution's case, which rested
on the argument that the men had illegally broken their contracts
on 30 June (a fact already recognised by the courts, for over 400 of
the company's employees had been prosecuted for this very offence),
and that they could hardly return to work on 17 July for the pur-

pose of handing in their notices to terminate contracts which had been ended nearly three weeks earlier.[54] The YMA was therefore supporting an illegal stoppage and was transgressing its own rules relating to the payment of strike and lock-out pay. What was surprising about the first hearing was not so much the court's verdict as the judge's marked bias against the miners. Lord Beveridge noted '. . . the bias, as it appeared to me, shown by the judge against the union'. At one point Judge Grantham openly declared that he wanted the strike bringing to an end by the cessation of strike pay.[55]

In the Appeal Court and the House of Lords there was a shift in legal emphasis, but before examining this aspect of the case the court action taken against the YMA must be placed in its correct perspective. Around the turn of the century there was a gradual attrition by judicial process of the favourable legal status procured for labour by the legislation of the 1870s. The court cases involving the Yorkshire miners must be seen in the light of the changing judicial climate *vis-à-vis* the trade unions in the late Victorian and early Edwardian period. The minority report of the Trade Unions Commission, 1869, which largely foreshadowed the Trade Union Act of 1871,[56] asserted that the time was not yet ripe for enabling trade unions to sue, and be sued, by their members, i.e. to recover contributions or fines from members, and be made liable to members for the benefits assured to them.[57] The incorporation of trade unions was also regarded by the report as being injurious and unpopular.[58] These recommendations were adopted by the Liberal government and included in the 1871 Act. In the Howden case the Act was said to be 'a remarkable relic of prejudice' and 'the result of great legislative timidity',[59] but in 1871 nothing more than a bare legitimation of trade union purposes was thought desirable or practicable. It was then considered beneficial to the unions and to society as a whole that not all internal and domestic arrangements of trade unions should be matters of judicial control and enforcement. By the late 1890s opinion in judicial and government circles had changed, and the Taff Vale decision rendered trade unions liable to quasi-corporate liabilities. Just as the Taff Vale decision illustrated a new hostility by the courts to the unions, and a partial revocation of the judicial conclusions formulated in 1871, so the Howden decision showed a desire to surmount some aspects of the 1871 Act and intensify, if not extend, the control of the courts over the internal affairs of trade unions.

Before 1871 trade unions were illegal at common law, and consequently members could not bring actions to enforce their rights *inter se*, nor could they succeed in the prosecution of officials for misappropriation of funds. The 1871 Act provided first (in section 2)[60] for the criminal prosecution of defaulting officers, whilst section 3 legalised trade unions, most of which were previously in unlawful restraint of trade in common law.[61] It was section 4 of the Act which contained the provisions for the vast majority of union rule books, and it was sub-section 3 of this section which was particularly relevant to the Howden case.[62] Section 4 provided that a union rule book, which was illegal in common law but which had been legalised by section 3, should contain certain rules that could not be actionable in damages or be directly enforceable in a court of law. The most notable of these rules were those 'concerning the conditions on which any members for the time being of such trade union shall or shall not . . . be employed'.[63] They included strike rules, rules not to work beyond maximum hours or for less than minimum wages, subscription rules, benefit rules and rules governing fines. This was a reflection of the judicial viewpoint of the 1870s that internal union organisation and discipline were matters for the unions themselves, not for the law courts. The question which the Appeal Court had to answer in January 1903 (before Lord Justices Vaughan Williams, Stirling and Mathew), and which faced the House of Lords in 1904-05, was whether YMA rule 72 relating to the distribution of strike and lock-out pay[64] coud be legally enforced, or whether sub-section 3 of section 4 of the 1871 Trade Union Act prevented its enforcement.

In the Court of Appeal and the House of Lords Rufus Isaacs,[65] defending the YMA, maintained that Howden's injunction contravened section 4, which clearly stated:

Nothing in this Act shall enable any Court to entertain any legal proceedings instituted with the object of directly enforcing or recovering damages for the breach of any of the following agreements, namely (cl. 3) . . . Any agreement for the application of the funds of a trade union: (*a*) To provide benefits to members.[66]

However, Montague Lush,[67] appearing for the plaintiff, argued that '. . . the object of the action is not directly to enforce an agreement for the application of the funds to provide benefits, but is an action to prevent the illegal payment of strike pay . . .'.[68] Lush's fine legal interpretation was upheld on both occasions, and in the House of

Lords Lord MacNaughton summarised the legal position as follows:

No administration or application of the funds of the union was sought or desired. The object of the litigation was simply to prevent misapplication of the funds of the union, not to administer those funds, or to apply them for the purpose of providing benefits to members.[69]

The decision of the House of Lords, that the purpose of the action was not to enforce a rule for the provision of strike benefit (under section 4 in a 'positive' sense), but to prevent strike benefit from being provided contrary to the benefit rule (in a 'negative' sense), was a fine distinction, but one which forcefully demonstrated the new-born desire of the courts at the turn of the century to increase their control over the internal affairs of unions. Howden's case, which remains the classic English illustration of breaking a strike by an internal action to enforce the union's own rule book, established the 'negative prevention rule of interpretation'. This significantly altered that area of trade union law which concerned the enforceability of union rule books. Once it was established that it was not a direct enforcement of a union's benefit rule merely to enjoin its breach, this negative prevention rule enabled injunctive actions to be brought in a wide variety of cases concerning the expenditure and transfer of union funds.[70]

## VI

local officials. Moreover the owners stated that they were bringing Two years before the Howden case was concluded the Denaby and Cadeby company simultaneously brought a further action against the YMA—or, more specifically, against some of its central and local officials—for damages for alleged conspiracy. In the first instance the company set out to recover £115,620, but on 1 January 1903 the employers claimed an additional £32,340. By the time the case had been laboriously debated in the King's Bench division, the Appeal Court and the House of Lords[71] the Association had amassed legal costs totalling £32,500. Therefore if the final decision of the House of Lords had gone against the Association in May 1906 the union would have been faced with a crippling burden of a bill of £180,460. Council for the Denaby and Cadeby Main Colliery Company claimed that the Yorkshire Association was liable in damages for the loss occasioned by the plaintiffs during the strike because the union was vicariously responsible for the actions of its the action against the YMA for conspiracy to induce the Denaby and Cadeby miners to break their existing contracts, for conspiracy to induce them not to enter in to new contracts, and also, as a separate cause of action, for conspiring to maintain the strike by unlawful means embracing intimidation, molestation and illegal payment of strike pay.

The defence for the YMA asserted that the union had not conspired to organise the stoppage and that the withdrawal of labour had been a spontaneous affair of which the Association had no prior knowledge.[72] In any event the Yorkshire Miners' Association argued that it was not legally responsible for the actions of its branch officials any more than Parliament was vicariously responsible for the actions of its MPs.[73] Accordingly the union claimed that it was not liable to compensate the company for the financial losses incurred by the latter during the dispute. Space does not allow an analysis of the evidence relating to the charges set out above,[74] but it is sufficient to note that the Association was found to be liable on all counts in the King's Bench division, and that this verdict was in turn quashed in the Appeal Court. The future fortunes of the Yorkshire miners therefore hinged on the decision of the House of Lords. The case was heard before the Lord Chancellor (Lord Loreburn),[75] Lords MacNaughton, Davey, James of Hereford, Robertson and Atkinson on seven days between 12 March and 14 May 1906.[76] Lord Loreburn declared that the breach of contract by the miners had been opposed by the Association and that there was no evidence that the union had conspired to create a stoppage.[77] It was stated that although Howden's case had decided that lock-out pay had been disbursed contrary to rules, this did not signify that the Association had engaged in a conspiracy, nor that the plaintiffs could sue the union for the illegal disbursement of funds.[78] The Lords also resolved that the district officials of the YMA had not planned, participated in or sanctioned unlawful behaviour, and moreover that the union was not vicariously responsible for the actions of its branch officials.[79] Finally, and most important, it was declared that if the Association was to be sued for financially supporting a dispute which caused a loss to the employers '. . . we should in effect be saying that every strike was an actionable wrong'.[80] In effect this was precisely what the Taff Vale decision had decided only a few years earlier.

In the summer of 1906 the Yorkshire miners were elated at the news of victory. Outside the Miners' offices a flag was hoisted, and a series of celebratory meetings were organised. For the previous four years the case had been *sub judice* but the miners' leaders now eagerly voiced their opinions. None of the YMA officials had any misconceptions about the ultimate objective of the Denaby and Cadeby colliery company; they considered that the employers had planned to destroy the union. In view of the extreme measures taken against the Yorkshire Miners' Association between 1902 and 1906 there seems little doubt that this was indeed the owners' intention. John Wadsworth[81] wrote later:

. . . our members and the general public must never forget that the Denaby and Cadeby Main people, assisted by other colliery owners,[82] did their level best, in my opinion, in the course they took to destroy the Yorkshire Miners' Association and its influence.[83]

At the annual gala and demonstration of 1906, which was held at Dewsbury, Fred Hall[84] claimed that he had evidence to support such assertions:

I want to say publicly that so far as these people who took the case into court are concerned, it was not so much to get the funds, but it was more a determination to break up the great organisation of which we are all members . . . I have some grounds for the statement I have made. Let me tell you that this colliery company endeavoured at the onset to get the colliery owners of South and West Yorkshire to adopt a similar aggressive attitude as themselves. (A voice: 'Be careful, Fred.') I need not be careful . . . I am free, but I have not been for the last four years . . . several letters were issued deliberately, copies of which are in our possession . . . signed by the colliery company,[85] telling other colliery companies that if they would but join with them in their cause in a year or two the miners of Yorkshire would be an 'undisciplined mob', and they would be able to do just as they liked with them as workpeople.[87]

## VII

Given the involvement of the YMA in the legal repercussions of the Taff Vale decision, it would have been surprising if the union had not been engaged in the campaign to implement a Trade Disputes Act which would reverse that judgement. The campaign involved the trade union movement at large, but the Association played its part, sending resolutions to the MFGB in support of the necessary legislation, and with Hall and Wadsworth working for a Trade Disputes Act both in and outside the Commons.[87] A House

of Lords decision in May 1906 delivered against one of the largest
trade unions in Britain,[88] and reinforcing the Taff Vale decision,
might have caused a temporary setback to the campaign for a
legislative reversal of the 1901 judgement. As it was, the Denaby
and Cadeby decision was diametrically opposed to the Taff Vale
verdict, and the four years' legal struggle fought by the Yorkshire
miners had helped make the 1901 judgement a controversial political issue. Indeed, the Howden and Denaby and Cadeby cases were
two of the most important legal actions considered by the Royal
Commission on Trade Disputes and Trade Combinations appointed
in 1903, with Lord Dunedin as chairman.[89] Both the majority and
minority reports of the Commission recommended the abrogation of
the Taff Vale judgement. The Denaby and Cadeby conspiracy case
therefore foreshadowed section 4 of the Trade Disputes Act, 1906,
which finally reversed the House of Lords' verdict of 1901.

In five years there had been a complete *volte-face* in an important section of trade union law. By way of a postscript it is interesting to note that it was to be over sixty years before another
reversal concerning vicarious liability occurred. The Industrial
Relations Act, 1971, made trade unions vicariously responsible for
the actions of even unofficial, non-union-paid shop stewards. The
YMA in 1906 was held not to be responsible for the actions of its
branch officials in a strike which it had officially supported for six
months. In 1972, in the Heaton's Transport case, the Transport and
General Workers' Union was held by the Industrial Relations Court
to be vicariously responsible for the unfair industrial practices of
its shop stewards, who were not union officials, who were acting
against the wishes of the union, and who had been specifically
ordered by the union to stop 'blacking' and picketing ports.[90] The
Industrial Relations Court turned down the pleas of Jack Jones,
the TGWU secretary, and fined the union £50,000. Such is the
chequered history of British trade union law.

## Notes

1  This chapter forms part of a paper previously presented at the Centre
   for the Study of Social History, University of Warwick. I am grateful
   to Professors C. Drake and A. J. Taylor for their comments on an
   earlier draft.
2  The Barnsley seam at Denaby Main Colliery was approximately nine
   feet thick, but only about six feet of this coal was mined. Approximately
   three feet of coal was left to provide a roof, and this coal was in two
   layers historically called the 'bags' and the 'day beds'. 'Bag muck' was

a layer of rock connected to the 'bags'. See Records of the YMA, *Howden* v. *Y.M.A.*, 1902–05, King's Bench division, 15 and 16 January 1903, p. 13. (At the offices of the NUM, Yorkshire Area, Barnsley.)

3 The case involved monetary claims of £180,000, compared with about £35,000 in the Taff Vale case. See below.

4 J. E. Williams, *The Derbyshire Miners; a Study in Industrial and Social History* (1962), pp. 388–9. *Cf.* A. R. Griffin, *The Miners of Nottinghamshire*, I, *1881–1914* (Nottingham, 1956), p. 149.

5 See R. G. Neville, 'The Yorkshire miners, 1881–1926: a study in labour and social history' (unpublished Ph.D. thesis, University of Leeds, 1974), pp. 152–9.

6 *Mexborough and Swinton Times*, 7 November 1902.

7 J. MacFarlane, 'Essay in oral history; Denaby Main—a South Yorkshire mining village', Society for the Study of Labour History, *Bulletin* No. 25 (1972), p. 100.

8 In addition to district disputes, strikes or lock-outs occurred at Denaby in 1869, 1875 (two), 1877, 1878–79 (October–January), 1880–81 (December–January), 1884–85 (December–August), 1886, 1889 and 1895.

9 YMA, *Howden* v. *Y.M.A.*, High Court of Justice, King's Bench division 15 January 1903, p. 38.

10 Miners' Federation of Great Britain (hereafter MFGB), *English and North Wales Conciliation Board, Agreements arising out of the Rosebery Conference*, 17 November 1893, p. 17.

11 YMA, *Howden* v. *Y.M.A.*, 15 January 1903, *op. cit.*, p. 38.

12 YMA *Minutes*, 30 July 1902.

13 *Barnsley Chronicle*, 12 July 1902.

14 *Rules of the YMA*, 1881, rule 29.

15 *Ibid.*, rule 67.

16 *Taff Vale Railway Company* v. *the Amalgamated Society of Railway Servants*, 1901.

17 S. and B. Webb, *The History of Trade Unionism, 1660–1920* (1920), p. 603.

18 Benjamin Pickard, 1842–1904, YMA General Secretary, President of the MFGB and the Yorkshire miners' first MP. See R. G. Neville, *op. cit.*, pp. 964–9, and J. Saville and J. M. Bellamy (eds.), *Dictionary of Labour Biography*, I (1972), pp. 268–70.

19 *Mexborough and Swinton Times*, 18 July 1902.

20 *Ibid.*, 25 July 1902.

21 YMA, *Howden* v. *Y.M.A.*, *op. cit.*, p. 27.

22 *Ibid.*, p. 28.

23 YMA *Minutes*, 24 July 1902.

24 The SYCTA membership encompassed the majority of colliery owners in south Yorkshire.

25 Letter from W. H. Chambers, one of the company's directors, printed in the *Barnsley Chronicle*, 19 July 1902. *Annual Report* of the SYCTA, 5 March 1903 (at Sheffield Public Library, M.D. 2699).

26 YMA, *Howden* v. *Y.M.A.*, *op. cit.*, pp. 31–2.

27 MFGB, *Denaby and Cadeby Collieries Ltd* v. *Y.M.A.*, House of Lords, 12 March 1906, pp. 38–9.

28 *Mexborough and Swinton Times*, 22 August 1902.
29 *Barnsley Chronicle*, 23 August 1902.
30 J. MacFarlane, *loc. cit.*, p. 99.
31 *Mexborough and Swinton Times*, 25 July, 29 August and 5 September 1902.
32 *Ibid.*, 5 September 1902.
33 Jesse Wilson, *The Story of the Great Struggle, 1902–03* (1904), pp. 16–19.
34 *Ibid.*, p. 11.
35 *Barnsley Chronicle*, 10 January 1903.
36 Professor Royden Harrison informs me that a film of the evictions was shown in Sheffield.
37 *Barnsley Chronicle*, 10 January 1903.
38 Jesse Wilson, *op. cit.*, p. 35.
39 Money raised by voluntary subscriptions.
40 Jesse Wilson, *op. cit.*, p. 46.
41 *Ibid.*, p. 15.
42 *Ibid.*, p. 42.
43 YMA, *Howden* v. *Y.M.A.*, *op. cit.*, pp. 160–6.
44 YMA *Minutes*, 2 February 1903.
45 *Barnsley Chronicle*, 28 March 1903.
46 C. Grunfeld, *Modern Trade Union Law* (1966), p. 171. The injunction was originally planned by F. Parker-Rhodes, the then secretary of the SYCTA; see *Annual Report* of the SYCTA, 1902.
47 YMA, *Howden* v. *Y.M.A.*, King's Bench division, *op. cit.*, pp. 39–41.
48 *Howden* v. *Y.M.A.* [1905] A.C. 256; 74 L.J.K.B. 511; 92 L.T. 701; 21 T.L.R. 431; 53 W.R. 667, H.L. affirming *sub nom. Howden* v. *Y.M.A.* [1903] K.B. 308, C.A.
49 YMA, *Howden* v. *Y.M.A.*, King's Bench division, *op. cit.*, p. 42.
50 SYCTA, *Annual Report*, 1902.
51 MFGB, *Report of the Denaby and Cadeby Main Case*, pp. 53 and 209–22.
52 Lord Beveridge, *Power and Influence* (1953), p. 11.
53 YMA, *Howden* v. *Y.M.A.*, K.B.D., *op. cit.*, p. 46.
54 *Ibid.*, p. 161.
55 *Ibid.*, p. 163.
56 R. Y. Hedges and A. Winterbottom, *The Legal History of Trade Unionism* (1930), p. 66.
57 *Minority Report of Trade Unions Commission*, 1869, p. 59.
58 R. Y. Hedges and A. Winterbottom, *op. cit.*, pp. 66–7.
59 *Howden* v. *Y.M.A.*, 1905 A.C., at p. 275, quoted by R. Y. Hedges and A. Winterbottom, *op. cit.*, p. 67.
60 See 1871 Trade Union Act, s. 2.
61 *Ibid.*, s. 3.
62 *Ibid.*, s. 4(3).
63 C. Grunfeld, *op. cit.*, p. 63.
64 The YMA rules relating to the distribution of strike pay have been discussed above.
65 First Marquess of Reading, 1860–1935, Lord Chief Justice of England, ambassador to the USA and Viceroy of India. A Liberal with a dazzling

career. See Lord Reading (Son), *Rufus Isaacs, First Marquess of Reading*, 1942–45. *Cf. The Times*, 31 December 1935; *Dictionary of National Biography*, 1931–40, pp. 462 ff.

66  YMA, *Howden* v. *Y.M.A.*, Appeal Court, 1905, p. 172.

67  Sir Charles Montague Lush, 1853–1930, one of the great judges of the first two decades of the twentieth century. See *The Times*, 23 June 1930. *Cf. Dictionary of National Biography*, 1922–30, pp. 524 f.

68  YMA, *Howden* v. *Y.M.A.*, House of Lords, 1905, pp. 569–70.

69  *Ibid.*, 14 April 1905, p. 639.

70  C. Grunfeld, *op. cit.*, p. 76.

71  *Denaby and Cadeby Main Collieries Co. Ltd* v. *Y.M.A.* [1906] A.C. 384; 75 L.J.K.B. 961; 95 L.T. 561; 22 T.L.R. 543, H.L. *Cf. The Times*, 28, 29, 30 January and 2–6, 9–10, 15 February 1904 and 20 May 1905.

72  MFGB, *Denaby and Cadeby Conspiracy Case*, 1904, *op. cit.*, p. 308.

73  *Ibid.*, p. 314.

74  For a full consideration of the evidence see R. G. Neville, *op. cit.*, chapter VI, pp. 332 *et seq.*

75  Sir R. T. Reid.

76  MFGB, *Denaby and Cadeby Conspiracy Case*, House of Lords, 1906, p. 3.

77  *Ibid.*, p. 434.

78  *Ibid.*, p. 438.

79  *Ibid.*, p. 437. For a full discussion of the legal history of the vicarious liability of trade unions for the tortious acts of their members see R. Hepple, 'Union responsibility for shop stewards', *Industrial Law Journal*, I, No. 4 (December 1972), especially pp. 204–7, which discusses the Denaby and Cadeby conspiracy case.

80  *Ibid.*, p. 439.

81  John Wadsworth, 1850–1921, General Secretary of the YMA, MP for Hallamshire; see R. G. Neville, *op. cit.*, pp. 998–1000.

82  The Denaby and Cadeby company received financial support from the SYCTA during the dispute.

83  YMA, *Annual Report*, 1906.

84  Frederick Hall, 1855–1933, agent of the YMA and MP for Normanton; see R. G. Neville, *op. cit.*, pp. 931–3.

85  Unfortunately I have been unable to trace any copies of this document.

86  YMA, *Report of the Y.M.A. Annual Demonstration*, 1906.

87  YMA, *Annual Report*, 1906; *Barnsley Chronicle*, 19 May 1906.

88  The YMA had over 62,000 members in 1906.

89  *Report of the Royal Commission on Trade Disputes and Trade Combinations*, 1906, Cd. 2825, pp. 9, 72–3 and 114.

90  *Heaton's Transport (St Helens)* v. *Transport and General Workers' Union; Craddock Brothers* v. *Same; Panalpina Services, Panalpina (Northern)* v. *Same*, 1972. 3 W.L.R. 431 [1972] 3 A11 E.R. 101, H.L. This case did not concern vicarious liability in tort, however. For a full discussion of the Heaton's Transport case see R. Hepple, *loc. cit.*

# Select critical bibliography

This select critical bibliography lists secondary works (and those which are only partly primary in nature) which examine the social and economic history of the Yorkshire coal industry. Studies of a purely geological or technological nature are omitted, but some of the more important works which consider the industry in a subsidiary fashion are included. The place of publication is London unless otherwise stated. Items marked with an asterisk are reprinted in the present volume.

1 Baernreither, J. M., *English Associations of Working Men*, 1893. Contains useful information on the West Riding Miners' Permanent Relief Fund.
2 Benson, J., 'The compensation of English coal-miners and their dependants for industrial accidents, 1860–1897', unpublished Ph.D. thesis (University of Leeds, 1974). Although not primarily concerned with Yorkshire, it examines the incidence of mining accidents in the county, the working of the Poor Law, the relief offered by Yorkshire colliery owners, the rise of the West Riding Miners' Permanent Relief Fund and the legislative and compensatory activities of the West and South Yorkshire Miners' Associations and of the Yorkshire Miners' Association.
3 Briggs, D. H. Currer, *A Merchant Banker and the Coal Trade, 1693–1971* (Dover, 1971).
4 Briggs, K. M., *Henry Briggs, Son and Company Limited, adapted from some historical notes—a History, 1860–1935* (n.d., place of publication unknown). Two short works dealing with the history of one of the most important colliery companies in West Yorkshire.
5 *Brodsworth Main Colliery 1905–55 Jubilee* (1955).
6 Bullock, J., *Them and Us* (1972). The autobiography of a Yorkshire miner who became president of the British Association of Colliery Management. Provides useful insights into the social history of the West Yorkshire coalfield after the turn of the century.
7 Clayton, A. K., 'Coal mining at Hoyland', *Transactions of the Hunter Archæological Society*, ix (1966).
8 Clayton, A. K., 'The Elsecar collieries under Joshua and Ben Biram'

(Hoyland Common, 1964). Typescript at Barnsley Library. It is hoped that this will soon be reprinted by the Doncaster Museums and Arts Service.

9  Coates, B. E. and Lewis, G. M., *The Doncaster Area* (Sheffield, 1966). Excellent on the geographical and geological background to the development of the Doncaster coalfield, it also contains a valuable comparison between living conditions in south and west Yorkshire.

10 Cox, R. M., 'The development of the coal industry in south Yorkshire before 1830', unpublished M.A. thesis (University of Sheffield, 1960).

11 Dennis, N., Henriques, F., and Slaughter, C., *Coal is our Life: an Analysis of a Yorkshire Mining Community* (1956). Although principally a sociological work, contains a wealth of historical information relating to all aspects of the life of the Yorkshire miner.

12 Davis, J. W., *History of the Yorkshire Geological and Polytechnic Society, 1837–1887. With Biographical Notices of Some of its Members* (Halifax, 1889). Includes biographical sketches of Henry Briggs, Joseph Charlesworth (senior and junior), Earl Fitzwilliam, Robert Hunt, Charles Morton and Thomas Wilson.

13 *Dictionary of Labour Biography,* ed. Joyce Bellamy and John Saville (continuing). Vol. I (1972) contains entries on Edward Bates Cowey, John Dixon (d. 1876), John Frith, John Normansell, Benjamin (Ben) Pickard and John Wadsworth. Vol. II (1974) contains entries on Fred Hall, Joseph Arthur Hall, William Lunn, William Parrott, John Samuel Potts, Herbert Smith and Thomas (Tom) Williams (Lord Williams of Barnburgh). Vol. III (forthcoming) will contain entries on Edward Dunn, William Gillis, George Arthur Griffiths, Thomas Walter Grundy, John Guest, George Henry Hirst, Edward Hough, Gabriel Price, Alfred Smith, George Sylvester and William Watson. Vol. IV (forthcoming) will include entries on Samuel Broadhead, Isaac Burns, John Dixon (d. 1914), John Hoskin, Thomas Oakey and Samuel Roebuck.

14 Duckham, H. and B., *Great Pit Disasters: Great Britain, 1700 to the Present Day* (Newton Abbot, 1973). A popular work which includes a chapter on the Oaks disaster, upon which is based Dr Duckham's contribution to the present volume.

15 Elliot, B. J., *The South Yorkshire Joint Railway* (Lingfield, 1971). Shows the expansion of the railway system in south Yorkshire and contains a short, but valuable, account of the development of the coalfield before 1914.

16 Evison, J., 'Conditions of labour in Yorkshire coal mines, 1870–1914', unpublished B.A. thesis (University of Birmingham, 1963). A sound introduction to the subject, with useful statistical data.

17 Evison, J., 'The opening up of the "central" region of the South

Yorkshire coalfield and the development of its townships as colliery communities, 1875–1905', unpublished M.Phil. thesis (University of Leeds, 1972).

18 Fox, W., *Coal Combines in Yorkshire* (Labour Research Department, 1935). An invaluable analysis of the structure of, and inter-relationships between, Yorkshire colliery companies.

19 Franks, D. L., *South Yorkshire Railway* (Leeds, 1971). Illustrates the relationship between railway and colliery development.

20 Goodchild, J., 'The first Mines Inspector in Yorkshire', part I, *South Yorkshire Journal of Economic and Social History*, part 3 (1971).

21 Goodchild, J., 'Some early Yorkshire coal masters' associations', *South Yorkshire Journal of Economic and Social History*, part 2 (1970). This short article provides the only published account of nineteenth-century Yorkshire colliery owners' associations.

22 Goodchild, J., 'Some notes on the early history of Denaby Main Colliery', *South Yorkshire Journal of Economic and Social History*, part 4 (1973).

23 *Gray, G. B. D., 'The South Yorkshire coalfield', *Geography*, XXXII (1947).

24 Greaves, P. C., *Black Diamonds: the Gleanings of Fifty Years in the West Yorkshire Coalfield* (Wakefield, 1938). A colliery owner's informative account of developments in the West Yorkshire coalfield. Greaves recounts his memories of trade union officials, industrial disputes, technological developments and of colliery owners who took a prominent role in the West Yorkshire Coal Owners' Association.

25 Gregory, R., *The Miners and British Politics, 1906–14* (Oxford, 1968). Contains a chapter examining the late transformation of the Yorkshire Miners' Association from Liberal–Labourism to parliamentary socialism.

26 Habershon, M. H., *Chapeltown Researches, Archæological and Historical, including old-time Memories of Thorncliffe, its Ironworks and Collieries and other Antecedents* (1893). Includes references to industrial disputes in the Chapeltown area of south Yorkshire.

27 Hallam, W., *Miners' Leaders—Thirty Portraits and Biographical Sketches* (1894). Provides biographical details of a number of Yorkshire miners' leaders.

28 Harris, A., 'The Ingleton coalfield', *Industrial Archæology*, 4 (1968).

29 Holland, J. L., 'Coal mining in Pontefract and district' (1967). (Typescript at Castleford Public Library.) Antiquarian in its approach.

30 Holmes, D. H., *The Mining and Quarrying Industries in the Huddersfield District* (Huddersfield, 1967). A recent revision (incorporating additional information) of Wray, D. A., *The Mining Industry*

*in the Huddersfield District* (Huddersfield, 1929).
31 Hopkinson, G. G., 'Development of lead mining and of the coal and iron industries in north Derbyshire and south Yorkshire, 1700–1850', unpublished Ph.D. thesis (University of Sheffield, 1958).
32 *Hopkinson, G. G., 'The development of the South Yorkshire and North Derbyshire coalfield, 1500–1775', *Transactions of the Hunter Archæological Society*, VII (1957).
33 Hopton, W., *Conversations on Mines, etc.* (Manchester, 1891). Contains an autobiographical study.
34 Hudson, S., *The Aberford Railway and the History of the Garforth Collieries* (Newton Abbot, 1971). Of wider interest than its title might suggest.
35 Jeffcock, J. T., *Parkin Jeffcock, Civil and Mining Engineer* (1867). The biography of one of the heroes of the Oaks disaster.
36 Jennings, B. (ed.), *A History of Nidderdale* (Huddersfield, 1967). Considers the history of the small-scale coal-mining operations of the region.
37 Jones, T. H., *Fingers in the Sky: a Miner's Life Story* (n.d., c 1950). The story of a Yorkshire miner's experiences in the South Yorkshire coalfield. His account of events during the 1926 dispute is particularly useful.
38 Lawson, J., *The Man in the Cap: the Life of Herbert Smith* (1941). This work, although written in a heroic style, presents the fascinating life story of one of Yorkshire's foremost miners' leaders.
39 Lee, C. E., 'The first steam railway: Brandling's colliery line between Leeds and Middleton', *Railway Magazine*, December 1937.
40 Lister, J., 'Coal mining in Halifax', *Old Yorkshire*, second ser., ed. Wheater, W. (1885).
41 Lodge, T. J., 'Lidgett Colliery', *Industrial Railway Record*, 54 (1974).
42 *MacFarlane, J., 'Denaby Main: a South Yorkshire mining village', *Bulletin of the Society for the study of Labour History*, 25 (1972).
43 *MacFarlane, J., 'Essay in oral history: Denaby Main—an addendum', *Bulletin of the Society for the study of Labour History*, 26 (1973).
44 Machin, F., *The Yorkshire Miners: a History,* vol. I (Barnsley, 1958). The best known account of Yorkshire mining trade unionism before the formation of the Yorkshire Miners' Association in 1881. It is, however, in the heroic mould of trade union histories and fails to take account of broad economic and social developments.
45 Manley, E. R., *Meet the Miner: a Study of the Yorkshire Miner at Work, at Home and in Public Life* (Lofthouse, 1947). A popular work introducing the Yorkshire collier to the non-mining community.
46 Mee, G., *Aristocratic Enterprise: the Fitzwilliam Industrial Under-*

*takings, 1795–1857* (Glasgow, 1975).

47 *The Monk Bretton Colliery Co., Barnsley* (n.d.). A slight company history.

48 Neave, D., 'The search for coal in the East Riding in the eighteenth century', *Yorkshire Archæological Journal*, XLV (1973).

49 Neville, R. G., 'The Yorkshire miners, 1881–1926: a study in industrial and social history', unpublished Ph.D. thesis (University of Leeds, 1974). The major theme of this study is the relationship between the activities of the Yorkshire Miners' Association and the economic situation of the coal industry. The work is not only concerned with wages, disputes and industrial policy, but political involvement, social and working conditions and union organisation and finance are also considered. Finally the careers of all district officials holding office between 1881 and 1926 are analysed in a separate appendix.

50 Newham, H. E. C., *Hull as a Coal Port and the Yorkshire, Derbyshire, Nottinghamshire Coalfields* (Hull, 1913). The only historical study of the export trade in Yorkshire coal.

51 *Occurrences and Events of Interest in Barnsley and District from 1229 to 1922* (Barnsley, 1922). Provides a catalogue of details relating to pit disasters and miners' trade unionism.

52 Offor, R., 'Two mining account books from Farnley Colliery, 1690–1720', *Transactions of the Yorkshire Dialect Society*, part XXXIV (1933).

53 Peace, K., 'Some changes in the coal-mining industry of southern Yorkshire, 1951–71', *Geography*, LVIII (1973). An extremely brief, though useful, survey.

54 Peck, J. A., *The Miners' Strike in South Yorkshire, 1926* (Sheffield, 1970). An elementary work but nonetheless soundly based on primary sources.

55 Rimmer, W. G., 'Middleton Colliery, near Leeds, 1770–1830', *Yorkshire Bulletin of Economic and Social Research*, VII (1955). Assesses the importance of the colliery in the development of Leeds and the West Yorkshire coalfield.

56 Rosenberg, J. J., *Life in a Model Coal-mining Village* (1947). An account by a 'Bevin boy' of life in 'Dashworth Colliery', south Yorkshire.

57 Rymer, E. A., *The Martyrdom of the Mine, or Sixty Years' Struggle for Life* (Monk Bretton, 1898). This pamphlet will be reprinted in two parts in *History Workshop Journal* during 1976, with an introduction and notes by R. G. Neville. The fascinating autobiography of a pioneering trade unionist, written from an experience of constant struggle and hardship. Rymer spent most of his life in Yorkshire, although he operated periodically in nearly all the other English coalfields from the 1850s until the late 1890s.

58 Slater, L., and Wandless, A., 'The Yorkshire coalfield', *Journal of The Institute of Fuel*, February 1948.
59 Smith, D., 'A study of the importance of working capital, and some of its sources, in the mining and metal industries, 1750–1830', unpublished M.A. thesis (University of Sheffield, 1974).
60 Sorby, E., 'Coal mining near Sheffield from 1773 to 1820', *Transactions of the Institute of Mining Engineers*, LXV (1923).
61 Stone, L., 'An Elizabethan coal mine', *Economic History Review*, second ser., III (1950–51). A detailed account of the small-scale mining operations on the Earl of Shrewsbury's estate in Sheffield Park.
62 *Souvenir Brochure to Celebrate the Opening of the Area Headquarters 100 Years Ago, 1874–1974* (Barnsley, National Union of Mineworkers, 1974). A popular work but contains reprints of interesting primary material, together with biographical details of the more important Yorkshire miners' leaders.
63 Teasdale, G. H., *Silkstone Coal and Collieries* (n.d., c. 1900). A valuable account of coal mining in the Silkstone area which contains numerous references to working conditions and miners' unions.
64 *The Tragedy of the Coalfields: West Riding Miners' Permanent Relief Fund Friendly Society, 1877–1927* (Barnsley, 1927). Slight and eulogistic, but the only existing account of this important institution.
65 Trigg, W. B., 'Halifax coalfield, Part II, The Shibden Hall pits', *Transactions of the Halifax Antiquarian Society* (1930).
66 Trigg, W. B., 'Halifax coalfield, Part III, Northowram Mines', *Transactions of the Halifax Antiquarian Society* (1931).
67 Trigg, W. B., 'Halifax coalfield, Part IV, Boothtown Mines', *Transactions of the Halifax Antiquarian Society* (1931).
68 Trigg, W. B., 'The Halifax coalfield', *Transactions of the Halifax Antiquarian Society* (1932). Considers the history of Sugden Head pit.
69 *Victoria County History, Yorkshire*, vol. II (1912). Contains: C. H. Vellacott, 'A history of Yorkshire mining and smelting (medieval)' and H. Perkin, 'Modern mining'.
70 Walters, J. Tudor, *The Building of Twelve Thousand Houses* (1927). Considers a scheme put forward by colliery companies, many of which were active in Yorkshire.
71 Ward, J. T., 'The Earls Fitzwilliam and the Wentworth estate in the nineteenth century', *Yorkshire Bulletin of Economic and Social Research*, XII (1960). Includes an examination of the South Yorkshire colliery interests of the Fitzwilliam family.
72 *Ward, J. T., 'West Riding landowners and mining in the nineteenth century', *Yorkshire Bulletin of Economic and Social Research*, XV (1963).

73 Ward, J. T., 'West Riding landowners and the railways', *Journal of Transport History*, IV (1960). Shows the part played by Yorkshire colliery owners in the promotion of railway development.

74 Whitelock, G. C. H., *250 Years in Coal: the History of Barber Walker & Co. Ltd* (Eastwood, 1956). Deals with the company's history in Nottinghamshire but also considers the expansion of the firm in the Doncaster area.

75 Williams, J. E., *The Derbyshire Miners: a Study in Industrial and Social History* (1962). Probably the best trade union history written since the second world war. Chapter IV considers in great depth the history of the South Yorkshire and North Derbyshire Miners' Association.

76 Wilson, J., *The Story of the Great Struggle, 1902–03* (1904). A garrulously biblical but invaluable account of the Denaby and Cadeby miners' strike.

77 *The Yorkshire Main Colliery Co. Ltd,* published by the company (1930). A short company history.

# Index